POVERTY
IS WHERE THE MONEY IS

Poverty

Is

Where the Money

Is

BY

SHIRLEY SCHEIBLA

ARLINGTON HOUSE

New Rochelle   *New York*

TO MY SON,

Louis C. Scheibla, III

Contents

Preface

The original intent in writing this book was to analyze the entire War on Poverty. It soon became apparent, however, that the dimensions were so staggering that a competent job could not be done in a single volume. Accordingly, a decision was made to concentrate on the basic premise on which the War on Poverty was launched and on the first weapons used—the Job Corps and community action. Even so, the Office of Economic Opportunity came up with so many innovations under community action that it was impossible to take in even that entire program. Nevertheless, what has been covered should provide a key to understanding the War on Poverty, the people involved, and the dangers.

I am indebted to Arlington House for awakening my interest in the subject; my boss, Robert M. Bleiberg, Editor of *Barron's National Business and Financial Weekly*, for his encouragement and contagious enthusiasm; my husband, Louis C. Scheibla, Jr., for his patience; my son, Louis C. Scheibla, III, for giving me his fresh young viewpoint; my typists, Judith Nee and Virginia Beazley, and the countless people who discussed the War on Poverty with me. Because the issues were so highly controversial, many of those who talked with me did so only upon receiving my promise that I would not use their names.

Introduction

As even the most casual newspaper reader must realize, the War on Poverty is one of the most expensive, scandal-ridden and revolutionary programs ever undertaken by the United States government. The total expense depends upon the figuring. Accounting only for the Office of Economic Opportunity (OEO), it ran a little better than one and a half billion dollars a year during fiscal years 1966 and 1967. But while OEO actually became the most confused, profligate and overpaid bureaucracy ever spawned by Congress, it was set up with the avowed aim of coordinating the War on Poverty waged by all the multifarious arms of the government. Considering all federal welfare expenditures, estimates of the cost of the War on Poverty ran as high as $35 billion a year. (This included Aid to Dependent Children, Medicare, Social Security, Unemployment Compensation, Aid to Appalachia and a host of other programs.)

The most revolutionary aspect of the War on Poverty is the making of a politically potent, and sometimes violent, group of the lower class. Whether Communists will take over the leadership of this class remains to be seen. Official investigations have proved that they already have infiltrated it.

One of the most Socialistic parts is the use of federal funds to undermine free enterprise. In addition the War on Poverty is altering the existing power structure by changing the political channels through which federal largesse is dispensed.

The scandals range from misspending of federal funds to stabbings and other forms of violence at Job Corps centers. As this study will show, they are largely the result of a poorly prepared program launched on a crash basis for political gain.

1

The Beginning
of the
War on Poverty

While the nation still was reeling from the shock of President Kennedy's assassination, Lyndon Johnson started work on the War on Poverty the day after he became President. He called it, "My kind of program." And indeed it was. It provided an issue—poverty in the midst of plenty —which could tug at the heartstrings and create national indignation. It also provided justification for massive new federal programs, and a vehicle for the rescue of a large number of Administration proposals, then moribund on Capitol Hill. Perhaps more important from the Johnson standpoint, however, was the prospect that it would give the Chief Executive unprecedented power which would stem from handing out federal money without going through established channels.

The build-up to the great Johnsonian discovery of poverty began as far back as 1949. The Congressional Joint Economic Committee put out a report on the subject that year, a mere three years after the Committee was created. Titled *Low-Income Families and Economic Stability*, the report studied "the number and circumstances of urban families having less than $2,000 of money income (per year) and of farm families having less than $1,000 of money income."

With amazing honesty, it stated, "The cash income levels . . . were selected only to designate an income group for intensive study and . . . are not intended to be and must not be interpreted to be a definition of low income." It also acknowledged that "The boundary line . . . between want and sufficiency is difficult to determine."

In 1948, the report said, 9.6 million families had incomes below $2,000 annually. Of the 3.3 million families who lived on farms, 1.7 million had incomes below $1,000.

The study came to a number of conclusions which never achieved immortality. Here are a few samples: "When the family is headed by a person who cannot work or who lacks the training or ability to command a good wage, the family is bound to suffer. . . . The type of work engaged in by the head is an important determinant of family income. . . ."

The document did make one statement, however, which later was to become part of the foundation for the War on Poverty. It declared, "The low income families have been left behind in the economic progress of America."

While the study itself, if not that sentence, has long been forgotten, it deserves a place in history as the grandfather of other studies and pseudo-studies, both in report and book form, which provided the basis for the War on Poverty.

John Kenneth Galbraith laid more of the foundation with his book, *The Affluent Society*, published in 1958. In one of the most freewheeling definitions of poverty yet, he said, "People are poverty-stricken when their income, even if adequate for survival, falls markedly behind that of the community."[1]

Then he leaped to the conclusion that "The most certain thing about modern poverty is that it is not efficiently remedied by a general and tolerably well-distributed advance in income."[2]

Professor Galbraith did not back up his "certain" conclusion with statistics, however. Instead he divided poverty into two categories, "case" and "insular." While his syntax left something to be desired, he made clear what he meant by "case poverty." He explained, "But some quality peculiar to the individual or family involved—mental deficiency, bad health, inability to adapt to the discipline of modern economic life, excessive procreation, alcohol, insufficient education, or perhaps a combination of several of these handicaps—have kept these individuals from participating in the general well-being."

Like the earlier committee study, and without any documentation, he assumed that greater general prosperity will not lessen the number of such people, say by making it possible for them to improve their education or health.

"Insular poverty," he said, occurs in islands of poor communities which lack adequate schools and health services so that subsequent generations will be ill prepared either for mastering the environment into which they are born or for migration to areas of higher income outside."

The economist also did not examine the possibility that greater general prosperity might lessen the number of such communities. A telling point he did make, however, was that in an affluent society, the poor had become a minority ignored by the politicians.

A study made for the Joint Economic Committee, and published a year after *The Affluent Society*, refuted claims

of both the book and the earlier Committee study that increases in general prosperity pass by the hard-core impoverished.

Acting as an outside consultant, Robert J. Lampman of
the University of Wisconsin prepared Study Paper No. 12
titled *The Low Income Population and Economic Growth*.
Figuring in 1957 dollars, he used the income of $2,500 for
a family of four as a poverty base. This, he said, was equiv-
alent to an income of $2,000 in 1949.

Professor Lampman found that the percentage of the
population with this "low income" fell from 26 to 19 in
the decade ended in 1957. This means, he said, that Professor Galbraith was wrong when he said general prosperity
passes by the very poor. Other decades of similar progress
would drop the low-income percentage to 14 in 1967 and
10 in 1977, Professor Lampman predicted. "With regard
to island poverty, the record suggests that movement (to a
new location) was a leading factor working for the reduction of numbers in low income status," he declared.

According to the Lampman findings, 32 million people
had low income in 1957, and as aforementioned, their number was dwindling. Moreover, there was no attempt to say
that all of these were impoverished, undoubtedly because
an undetermined number of people live well without salary
or wages, the sole determinant of low income. They include those receiving their income from stocks and bonds,
and/or sale of real estate and other assets.

It was Socialist Michael Harrington who fired the White
House to action with his writing about poverty. In his
book *The Other America*, published in 1962, he dwelt at
length on descriptions of the poor he knew while living on
Skid Row of New York's Bowery as a social worker. The
poor he encountered in trips to Appalachia and elsewhere
also came in for their share of handwringing descriptions.
The existence of such deprivation and degradation in the

midst of plenty is a national scandal and calls for drastic federal action, he maintained.

To justify this, it was necessary somehow to define and count the poor. In doing so, Mr. Harrington frankly declared, "If my interpretation . . . overstates the case slightly, that is intentional."

The author discarded the low-income base of $2,500 used by Professor Lampman. The former said it should be more like $4,000 a year, the income deemed necessary to afford the "modest but adequate budget" for a family of four which is used to make up the Consumer Price Index compiled by the Labor Department's Bureau of Labor Statistics (BLS) and loosely referred to as the Cost of Living Index. What Mr. Harrington didn't mention is that the "modest" budget includes such items as golf fees, film developing, piano lessons, TV tubes, phonograph records, dog food, parking charges, bus and taxi fares, airline tickets, earrings, baby-sitters, power lawnmowers and air conditioners.

There are fifty million people without salaries or wages adequate to afford the BLS budget, Mr. Harrington said. But he added, "If some statistician should find an error in technical approach, if he could say there are ten million less poor, that would not really be important."

Admitting that those he called poor would not be judged so by foreign standards, he declared, "The American poor are not poor in Hong Kong—They are dispossessed in terms of what the rest of the nation enjoys, in terms of what the society could provide if it had the will." He added, "To have one bowl of rice in a society where all other people have half a bowl may well be a sign of achievement and intelligence. . . . To have five bowls of rice in a society where the majority have a decent, balanced diet is a tragedy."

Thus, by Mr. Harrington's definition, the poor indeed

will always be with us because they will be those who have less than the majority.

Mr. Harrington did not say how he arrived at most of his major conclusions regarding the specific problems of poverty. He ignored the findings of Professor Lampman and offered no documentation of his own. This was glaringly obvious when Mr. Harrington said that in good times "the familiar America of high living standards moves upward; the other America of poverty continues to move downward."

He declared that poverty keeps people from moving, but at another point discussed the migration of the poor Southern Negroes to Harlem. Nowhere in the book did he reconcile the two statements or explain how it was that poverty did not keep Negroes from moving to Harlem.

Without supporting facts or figures, he assumed that automation causes unemployment. Two major studies have shown, however, that while automation eliminates some jobs and causes some temporary displacement of workers, it does not reduce the total jobs available.

The National Commission on Technology, Automation and Economic Progress found that "the persistence of a high general level of unemployment in the years following the Korean War was not the result of accelerated technological progress." It concluded that "technology eliminates jobs, not work."

Here is a warning the General Electric Company issued after studying the situation and reaching a similar conclusion: "The day that displacements cease to occur because of the improved methods of production—that day will mark the start of a failing economic system which no longer permits a rising standard of living and the power to compete successfully with other economic and political systems. Also on the day that technological displacements do not occur or jobs do not 'disappear,' we will no longer have sufficient labor to shift from declining products to growth products as has taken place in the past."[3]

The facts also refute Mr. Harrington's claim that unemployment is building up in a relatively few areas. Consider what has happened since 1960. In that year, 92 of the 150 major labor markets had less than 6% unemployment. By 1963 the figure rose to 109, and by 1964, it was 120.[4]

With all his challengeable statements, Mr. Harrington did make one potent point—the poor are a new minority group without a political voice. Professor Galbraith, as noted, had made the same point in *The Affluent Society*. Mr. Harrington, however, made it more forcefully. He declared, "The people of the other America do not, by far and large, belong to unions, to fraternal organizations, or to political parties. They are without lobbies of their own; they put forward no legislative program. As a group, they are atomized. They have no face; they have no voice."

Moreover, Mr. Harrington told the politicians how to take advantage of the situation. Publicizing two phrases which will be long remembered, he suggested organizing this minority through a War on Poverty to lift them up into the Great Society. This made some political sense. As any good politician knows, a well-organized minority can be more powerful than an unorganized majority.

Mr. Harrington used a curious route to arrive at the conclusion that the federal government should do the job. First, he said, "If there is to be a way out [of the culture of poverty] it will come from human action, from political change, not from automatic processes."

Next he said that private charitable contributions don't work, city governments don't have a sufficient tax base and "state governments are notoriously weighted in the direction of caution, pinchpenny economics and indifference to the plight of the urban millions."

Then the grand conclusion—"there is only one institution in the society capable of acting to abolish poverty. That is the federal government."

Never was there a more flamboyant display of inverse reasoning. Mr. Harrington had admitted that the U.S. has the most prosperous economy in the world and has achieved the distinction of having the poor in the minority. Moreover, he also admitted that the poor in the U.S. would not be considered so in many other areas of the world.

What he failed to admit was that this has come about under private enterprise, the system which has made America great. Instead, he reasoned that because there is any poverty at all in a prosperous country, it is a national disgrace which calls for drastic federal action.

Since Mr. Harrington is a Socialist, it is not surprising to hear such reasoning from him. What is surprising is the enthusiastic reception his book received in high places.

Shortly after publication of *The Other America*, Dr. Walter W. Heller, then Chairman of the Council of Economic Advisers, gave a copy to President Kennedy. Dr. Heller states the Chief Executive was so fascinated that he never returned it.

At this point it seems appropriate to take a close look at Michael Harrington, the man who did the most to inspire the War on Poverty. He has worked for the Fund for the Republic which was investigated by the House Committee on Un-American Activities and found to be a hindrance in the battle against Communism. The Committee specifically found the Fund engaged in propaganda against Congressional investigations of Communism, government security procedures, loyalty oaths and regulation of immigration. The Fund spent several million dollars opposing the denial of employment to security risks in government, defense and other industries.[5]

Mr. Harrington also was Organizational Secretary for

the Workers Defense League[6] which, according to Congressional testimony, was formed by leading members of the Socialist Party.[7]

More recently Mr. Harrington has written the introduction for the book, *Poverty in America*, published in 1965 by the University of Michigan Press. The book is dedicated to the favorite Socialist Party candidate for President, "Norman Thomas in his eighty-first year in tribute to a lifetime of crusading against the causes of poverty."

In his introduction, Mr. Harrington leaves no doubt that he sees the War on Poverty as an instrument of Socialism. It will mean widespread federal intervention in the economy and "national economic planning," according to Mr. Harrington. Pooh-poohing any connection between economic planning and the loss of freedom, he declared, "The United States is a curious exception in the world, because the typical American reaction to the word 'planning' is that it equals red revolution and bringing Brezhnev to the White House, and having some bureaucrats determine the brand of toothpaste which the citizens use. We are the only people who think this way."

In addition he said, "The causes of the riots in the summer of 1964 were not to be found in the Communists, the Nationalists, or any other organized group, but rather in the unspeakable conditions under which Negroes live, north and south."

Mr. Harrington also denounced the profit motive, neglecting to note that it has been responsible for this country's present affluence. Future economic decisions should be made by the government and should be based on need rather than profit, the author argued. He called for an "ideological struggle to make human need, rather than private profit, the criterion for economic decisions."

Moreover, Mr. Harrington made the following ominous statement: "The President is saying that we are going to have a revolution without the painful inconvenience of changing basic institutions and the reason we can do so is that now we live in a society which is so abundant that it need no longer have class conflict in order to make economic decisions, because all reasonable claims can now be satisfied and politics will now proceed by way of consensus rather than by way of conflict.

"It seems to me that this view of reality fails because if we are going to eliminate poverty and create a qualitatively new society, we are in for some radical changes. There are going to be more than a few conflicts when we throw so much of the conventional and outlived wisdom overboard and start acting a new way."

Mr. Harrington was more subtle in writing *The Other America*. After reading the book, President Kennedy asked Dr. Heller for more information on the poverty problem. By this time Professor Lampman had joined the staff of the Council of Economic Advisers (CEA), and Dr. Heller asked him to update his old study. The resulting work has never been made public. Shortly thereafter, however, on May 1, 1963, Dr. Heller drafted a memo to President Kennedy showing alarm:

"Updating the 1957 data on poverty gives distressing results—they offer one more demonstration of the cost of economic slack. . . . Table IA shows the drastic slowdown in the rate in which the economy is taking people out of poverty. The rate in the past five years is far below that of the earlier postwar years—In the decade from 1947 to 1956, the percent of families with less than $3,000 total money income (in 1961 dollars) declined by 10 percentage points, from 33% of the population to 23%. But in the five years from 1956 to 1961, it declined only two points."[8]

In his advocacy of the War on Poverty, however, Dr. Heller chose to ignore, at least publicly, a number of significant Lampman findings. One was that the Lampman estimate of 9.3 million poor families was too high because it failed to account for non-money income, spending savings, receipt of gifts, borrowing and consumption of assets. Another was that all those counted as poor were not desperately seeking good job opportunities since one-third of them were children and between one-fourth and one-fifth were elderly.[9]

President Kennedy, however, saw only the Heller memo and not the original Lampman findings. Here, in Dr. Heller's own words, is what happened next:

"By October, President Kennedy had given us a green light to pull together a set of proposals for a 1964 attack on poverty. . . . I had a crew working on gathering anti-poverty proposals from all over government. The President had as yet given us no guidelines but had said, 'Go ahead and work on it.' I was not entirely sure he was going to put it in his 1964 program until about 7:30 the evening of the 19th.

"I called Mrs. Lincoln [Secretary to President Kennedy] and asked whether I could see the President for a moment. She said, 'Sure, if you hurry.' When I got there, John-John followed me into the President's office. After we shooed him out, I asked the President whether he wanted our work to go forward on the assumption that the anti-poverty measures would be part of his 1964 legislative program. His answer was an unhesitating, 'Yes, and let me see your proposals within a couple of weeks.'

"Four tragic days later, on the evening of November 23 [President Kennedy was killed November 22], the very first matter that I took up with President Johnson was the anti-poverty program. His immediate response was, 'That's my kind of program. I want you to move full speed ahead on it.'"

Dr. Heller indeed moved like the wind. He consulted virtually every government agency to see if it had any

legislation stalled on Capitol Hill which might slide through
Congress in an anti-poverty package. Thus he acquired
quickly a large legislative bundle. The only really new
idea for legislation evolved from conversations Dr. Heller
had with Attorney General Robert Kennedy, Budget Bureau Director Kermit Gordon and Special Assistant to the
President Theodore Sorensen. They talked of having Community Action Centers to coordinate federal facilities at
the local level and give the local poor a voice.

This was enough for the new President. Immediately he
began laying battle plans. Dr. Heller's role was to provide
ideas and justification. Others, as will be shown later, were
to help refine and sell the grand design.

By January 8, 1964, the crash program was moving so
fast that President Johnson declared War on Poverty in
his State of the Union Message. A few days later he explained, "We are going to try to take all of the money that
we think is unnecessarily being spent and take it from the
'haves' and give it to the 'have nots' that need it so much."[10]

A few days after the Message, the Council of Economic
Advisers issued its now-famous Annual Report in which it
said that any family of four with a yearly income below
$3,000 is in poverty. For this figure, the Council relied on
a study by Mollie Orshansky of the Social Security Administration issued in July 1963.

As an admittedly "crude criterion of income adequacy,"
she selected the "economy" and "low cost" food budgets
devised by the Department of Agriculture, estimated their
cost and the percentage of income they should represent.
From this she arrived at the conclusion that an economy
budget for an urban couple with two children should be
$3,165, and a low-cost budget, $3,955.

While Miss Orshansky was careful to say that the figures
did not apply to farm families, the Council failed to mention it when it cited her figures. It added, "Other studies

have used different market baskets, many of them costing more. On balance, they provide support for using as a boundary, a family whose annual money income from all sources was $3,000. . ."

Subsequently the Task Force on Economic Growth and Opportunity of the U.S. Chamber of Commerce declared, "Because of regional differences in the cost of living and other factors, this definition includes many Americans who are not poor by any standard and would be insulted to be identified as such."[11]

Here's how Herman P. Miller, Special Assistant to the Director of the U.S. Census Bureau, pointed out regional differences in the poverty line:

"Consider, for example, Tunica County, Mississippi, the poorest county in the poorest state. About 8 out of every 10 families in this county have incomes under $3,000 which makes them poor by currently used national standards; yet, 52% own television sets, 46% own automobiles, and 37% own washing machines. These families may be deprived of hope and poor in spirit; but their material possessions, though low by American standards, would be the envy of the great majority of mankind in the world today."

Mr. Miller added the following:

"The national picture shows even more affluence among families with incomes under $3,000 than the above figures suggest. Consider the following facts:

79% own a television set
51% own both a television set and a telephone
73% own a washing machine
19% own a home freezer
65% have a dwelling unit that is not dilapidated and has hot running water and a toilet and a bath for their exclusive use
14% bought a car last year."

Asked about the $3,000 poverty line, one top government economist (not Mr. Miller) declared, "The figure almost literally was picked out of a hat."

Not foreseeing how widely the figure would be used, the Council itself admitted, "No measure of poverty as simple as the one used here would be suitable for determining eligibility for particular benefits or participation in particular programs. [Subsequently it was, many times.] Nevertheless, it provides a valid benchmark for assessing the dimensions of the task of eliminating poverty, setting the broad goals of policy, and measuring our past and future progress toward their achievement."

For 1962 the Council reported that one-fifth of the nation's families, 30 million persons, had incomes below $3,000. This admittedly shaky statistic was the basis for the sweeping statement by President Johnson to the Congress March 16, 1964 that "There are millions of Americans— one fifth of our people—who have not shared in the abundance which has been granted to most of us, and on whom the gates of opportunity have been closed." The Chief Executive did not explain how he arrived at the conclusion that all those with incomes below $3,000 lacked opportunity, or why those with incomes below $3,000 are required to pay income taxes, or why Social Security benefits are cut off before income reaches $3,000, or why over a million members of the U.S. armed forces have incomes under $3,000.

According to the Department of Defense figures, 1,049,248 members of the U.S. armed forces had less than $3,000 yearly income in 1961, including all allowances for food, clothing, shelter, plus the value of federal income tax exemptions.[12] Publication of the Defense Department statistics prompted Senators Barry Goldwater (R., Ariz.) and John G. Tower (R., Tex.) to ask, "Are we to believe that a substantial proportion of our servicemen are among those whom Mr. Johnson claims are engaged in a daily struggle to barely exist?"[13]

Finally, Sargent Shriver (after he had become Director of the Office of Economic Opportunity) conceded, "The definition or the cutoff point that the Council of Economic Advisers has used, of the $3,000, is the subject of criticism, because there is no question about the fact that some people who have an income of more than $3,000 in a particular year are poor, and some people who have less than an income of $3,000 in a particular year are not poor."[14]

Three years later, however, the discredited poverty arithmetic was to inspire this statement from Hyman H. Bookbinder, Assistant Director of the Office of Economic Opportunity:

"The American people now believe what they didn't believe when [Michael] Harrington first wrote his remarkable book, *The Other America*. They know there is an 'other America' of more than 30 million people living in abject poverty. . . ."[15]

A few months later during House debate on 1966 anti-poverty legislation, a Republican, Representative Ogden R. Reid (N.Y.), told his fellow legislators, "There has not been sufficient talk today of the fact that in these United States there are still 32 million Americans living in abject poverty. . . ."[16]

For its part, the Social Security Administration worked on further refinements and justifications of the $3,000 benchmark. It also scrutinized those it had declared "in poverty." By February 1964 it declared that of the 30 million persons with incomes below $3,000, over 11 million were children.

"Particularly alarming," it said, "is the fact that one-third of the children of poor families have less than a grade school education." Without examining the faults of free compulsory education in this connection, the Administration declared, "Unless measures are taken to provide them with further education and training, they will probably perpetuate the poverty of their parents." Thus it echoed

Michael Harrington and provided one of the raisons d'être for the War on Poverty.[17]

By January 1965 Mollie Orshansky discovered the "hidden poor, the 1.7 million elderly and the 1.1 million members of subfamilies, including 600,000 children, whose own income does not permit independent living at a minimum standard but who escape poverty by living in a household with relatives whose combined income is adequate for all."[18]

The following May, Miss Orshansky discovered the "near poor." These include, she said, 15¾ million persons with "incomes above the poverty threshold but still low enough to be considered near poor."[19]

While Dr. Heller and his "experts" struggled with ideas and the justification for the War on Poverty, President Johnson wanted someone to help shape and sell it. He remembered the young and handsome Sargent Shriver. The latter had come to him when Mr. Johnson was Vice President for advice on how to obtain Congressional approval for the Peace Corps. Mr. Shriver had not only carried through brilliantly but was a member of the Kennedy clan by virtue of being married to President Kennedy's sister. Thus President Johnson saw Mr. Shriver as both a good salesman and one who could provide a bridge between the Kennedy and Johnson Administrations. The result was that two weeks after the Kennedy funeral, Sargent Shriver agreed to tackle the War on Poverty.

Having recruited Secretary of Defense Robert S. McNamara and his Whiz Kids to government originally, Mr. Shriver turned to them first and borrowed the Number One Kid, Adam Yarmolinsky, who then bore the title of Special Assistant to the Secretary of Defense.

Between the two of them, Messrs. Shriver and Yarmolinsky put together a so-called Anti-Poverty Task Force to shape and sell the War on Poverty. Some who served on it told me that the original plan was to have Mr. Yarmolinsky head the War on Poverty, thereby leaving Mr. Shriver free to remain as head of the Peace Corps. Others said the former was lined up by members of the Task Force and the White House to be first deputy to Mr. Shriver at anti-poverty headquarters.

Meantime, however, Mr. Yarmolinsky had proposed a Pentagon regulation which would have forbidden personnel at military bases to patronize nearby communities unless they were racially integrated. This incurred so much wrath from influential Southern members of Congress that the Administration sent Mr. Yarmolinsky back to the Pentagon after he had completed his work on the Task Force. It was feared that designating him as an anti-poverty chieftain would have jeopardized Congressional support for the War on Poverty.

Despite its interesting composition, no official list of the membership of the Task Force ever was published. Among the first hired was Richard Boone, then on the White House Special Projects Staff, acting as a consultant to the President's Committee on Juvenile Delinquency. Earlier he had been a Chicago police captain, directing a street gangs program, which he said meant "working with fighting gangs in Chicago." He also had set up a new juvenile bureau system at the Illinois State Reformatory while serving as administrative assistant to the superintendent.

Mr. Boone was one of the most important members of the Task Force because he was in charge of the community action part, which, as noted, was the only really new concept. In addition, as will be shown later, it is the most politically potent and dangerous part of the War on Poverty. The idea was to mobilize all resources and the poor themselves for concerted attacks on poverty and its causes.

Those who gave Mr. Boone the necessary go-ahead signal on community action were Messrs. Theodore Sorensen, Kermit Gordon and Robert Kennedy.

Later Mr. Boone became Executive Director of the Citizens' Crusade Against Poverty, which achieved nation-wide notoriety in April 1965 in Washington when it booed Sargent Shriver out of a meeting and staged a near-riot. After that the CCAP began advancing to its announced goal of preparing a thousand workers to train the poor to demonstrate, agitate and otherwise participate in political action. The organization hopes ultimately to establish a nation-wide network of political cadres of the poor.

At the same time that Mr. Boone worked on the legislative proposals for community action, Jack Conway of the Industrial Union Department of the AFL-CIO drew up programs for administration, assuming the proposals would become law. As Mr. Conway himself told it, "We have participated in CCAP since the beginning."[20] Indeed, in mid-December 1966 CCAP named Mr. Conway to the steering committee for a National Grievance and Information Center with the avowed aim of providing information to the poor on the availability of federal money and how to challenge "arbitrary" decisions in dispensing it.[21]

Before becoming involved with the CCAP, however, Messrs. Boone and Conway served as Office of Economic Opportunity officials immediately after the agency was created. Mr. Conway became OEO Deputy Director and Mr. Boone was Director of Program Policy and Development for the Community Action Program.

Indeed, the Task Force provided the nucleus of the top staff of OEO, with most of them earning $27,000 a year. William P. Kelly, who was responsible for obtaining facilities and services for the Task Force, became Assistant OEO Director for Management. Glenn Ferguson worked on VISTA (Volunteers in Service to America) on the Task Force and left the Peace Corps to become Assistant OEO Director for VISTA.

Frederick O'R. Hayes, who had worked with Mr. Boone

on community action on the Task Force, left the Urban Renewal Administration to become Associate OEO Director of the Community Action Program.

Another Force member, Edgar May, became Assistant Director for Inspection, having previously held the post of Director of Public Welfare Projects for the State Charities Aid Association of New York, a private organization. This is the same Mr. May who wrote, "Negroes will have to furnish more than civil rights demonstrations to make this [integration] 'necessity' both obtainable and, more importantly, workable. The void of Negro leadership in the slums of many communities will have to be filled. There has been too little effort expended by Negroes for Negroes."[22]

Mr. May also was a vocal exponent of the idea that the federal government should stimulate the economy to relieve poverty. In his book *The Wasted Americans*, published in 1964, Mr. May wrote, "For the economists who have examined poverty, the key answer is within the nation's economic growth rate ... There is little doubt that America's industrial system must expand at a faster rate than it has if the war babies grown to manhood and the widening shadow of automation are not to overtake it."

By March 1966, Administration implementation of this theory had led to so much trouble that President Johnson appealed to industry leaders to cut their investment for expansion because of inflationary competition for labor and materials.

The Task Force member responsible for the Job Corps was Daniel Moynihan, then Assistant Secretary of Labor. Mr. Moynihan is the author of the famous Labor Department study, *The Negro Family*, which declared, "The family structure of lower class Negroes is highly unstable, and in many urban centers is approaching complete breakdown." Strange as it may seem, this statement was by the same man who recommended the establishment of job camps where youngsters remain in residence, away from their families, for as long as two years.

Careful reading of Mr. Moynihan's study gives a hint of his leftist political thinking. He said the U.S. must give Negroes more than equality of opportunity because "to the extent that winners imply losers, equality of opportunity almost insures inequality of results." According to Mr. Moynihan, "The principal challenge of the next phase of the Negro revolution is to make certain that equality of results will now follow. If we do not, there will be no social peace in the United States for generations."

Subsequently, Mr. Moynihan declared on a national television show, "The sad fact of life is that violence works sometimes."

On the same program, Daniel H. Watts, editor of *Liberator*, said, "Let the whites keep civil rights and give me money and power instead. . . . What happened in Watts is just a prologue."

To this statement, Mr. Moynihan responded, "The things Watts asks for are not things a person shouldn't ask for. We don't need the trouble he threatens because we can give him what he asks for."

Later Mr. Moynihan told a Senate subcommittee that government programs were "too much concentrated on doing things for the poor and not on giving them money" to work out their own lives. He advocated a national allowance for poor families at an estimated cost of $9 billion a year.[23]

The Task Force borrowed Stephen J. Pollak from the Civil Rights Division of the Justice Department to draft the VISTA portion of the OEO bill. The idea was to have a domestic version of the Peace Corps to help the poor. It was the brainstorm of Bobby Kennedy and had been promoted unsuccessfully as a National Service Corps back in

1963 by the President's Task Force on a National Service Program. Mr. Pollak said he accepted the suggestion of Representative Frank Thompson, Jr. (D., N.J.) to change the name to VISTA.

James L. Sundquist, then Deputy Under Secretary of Labor and former Administrative Assistant to Senator Joseph S. Clark (D., Pa.), spearheaded the Task Force work on rural poverty. Since other Task Force leaders were interested primarily in urban problems, Mr. Sundquist and his assistants worked alone most of the time. The latter included James Patton, President of the Farmers Union, and Joseph C. Doherty, then Administrative Assistant to Howard Bertsch, head of the Farmers Home Administration.

The recommendations they came up with were so far out, even for the other Task Force members, that the latter left it to the rural experts to sell their program on Capitol Hill. For instance, in a scheme reminiscent of Communistic land reform, they proposed to have the Agriculture Department purchase land and redistribute it to the poor. Congress turned down the idea.

The Farmers Union was the only farm organization the Task Force asked for ideas; it did not approach others like the American Farm Bureau or the National Grange. The Farmers Union is considered the most liberal of these three major farm groups.

Asked why the Task Force never issued a formal report, one member declared, "We were working under such forced draft that there wasn't time; we were running our papers to Capitol Hill as fast as they came out of the typewriters."

As a matter of fact, the House Education and Labor Committee did not see the complete Economic Opportunity bill until the day it opened hearings on it, March 17, 1964. The usual Congressional procedure is to make a pro-

posed law available for several days in advance of hearings
to allow time for study, particularly for a complicated one
like the anti-poverty bill. It ran 70-odd pages, had seven
titles, nine separate programs and established a new bureaucratic apparatus. Its scope was vast enough to affect every
section, community and person in the U.S.

With the exception of the interruption of the Easter
recess, the Committee held six weeks of hearings on the bill,
starting at 9 a.m. instead of the usual 10 a.m., and several
times going on until 8 p.m.

Mr. Shriver was the first Administration witness. Rather
than follow the tradition of rotating between Democrats
and Republicans for questioning, the Committee Chairman
went straight down the line of Democrats. After letting
each one use 20 to 25 minutes, he restricted each Republican to five minutes.[24]

Representative Peter Freylinghusen (R., N.J.), ranking
minority member of the Committee, complained that "on
numerous occasions Republicans were ruthlessly denied an
adequate opportunity to question witnesses."[25]

In all those six weeks, no Republican witnesses were
allowed. Finally, after great insistence, the Republicans
were allotted three days for all their witnesses to testify.
This was the same length of time the bill's single leading
proponent, Mr. Shriver, spent in testimony. This led Representative Freylinghuysen to voice this complaint to the
House:

"In the course of this rush, we were obliged to refuse the
requests of witnesses to appear. Some who had been offered
an opportunity to testify did not have that opportunity.
They were simply stricken from the witness list. A number
of others who sought the opportunity were not given it."[26]

Following the conclusion of the open hearings, the
Democrats met in caucus to consider the bill. At this point
the Republican members complained that it was in reality

an executive session for putting the bill in a final form on which the Committee could agree before reporting it out. They contended that they should not be excluded from this so-called "marking-up" session because the minority wouldn't have the strength to keep the bill from being reported favorably after such majority action. When the Republicans got nowhere with this argument, the first demonstration in the War on Poverty took place. The Republicans sat in chairs outside the Committee chamber and notified the press that they were waiting to be called to the Committee meeting.

The maneuver was to no avail, however. By the time the Republicans got in, the Democrats already had marked up the bill, and they then presented it to the Republicans as a fait accompli. Since the latter naturally constituted a minority, they lacked the votes to overturn the action of the majority.

Representative Freylinghuysen commented later, "The executive sessions on the bill . . . were marked by a virtual absence of meaningful debate and discussion, the indiscriminate invoking of the previous question, the one-sided rejection of all substantive Republican amendments, and the equally one-sided approval of numerous Democratic amendments. The whole performance of the committee from beginning to end has been marked by extreme and ill-considered partisanship on the part of the chairman of the committee and his Democratic majority."[27]

The Committee even refused to issue a print showing the changes it made in the original bill. Commented Representative Freylinghuysen, "Since almost 100 amendments have been made in the text of the original bill—many of them six pages or longer—this latest move makes it impossible for any member of the committee, much less any member of the Congress, to say with certainty and in what manner the original bill has been altered. In all my years in Congress this is the first committee action of this type that I've ever witnessed."[28]

The Senate gave the bill even more abbreviated treatment. Only two Administration witnesses testified before the Senate Labor Committee. Mr. Shriver presented a one-page statement explaining the bill, and then spent portions of three days answering questions. Secretary W. Willard Wirtz completed his testimony in fifteen minutes. After a single executive session, the Committee hurried the bill to the Senate calendar.[29]

Neither the Banking and Currency Committee nor the Agriculture Committee ever considered the bill. Here is what Senators Barry Goldwater (R., Ariz.) and John G. Tower (R., Tex.) said about that in their minority views:

"At least two of the key titles of the bill do not properly fall within the jurisdiction of this [Labor] committee. Title IV, the employment and investment incentives program, is to be administered by the Small Business Administration. The SBA, and legislation regarding it, comes within the purview of the Banking and Currency Committee. Nevertheless, this committee's lack of expertise in this area did not prevent the administration from throwing the small business program in with the rest of the poverty grab bag for our consideration.

"Perhaps a more flagrant perversion of the functions of the committee system can be observed in the bill's inclusion of Title III; Special Programs to Combat Poverty in Rural Areas. The proposals included within this title infringe upon important federal agricultural programs and would affect our entire agricultural economy. The Agriculture Committee, whose members are knowledgeable in this complex and specialized area, should, if any rational procedure was followed, have considered this title. That the proper committee was bypassed and our committee, whose members do not include a single Agriculture Committee member, undertook to legislate a farm program is symptomatic of the errors which can infect those who act in haste. In short, this legislative bungle illustrates that almost 'anything goes' where President Johnson's War on Poverty is concerned."[30]

The protesting senators acquired few followers, however, despite the momentous and dangerous proposals of the War on Poverty. Representative William B. Widnall (R., N. J.) undoubtedly gave a clue for the reason when he said, "Anybody who gets up and speaks against a slogan like that is considered automatically a man without a heart, without humanitarianism, without any concern for the people who are the underprivileged."[31]

A couple of years later Representative B. F. Sisk (D., Calif.) admitted on the floor of the House, "Lord knows, no politician is crazy enough to oppose the poor."[32]

2

The Beginning of OEO

A few short months after President Johnson gave the go-ahead, the War on Poverty became part of the laws of the land with passage of the Economic Opportunity Act on August 11, 1964, and subsequent quick Presidential approval. Because of inadequate study by Congress, many members obviously did not understand what they had voted for.

The act authorized establishment of the Office of Economic Opportunity (OEO) within the Executive Office of the President to operate a host of programs on its own and oversee others operated by various federal agencies. As will be shown later, it launched a flood of uncoordinated and untried programs on a crash basis and gave unprecedented power to the OEO Director.

While formal establishment of OEO had to await a Congressional appropriation (which was given in October 1964 for $793 million), this didn't stop the crash program. The official assignment of the Task Force ended with the legislative recommendations, but members and staff, totaling about two hundred, stayed on to prepare the way for OEO. This was a remarkable feat in view of the fact that Congress had appropriated no funds for that purpose. The

Administration felt that a technicality like that could not be allowed to delay the War on Poverty.

The Force squatted in free makeshift quarters in the abandoned old Court of Claims building at 17th Street and Pennsylvania Avenue, N.W. until the roof literally fell in because of excavation next door (no casualties). After that it persuaded the U.S. Information Agency to let it borrow space the latter held in the old Emergency Hospital at New York Avenue and 17 Street, N.W., then being rehabilitated. Since most of the partitions had been torn out, desks were set up in open bays.

Finally the Force persuaded the General Services Administration (GSA) to let it take over the New Colonial Hotel at M and 15 Streets, N.W. which actually was very old. Said one member of the Force, "They had it under lease and couldn't get anybody else to occupy it except the Board of Geographic Names which didn't need all of it like we did. We almost literally dragged the Board out screaming and took over our new free space."

The Force also was able to establish a line of credit and borrow typewriters from IBM, Remington Rand and Smith Corona and calculators from Friden. Then it all but emptied the GSA surplus warehouse in nearby Alexandria, Va., even taking desks of 1930 vintage with stuck drawers.

The various members and their staff were on loan from their parent agencies which meant that they were receiving their salaries from other arms of the government while working for the Task Force. The Defense Department was paying Mr. Yarmolinsky at the rate of $20,000 a year during all the months he served as Deputy Director of the Task Force.

Mr. Kelly, who showed ingenuity in finding facilities and services for the Task Force, carried out this responsibility on a full-time basis starting in May 1964, but drew pay at an annual rate of $24,500 from the Agency for Interna-

tional Development until January 1965 when he went on
the Office of Economic Opportunity payroll at $27,000 a
year as Assistant Director for Management.

While the aforementioned Mr. Sundquist worked full
time on the Task Force, he was drawing pay at the rate of
$24,500 as Deputy Under Secretary of Agriculture.

So it went. Even the secretarial staff was paid out of
funds for other agencies. The General Accounting Office
raised the question of the propriety of government employees doing one thing while being paid for another. The
answer from the White House was that it has authority to
detail employees from interested agencies to work on the
development of programs. Where an agency's interest is
questioned, the employees can be paid out of the President's
Emergency Fund, it was maintained.

The GAO accepted the answer. It did not raise the further question of the right of employees to continue to work
on detail after programs have been recommended and before Congress has authorized them. No one questioned the
legitimate interest of the Defense Department and AID in
the War on Poverty.

Thus the Task Force is the reason the OEO was able to
spring into action with remarkably short lead time.

The first, biggest and most urgent problem OEO faced
when it officially started was to sell its programs. Obviously
it could get nowhere without requests for the largesse it
was ready to dispense. As has been noted, however, it had
an enormously complicated statute which even some law-
makers did not understand. The big question was how to
sell it to local governments and the impoverished, many of
whom were not even literate.

Secretary of Defense McNamara, Mr. Shriver's recruit to
government, suggested that the latter toss the problem to
Holmes Brown who had worked under Mr. McNamara as
Director of Public Relations for the Ford Division at Ford

Motor Co. and then held a similar post at Martin Marietta. Together, Messrs. McNamara and Shriver persuaded Mr. Brown to leave Martin Marietta to become Director of Public Affairs for OEO. The result was that Mr. Brown was at OEO and ready for action the moment everything became legal and official.

Mr. Brown was very proud of what he did. As this was being written, he held the post of Vice President of American Airlines. When I asked him to explain his role in the War on Poverty, he was eager to do so. He flew down to Washington from his New York offices and spent hours talking with me at the Admirals' Club at Washington National Airport. He told me that OEO felt that quick action and nation-wide publicity would sell the War on Poverty. In his quiet, almost shy manner, the master publicist explained how he got the agency what it wanted.

Showing extraordinary savoir faire in the business of obtaining federal funds, Detroit had started preparing a community action program while the legislation was pending. Thus, at passage, it was ready to make use of OEO money.

For the first big OEO announcement, Messrs. Shriver and Brown flew down to the Texas White House to announce a community action grant to Detroit. They felt that the entourage of reporters accompanying the President would ensure nation-wide publicity, and they were right. The subtle message here was that if other cities wanted to get similar grants, they should get on the ball quickly, like Detroit, before the money ran out.

Nevertheless, the requests did not come in fast enough to suit OEO. Was this simply because potential applicants didn't know about the program? Or was it because they recognized the Community Action Program (CAP) as the most dangerous part of the War on Poverty because of its potential for creating a new militant political group of the poor, as advocated by Socialist Michael Harrington? The

answers probably never will be known. (But the alacrity
with which communities later jumped on the grant wagon
indicated that many of those who had fears managed to
overcome them at the prospect of free federal money.)

At any rate, what OEO officials did next was to examine
Census figures to locate the nation's "poverty pockets."
Said Mr. Brown, "We tried to spark some communities in
desperate shape just by things like personal phone calls. The
area around Akron was a case in point. We got somebody
who had worked at Ohio University to call someone in
Akron, who took a bus to Washington and got told what
to do."

Then OEO used 100 college students who were working
as volunteer "government interns" during the summer to
learn the processes of government. The interns fanned out
to the "pockets" on weekends and literally knocked on
doors to spread the word that there was money in Washington just for the asking to pay for 90% of community
action programs if someone, anyone, could guarantee 10%
local funding which could be in the form of facilities instead of money. Eventually the pioneering work of these
"interns" was taken up by half a million volunteers.

Still, the promoters encountered some resistance, particularly in the rural South. In the view of Mr. Brown this was
because "almost every rural county is run by about four
people, and they were not about to let anybody break up
their power structure."

The OEO got around this problem to some extent by
putting together programs based on four or five counties.
By getting one liberal from each county, it frequently obtained a group adequate to guarantee the 10% local contribution and get a CAP started. Mr. Brown estimated that
in the early days OEO put together about 20 or 30 of such
groups.

Once the time came to announce the new CAP grants,

Mr. Brown realized that if the agency announced them one at a time, it would get nothing more than a play by the local press concerned. His goal, however, was nation-wide publicity which would spur other areas to apply for CAP's.

Accordingly, he explained, "We decided to bunch our hits and make a major announcement every month of all the local programs." The next few announcements came from the White House in Washington, with details supplied at the anti-poverty headquarters in the impoverished-looking New Colonial Hotel. This worked until irate Congressmen insisted upon making the announcements themselves first to their constituents. OEO, however, continued to make its announcements in bunches, hoping for maximum nation-wide publicity, and reducing the need to supply many details on individual programs.

While the initial community action programs were being ballyhooed, OEO was working out a much more elaborate public relations campaign. For the sake of simplicity, Mr. Brown decided that initially it should concentrate on the Job Corps. Here he saw the possibility for simple appeals which everyone could understand—for the general public, the opportunity to give a chance to youngsters who had never had a chance before; for the youngsters themselves, a chance to be somebody.

The stumbling block to putting thees ideas across, however, was that OEO did not feel it could legally spend money for advertising. Remembering how the Advertising Council had promoted government bonds without charge, Mr. Brown appealed to it to advertise the Job Corps. He was turned down on the grounds that the War on Poverty was political.

In desperation, he went directly to the television, radio, newspaper and billboard industries, to movie stars, athletes and business leaders. Appealing both to patriotism and humanitarianism, he asked them to donate some of their time and/or space to help the first phase of the War on Poverty by urging boys to join the Job Corps.

Said Mr. Brown, "Nobody had ever tried before to get the full-fledged participation of American business in such a campaign except in war, but this was war, War on Poverty, and we had no trouble in marshalling the forces." Movie and television stars who donated their time for TV film clips promoting the Job Corps included Jackie Gleason, Donna Reed, Betty Furness, Andy Williams, Andy Griffith, Danny Kaye, Dick Van Dyke and Harry Belafonte. Even rock and roller Murray the K (Murray Kaufman) contributed his services, and Columbia Broadcasting System gave him an hour of free network time to promote the Job Corps.

Athletes included Johnny Unitas, Sandy Koufax and Rocky Marciano. Business leaders included Keith Funston of the New York Stock Exchange, Edgar Kaiser of Kaiser Industries, Roger Sonnabend of the Hotel Corporation of America, Robert Brooker of Montgomery Ward & Co., Harold Geneen of International Telephone & Telegraph and Sol M. Linowitz of Xerox Corp.

The Brown approach was to tell these people that there were 30 million poverty-stricken people in the country and that the teenagers among them particularly deserved a chance for a better life. The Job Corps would give this chance by providing the technical tools to get and hold a job, he said. Without this, he warned, they would probably spend their lives on welfare at a cost of $125,000 for each family.

That was enough. Mr. Brown says he can't recall a single person he approached ever having asked for details about how the Job Corps would operate. Outlining the problem was enough to obtain their help.

OEO estimated that well over $4.5 million worth of talent was donated for spot Job Corps announcements for

700 TV stations and 4,200 radio stations. The stations donated their facilities for making and broadcasting the spots, and some still ran them a year later when they had blank time. The only cost to OEO was the manufacture and mailing of the film strips which was "peanuts," according to Mr. Brown.

Even the Orange Bowl in Miami agreed to a free TV Job Corps commercial in color. Without cost, billboards across the country also blatantly boosted the Corps.

Newspapers ran full-page ads free. Facetiously the *Daily Princetonian*, the student newspaper at Princeton University, obliged by running a free ad urging its readers to join the Job Corps. "That, of course, was ridiculous," said Mr. Brown, "but we simply made the request to every paper in the U.S."

Job Corps posters in YMCA's all over the country carried a straightforward and simple exhortation, "Be somebody. Join the Job Corps." Stacks of application cards were placed near each poster and pre-addressed to The White House, U.S.A. The Post Office Department nearly flipped over this, but simmered down when Mr. Brown agreed to include a zip code in small print so that the cards would indeed reach the OEO which isn't in the White House at all.

The upshot of all the activity was that OEO was snowed under with applications for the Job Corps. Within one month it received 200,000, and, in the words of Mr. Brown, "Nobody knew what the hell to do with them."

OEO never got around to distributing a Li'l Abner comic book promoting the Job Corps, created gratis by Al Capp. The agency had 435,000 copies of *Li'l Abner and the Creatures from Drop-Outer Space* printed at a cost of $25,000 and then stored at $125 a month.[1]

Other developments involving the Job Corps are discussed in the chapter on that subject.

Next Mr. Brown refocused his attention on community action and told Mr. Shriver he wanted a simple success story to sell it. In response, the latter came up with the idea of Head Start, pre-school training for poor youngsters. He figured that the Economic Opportunity Act permitted this even though it did not specifically mention it. Public acceptance seemed certain, Messrs. Shriver and Brown figured, because nobody would oppose help for poor little children. Moreover, OEO hoped to use the children as a means of getting the parents interested in participating in community action.

Here again the agency faced the problem of obtaining applications. In this case Mr. Brown ignored the legislative ban on paying for advertising and turned to robotyping which can produce thousands of letters with the appearance of an original. During one weekend, he says, OEO engaged virtually every robotyper on the Eastern Seaboard and turned out 50,000 Head Start letters.

Under the signature of Mr. Shriver, these went to every mayor in the country and every school superintendent, grade school principal, county supervisor, health commissioner and welfare commissioner. The message they carried was that OEO would pay 90% of the costs of pre-school training for impoverished children if the communities would pay 10%. It added that the 10% could be in the form of school space and that the program would be conducted in the summer when much such space was unused.

Each letter requested the recipient to fill out and return an accompanying card immediately and warned that those who failed to qualify within three weeks might lose out altogether. It asked for estimates of the number of poor children in the city, whether the official wanted Head Start, and whether he wanted more information.[2]

At the same time the letters and cards were going out, Mrs. Lady Bird Johnson held a White House Conference on Head Start, to which she invited 300 women, including the wives of the governors of every state in the union and the heads of various women's organizations like the Women's Clubs and the American Legion Auxiliary. She asked them to hold similar conferences after they went home.

Mrs. Johnson succeeded so well that Mrs. Orval Faubus went home to Arkansas and held the first integrated meeting at the Governor's mansion, and women came from all over the state to start the ball rolling for Head Start. Up North, Mrs. William Scranton, wife of the Republican Governor of Pennsylvania, held a similar conference.

Then the cards started pouring in. The offer of something for nothing held its age-old appeal. OEO, which figured it had funds sufficient for Head Start programs in 300 communities, got back 7,500 cards.

Twice OEO went directly to the White House over the head of the Budget Bureau, saying the demand for Head Start was so great that it needed more money. It made Mrs. Johnson Honorary Chairman of Head Start, and ended up with $100 million to begin programs in 1,000 communities, instead of the $19 million originally budgeted for 300 communities.

Still OEO could not honor all requests for Head Start programs. To get maximum Congressional support, it aimed at approving programs in every state and nearly every Congressional district.

The next problem was to persuade parents to enroll their children in the program. Again Mr. Brown used the TV ballyhoo technique, even persuading the famous pediatrician-author, Dr. Benjamin Spock, to make a free TV film clip urging parents to enroll their little ones. Again Mr. Brown also sent out the volunteers to knock on doors.

What happened in Chicago shows the desperate measures to which OEO resorted. About ten days before the Head

Start program was due to begin there, the agency, which had been counting on having 24,000 children enrolled, discovered that the actual figure was only four thousand.

With the help of Chicago Mayor Richard J. Daley, OEO launched a ten-day enrollment drive, using all city employees, including policemen, social workers and teachers. These personally contacted parents and urged them to enroll their children in Head Start. Some of the press was highly critical of this maneuver at the time, charging that parents feared reprisals should they not follow the advice of city employees, particularly the policemen and social workers.

At any rate, the scheme worked, and within the ten-day schedule, Chicago enrollment zoomed from 4,000 to 23,804. The upshot, however, was that 28% of the children who took part in the Chicago program were not poor.* Moreover, Republican Congressional investigators found that in 20% of the cases, administrators did not even know the family income.[3] According to Republican members of the House Poverty Subcommittee, "Very little solicitation was done in several hard-core poverty areas because teachers were afraid to enter those sections of the city."[4]

Nationwide, to make sure that those who enrolled actually showed up, the volunteers went so far as to drive the children to and from the Head Start classes.

Again trying to obtain maximum publicity, OEO scheduled Head Start openings nationwide for Independence Day. Mr. Brown persuaded Xerox Corporation to pay for special Head Start flags which were raised with great fanfare at the openings. Rather than rely on the local folks to publicize this, OEO sent special press packets to all the news media in every Head Start community.

Thus the War on Poverty began on the premise that

---

* Annual income of $3,000 or less for a family of three and $500 extra for each additional member, up to $6,000.

poverty in the most prosperous nation in the world constituted an overwhelming problem which had to be dealt with on a crash basis even though no one could be sure of the number of the poor, the causes of their poverty, or the means of ending it. Both the executive and legislative branches of government ostensibly assumed that expensive federal action was essential to deal with a problem on which they had inadequate knowledge. How many actually believed this assumption and how many used poverty as an excuse for fostering Socialism probably will never be known.

At any rate, the nation plunged pell mell into a crash program to carry out untried and revolutionary ideas without adequate consideration or even preliminary testing on a small scale.

3

The Beginning
of the
Job Corps

In gathering up moribund bills for the anti-poverty package, the Task Force resurrected the Youth Conservation Corps bill Vice President Hubert H. Humphrey had introduced in 1956 when he was a Senator. It called for establishment of camps like those of the Civilian Conservation Corps, spawned by the New Deal during the Great Depression. While the measure had won Senate passage in 1959, it failed to reach the floor of either the Senate or House in subsequent years.

From this bill the Task Force borrowed the idea of residential camps for boys aged 16 to 22 years to receive on-the-job training, work experience and education. The conservation part, however, was dropped since emphasis was to be on training the boys could use when they returned home.

Subsequently, when prospects for passage appeared dismal, conservation was put back in the bill. Representative

John P. Saylor (R., Pa.) then introduced an amendment specifying that the Youth Conservation Corps must constitute 40% of Job Corps enrollees. This won the vitally necessary votes of the conservationists and resulted in passage of the Job Corps legislation. (To pick up all possible votes the House Education and Labor Committee had the bill cover girls as well as boys.)

Proponents attempted to justify the program by saying the nation had one million unemployed teenagers who needed help right away. Over and over I was told, "Those kids won't wait, and there are a million of 'em!"

Of that million, however, the majority were dependents, and only 141,000 were members of families with incomes below the poverty line of $3,000.[1] Nevertheless, they were the basis for a program aimed at enrolling 100,000 in the Job Corps.

In addition, the new bill failed to meet objections which had been voiced to the Humphrey bill. What is more, it used an approach devised about three decades ago when employment demands and training needs for young people were appreciably different. Also, the vocational training offered was insufficient to meet modern needs.

The make-work conservation program would take boys off the streets for six months to two years and then send them back with no better skills than they had before. Moreover, the educational portion put the federal government in direct charge of schooling at the camps.

As with the Humphrey bill, the argument was given that the measure was needed because of lack of local funds to help the boys. Job Corps projects, however, were not confined to areas lacking the financial resources.

Representatives Albert H. Quie (R., Minn.) and Charles E. Goodell (R., N. Y.), leading the Republican opposition, urged Congress to try the Job Corps on an experimental basis first with a residential training center right in Washington. But the Congress and President Johnson were more interested in fast, impressive action. Indeed, Mr. Yarmolinsky had stated that, before the November elections, the Administration felt "the necessity of starting the Job Corps in a clearly visible way through the country."[2]

The result was that Congress rushed out the Job Corps legislation with the stated purpose "to prepare for the responsibilities of citizenship and to increase the employability of young men and young women aged 16 through 21 by providing them in rural and urban residential centers with education, vocational training, useful work experience, including work directed toward the conservation of natural resources and other appropriate activities."

"Just picture me," said Otis Singletary, the first Job Corps Director. "There I was with a desk, a secretary and a bill requiring OEO not only to increase the employability of youngsters but to prepare them for the responsibilities of citizenship. This latter requirement was so vague that I was not certain how I was supposed to do it or how anyone could measure my success."

Because of White House orders for fast action, and the problems connected with speed and vague legislation, several OEO officials admitted that they were able to take care only of what they considered "crisis items." This meant they had no time at all for evaluating what they were doing, finding employment for Job Corpsmen and examining results. Moreover, they gave totally inadequate time to estimating costs and obtaining approval of local communities for establishment of Job Corps centers in their midsts.

The new law authorized the OEO Director to make any arrangements he desired regarding selection of enrollees, discipline, removal, quarters, equipment, services, transportation and "other expenses as the Director may deem necessary or appropriate for their needs." Thus Aristocrat

Shriver was given unprecedented power in dealing with boys and girls with whom he had had virtually no contact. His experience as Director of the Peace Corps was cited as qualifying him for the new chore. The Peace Corps youngsters, however, were not impoverished and with nowhere else to go. Whether he realized it or not, he had an entirely different problem.

Mr. Shriver, however, lived up to his reputation as a promoter and man of action. He also gained a new one through misuse of his unprecedented powers.

As noted earlier, the nationwide ballyhoo for the Job Corps resulted in such an avalanche of applications that nobody knew what to do with them. No decision was made then on whether to take youngsters from the bottom of the barrel or to select those with the greatest promise. (Indeed, in the summer of 1966 such a decision still had not been made.) Illiterates and those with several years of high school education, hardened criminals and boy scouts, men of 21 and boys of 16, all were put together in the same groups.

OEO paid $80 a head for screening applicants, with the result that the applications were rushed through in record time. Information supplied in applications was not checked until after the applicants had taken up residence. If they chose not to make known their criminal records, OEO and its centers remained in the dark. Even when boys with criminal records were knowingly accepted, the centers to which they were assigned were not informed of the nature of their crimes. In many instances it was impossible to check the criminal records because state laws prohibited releasing such information on juveniles.

OEO denied disciplinary authority to the centers, preferring to handle disciplinary problems directly from Washington in its slow, bureaucratic, bungling way. When this resulted in complete breakdowns of discipline at many centers and in outbreaks of violence, OEO paid for lawyers, fines and other costs of the Job Corps criminals.

OEO turned down repeated suggestions for setting up screening centers which would have given the organization time to check on the background of the youths, to screen out the misfits and serious troublemakers and to orient the enrollees to camp life, besides outfitting them and giving them medical examinations. OEO wanted to get the show on the road right away and turned down screening centers as too expensive and time-consuming. It failed to balance this expense against the expense of the disasters (which should have been foreseen) occurring because of improper screening.

Also turned down as too slow were regular Civil Service procedures for hiring staffs for the centers. As in the case of the enrollees, the information supplied in their applications was not checked until after they started work. As a result, in some instances criminals ended up on the staffs. OEO extended them the same courtesies as the enrollees; when instructors were arrested, OEO paid their costs.

The excuse for the crash Job Corps program and slipshod enrollment and hiring methods was that there was an urgent need to give the youths sorely needed vocational training. In determining what training was sorely needed, however, OEO relied on the Bureau of Labor Statistics which published employment and unemployment figures but had no information on job vacancies. This inspired Representative Thomas B. Curtis (R., Mo.) to comment that he didn't see how Sargent Shriver could conduct a War on Poverty without obtaining such information.[3]

In the great rush OEO also neglected to set any minimum requirements for the training. (Two years later it still had not done so.) Moreover, many centers opened before they were equipped to give any vocational training at all. Thus, many law-abiding enrollees with promise found they were in danger of their lives, hundreds of miles from home in a hostile environment, without the superb vocational training they had been promised and with little to do with their leisure time.

Pre-entrance medical examinations were so inadequate that the government paid plane fare to the training centers for many who were physically unable to take part in the Job Corps. Others had communicable diseases which they transmitted to other enrollees before being examined at the centers. Still others had severe emotional problems which not only made it impossible for them to benefit from the Job Corps but also disrupted the centers to which they were assigned.

The Job Corps center at Mountain Home, Idaho, provides a classic example of what was wrong with the program. Ostensibly operated as a conservation camp by the Bureau of Land Management, it was actually under the immediate control of OEO.

Based upon what recruiters had told them, the youths expected to do welding and to work with other tools. However, the center opened without any vocational workshops. In desperation, it rented a warehouse and put the boys to work in it making signs.

Since, like all conservation camps, it was out in the country, transportation for the boys was important. Buses ordered were not delivered for months after the opening, however. This made it extremely important to have recreational facilities at the center. These were practically nonexistent. The recreation room was too small to accommodate all the boys; the gym was not built until many months after the opening. The only gym available to the boys was the one at the Mountain Home Air Force Base, fifteen miles away, which they used at the convenience of the Air Force—when transportation was available.

This would have meant a difficult situation for the best of boys. But of the first 35 enrolled at Mountain Home, eighteen had criminal records. Charles H. Stoddard, Director of the Bureau of Land Management (BLM) which operated the camp under the direction of OEO, received the following information on the eighteen, on October 19, 1965:

1. First offense 5/23/60, indecent assault—disposition, delinquent ward, probation until further order.
   Second offense—runaway, 9/25/63, probation.
   Third offense—malicious conversion and runaway.
   Fourth offense—auto theft, 3/65, probation.
   Fifth offense—runaway, 4/65, probation.

2. Burglary, robbery, malicious conduct 11/19/62. Committed Hawaiian youth correctional facility. Released on parole 2/5/64. Evidently still on parole.

3. Drunk minor 10/21/62, released. Carrying concealed weapon 10/7/63, released. Burglary first degree 4/22/64. Three-year probation, disturbing the peace 9/26/64, arrested. Disturbing the peace 9/28/65, $29 fine. Still on probation until 4/21/67.

4. Auto theft 8/7/59, dismissed when family moved. Discharging pistol in city limits 5/27/60, probation. Battery 9/30/60, committed to Fouts Springs Boys Ranch. Released from probation 2/15/62. Probation officer recommended rejection by Job Corps.

5. Petty theft 5/28/62, wardship and probation. Incorrigible 10/30/62, probation. Intoxication at school 12/20/62, committed to McMillan School, released 7/16/63. Curfew violation 4/17/64, probation. Smoking in high school 2/26/65, $100 fine and probation. May 16, 1965, the Orange County juvenile court authorized him to enter the Job Corps and said that at the time of entrance custody will be taken from his mother and invested in the Job Corps.

6. Offense—burglary of car, disposition—2 years probation 11/27/64.

7. Burglary of a school 3/17/64, dismissed. Beyond control of parents. Burglary 3/5/65, sustained according to the deputy probation officer; boy is still a ward of juvenile court.

8. Grand larceny, 8/12/63, Nolle prosequi. Undesirable discharge from Army 12/63.

9. Two break-ins, grand larceny 3/11/63, 5 years probation. Release date from probation 3/11/68.

10. Truancy 3/8/61, ward and probation. Burglary 12/26/61, continue as ward. Released from probation 10/26/64.

11. Larceny, second degree 3/1/63, disposition—delinquent ward, probation. Off probation 3/6/64.

12. Larceny, second degree 7/27/62, settled without petition.

13. Auto theft 4/2/63. Subject was never brought before court since his attorney managed to get many continuances.

14. Joy riding in auto 12/10/63, commitment to Department of Correction, Minnesota. Released on parole 8/11/64, subject to review 5/65.

15. Burglary 4/59 pending. Indecent exposure, 8/6/64, probation. Out of control of parents 10/18/63.

16. Petty theft, probation 9/19/62.

17. Larceny 12/12/64, bound over to grand jury 12/14/64. Remanded back to city court 3/16/65, dismissed.

18. Malicious destruction of private property 4/2/65, $100 or 30 days, suspended.

Both the Mountain Home Director and the Job Corps staff of the Interior Department appealed to OEO for permission to reject the criminals. However, in Mr. Stoddard's words, "OEO proceeded with the scheduled input."

The following month, one of the enrollees Mountain Home wanted to reject, Paul Dennis Jones, beat up a fellow corpsman and plunged a knife into his abdomen. (The victim ended up in a hospital and subsequently resigned from the Corps.)[4] When members of Congress protested to the OEO, officials there professed to be surprised to learn that Corpsman Jones was a three-time (felony) loser, including a conviction for attempted murder.

Mr. Stoddard thought that the stabbing incident, with the attendant notoriety, would wake OEO up to what was happening and result in better screening. Instead, however, the agency paid for an attorney for the stabber and wired the Court at the time of sentencing that he would be re-accepted in the Job Corps.[5]

At one Bureau of Land Management center a sex deviate caused problems. Here is how Mr. Stoddard described the situation:

"We discovered in our center at Tillsmook, Oregon a youngster who is transvestite in character. This fact we were able to keep from the other corpsmen for several months while members of the center staff counseled the youth, and he was given psychiatric treatment at a nearby city. When other corpsmen did learn of his character, they became upset and general bedlam reigned at the center until he was discharged and committed to an institution in New Jersey. The process of removing and committing the youngster used the time of the center counselor for one full week. Additionally, he learned in New Jersey that it was common knowledge the youth was and had been so afflicted for as long as 10 years past. Proper screening procedures would have revealed this information and proper psychiatric treatment might have been administered to him before coming to a conservation center."

Just on the basis of this one case it is not hard to understand why Mr. Stoddard wanted better screening. Here, in part, is a statement he sent to OEO on the matter:

"All of our directors agree with me that the screening process was very poorly administered. Few of the corpsmen knew what type of camp they were coming to, or what to expect when they arrived. Most had signed up because the promotional film strip shown them gave them the idea they were going to be trained immediately as mechanics, radio repairmen, welders, etc. . . .

"Our local communities, in good faith, have been promised that the Corps would not take boys with criminal records—yet we had several with histories of arrest and conviction."

In pressing OEO to screen more carefully, Mr. Stoddard was not alone. Also urging the agency to do this were Litton Industries, Federal Electric Corporation and U.S. Industries, Inc., all of whom operated Job Corps centers for the agency under contract. They advocated special reception centers which could have employees who specialized in screening. Such centers, they argued, also could do better jobs in such matters as medical examinations.

Representative Charles E. Goodell (R., N.Y.) asked Job Corps officials why they didn't do a better job of screening and reported they told him they had no way of checking whether a man was on parole or probation when he applied. Said the Congressman, "They shy away from fingerprinting their applicants, apparently because they believe such a procedure is a personal indignity. . . . Of course, all of our boys who go into military service are automatically fingerprinted. [He could have added that all members of the press who go to the White House also are fingerprinted.] A quick check with the FBI could give them a full criminal background on every applicant."

In addition to turning down the screening advice, OEO sent these instructions to its Job Corps centers for handling trouble:

"Courteously but firmly direct the corpsman's attention to the deviant behavior and suggest remedial action; if the

corpsman fails to act upon constructive suggestion, request
ID card of the corpsman; write a brief report of the incident and forward same to the guidance director; if the
corpsman refuses to surrender ID card . . . attempt to secure
identification from bystanders . . . .

"No dismissals from Job Corps can be made by centers
without getting prior approval from Job Corps headquarters. . . . Under no circumstances, explicit or implicit, should
a resignation be asked for or the opportunity to resign
offered."[6]

This is Mr. Stoddard's reaction:

"When there is a corpsman who flouts authority and
undermines discipline in a camp, and also endangers the
welfare of others, it is intolerable that a director must first
get clearance from Washington before he can send the
troublemaker home. If our directors are to have responsibility for the successful operation of the camps, they must
have the right to act on their own best judgment when a
situation calls for immediate action. They can maintain no
discipline if they are to be mere call-boys when the chips
are down! Either we are to have confidence in our directors, and show it by giving them authority that must
accompany responsibility, or we will have to operate each
of our camps directly from Washington."

After fruitlessly pleading with OEO for the right to
reject criminals and/or discipline corpsmen, on February
24, 1966 he sent the following teletype message to all Job
Corps Conservation Centers operated by BLM:

"It is apparent from continuing incidents at your centers
that poor screening of candidates for enrollment in the
program had and is having a deleterious affect on the program. Additionally, your lack of authority to immediately
discharge unsuitable corpsmen has led to serious troubles in
maintaining discipline. For above reasons I direct you to

review records you now have on your corpsmen and to discharge immediately any who show a history of serious and repeated offenses against persons or property, extreme sexual deviation or emotional disturbances. You will take this action without regard to procedures established by OEO when delay will cause overburdening of your staff, adverse community relations, escalation of discipline problems with other corpsmen, or serious morale problems at your center. As you receive additional new enrollees, and advance records indicate problems of the stature stated above, you will not accept delivery of corpsmen but will return them to their homes immediately.

"Should you be questioned from any source as to your authority to take the above actions, you will quote this communication from me."

In a memorandum to Secretary of the Interior Stewart L. Udall explaining the reasons for the teletype message, Mr. Stoddard said, "If OEO will establish reception centers and delegate adequate disciplinary authority to Job Corps camp directors, these easily preventable situations will not occur. As soon as this is done, I will be glad to rescind my order of February 24. Furthermore, I will request a leave of absence ... to direct this program into a successful operation."

Mr. Stoddard obviously was sincerely interested in the welfare of the program. He had been an advocate of the conservation camps as far back as 1954 when he wrote up the proposal for a speech then Senator Humphrey gave in Grand Rapids, Minn. during a re-election campaign. Indeed, Mr. Stoddard had assisted in drafting the aforementioned Youth Conservation Corps bill which inspired the Job Corps legislation.

Here's what happened to him for trying to set things right at the Job Corps centers: He was ordered to rescind his teletyped order. His offer to take a leave of absence to help with the program was turned down. Finally, he was removed from his job as BLM Director, by personal order of President Johnson, and demoted to Interior's Program Planning staff. Mr. Stoddard took the hint and resigned from the government.

While Mr. Stoddard knew firsthand only about cases involving his Bureau of Land Management, trouble was not confined to centers operated by that Bureau. When one corpsman left Camp Kilmer, New Jersey (run by Federal Electric) in terror, he declared, "Many youths sent to court for a minor crime were given a choice between the Job Corps and reform school."[7]

The residents of Edison, New Jersey, the location of Camp Kilmer, petitioned the Job Corps to leave after corpsmen were accused of drunkenness, using narcotics, assaulting local residents and stoning cars on a highway that passed through the camp.[8] The Job Corps stayed.

John W. Deinema, Associate Director of Job Corps Conservation Centers for OEO, made it clear that violating the law did not bar service in the Job Corps. Enrollees who got into misdemeanor trouble could expect to have their fines paid by OEO, provided they later reimbursed it from their Job Corps pay, he declared.[9]

When two corpsmen from Camp Atterbury, in Indiana, were arrested and charged with possession of marijuana, the camp posted bonds of $1,000 for each of them. Two other boys from Atterbury received fines and suspended jail terms for allegedly beating two Job Corps officials.[10]

The Worcester, Massachusetts *Gazette* quoted William A. Boulanger, Jr. of Spencer, Massachusetts, who left Camp Atterbury in disgust, as saying, "Liquor, narcotics, sex—all these things were normal. It was a madhouse."

When James W. Neely and Claudell Hughes, corpsmen from Camp Gary at San Antonio, Texas, were arrested on charges of robbery, OEO hired a separate lawyer for each and posted bonds and accepted them back at camp. They eventually had to leave, however, because they were found guilty. Mr. Neely was sentenced to eight years in prison, and Mr. Hughes to four years.[11]

Danny and Dana Harrison, eighteen-year-old twins from Kingsport, Tennessee, had wrecked their cells after being arrested for public drunkenness. According to local newspapers only Job Corps assignments saved them from lengthy terms for destroying prison property.[12] Dana went to the Colconda Camp, 30 miles south of Harrisburg, Illinois and Danny went to the Crab Orchard Center at Carterville, Illinois.

When the twins departed, fresh warrants were outstanding against them, charging felonious assault. According to the *Times-News* of Kingsport, "the warrants resulted from a Sunday night going-away party in which the twins allegedly bludgeoned Arthur Clark and Billy Carnes with a lead pipe." The paper said, "Both youths have been in trouble since they were nine years old." Within less than a month the boys resigned from the Job Corps and Dana was found guilty and jailed for disorderly conduct, public profanity, public drunkenness and carrying a concealed weapon.[13]

By April 28, 1966 affairs had come to such a pass that Senate Majority Leader Mike Mansfield took to the Senate floor to declare, "Everyone was in too big a hurry to get the first camps operating. Too little time was given to the screening of the Job Corps applicants. There is need to be more selective . . . It was not my intention to support the establishment of three reformatories in my state."

Senator Mansfield described an incident which illustrated his cause for concern. A boy from Billings, Montana had enrolled in the Job Corps. Before leaving for camp in Kentucky, however, he was involved in a barroom brawl and shot a patron. Job Corps officials, rather than reject him on such grounds, took over his defense and paid for his plane transportation back to Billings, when required by the court. Later he escaped from the camp, stole a car and was involved in an auto accident that took the lives of two people and hospitalized others in critical conditions, including himself. Subsequently Representative Paul A. Fino (R., N.Y.) disclosed that the Job Corps had posted $2,500 bond for the boy in the shooting.[14]

After two trainees at the Job Corps center at Casper, Wyoming were involved in stealing a car, an investigation revealed that they had arrest records in other states. Senator Milward L. Simpson (R., Wyo.) said the people of Casper approved the establishment of a Job Corps center only on OEO's assurance that it would not serve as a rehabilitation area for youths with prior law violation records. Then he quoted the local county attorney, John Burk, as terming the camp "a junior penal farm."

Residents of New Bedford, Massachusetts became upset over the Job Corps to such an extent that they formed the Citizens' Ad Hoc Committee for Study of Rodman Job Corps Center (located at New Bedford). In a report dated September 26, 1966, the Committee found the same faults which had been apparent at other centers—inadequate screening, acceptance of criminals, poor discipline, unlawful behavior by the trainees, and other faults (to be discussed later).

Said the report: "We are concerned that OEO has developed no clear standards for admission into the program . . . We learned that in April 1966 a crash program of recruitment went into effect, leading to loose standards . . . We wonder why there is a need for crash recruitment and are critical of this approach. We also are critical of practices whereby some agencies and law enforcement officials refer social and behavior problems to the Job Corps for rehabilitation."

The Rodman corpsmen included 91 who had been convicted before enrolling of crimes including theft, larceny,
burglary, breaking and entering, intoxication, disorderly
conduct and assault.

Within one year the New Bedford police had arrested
56 Job Corps youths. One of the 56 was Willie Biggins
who was charged with stabbing Corpsman Charles Beaver
in the chest. The latter ended up in the hospital on the
danger list. The Committee did not reveal the name of the
corpsman who allegedly slashed enrollee Linzell Sykes
three times with a razor, inflicting wounds which required
35 stitches. New Bedford police arrested four Rodman
enrollees April 29 when they allegedly interfered with the
arrest of another corpsman for disorderly conduct.

One episode revealed by the Committee resulted in no
arrests. It was a riot of nearly 200 corpsmen in New Bedford. Getting them back into the center required around
40 policemen. Once inside the main gate, youths began
pelting police cars and the paddy wagon with rocks, iron
pipes and other objects.

As a rule, the Committee said, the policemen were denied
access to the Center when they attempted to question enrollees who had returned to it.

(While the report clearly defined the disturbance as a
riot, the month after it came out Sargent Shriver told a
House Appropriations Subcommittee that there had been
no riots in Job Corps centers during the entire life of the
Job Corps. Saying that this was a period "when the nation
was extremely preoccupied by riots in the cities allegedly
run by teenagers," he contended, "to me this indicates that
somehow or other these centers are in fact modifying the
behavior and the attitude of these youngsters.")[15]

In addition, the Committee report said the following:

"Residents near the Rodman Center are critical of the
yelling and noise that comes from corpsmen on and near

the base day and night, particularly after curfew hours. They object to vulgar language used by the boys, sometimes directed at them personally as the students pass their homes. They object to boys trespassing on their property day and night . . .

"Fire Chief Richard T. Gaughan reported seven false alarms from Rodman . . . (in three months). He said this might lead to the Department cutting off the automatic alarm system service to the Center."

In a private meeting with the Committee at Rodman on July 18, 1966, Sargent Shriver, according to the report, "said there is a difference of opinion among Job Corps officials whether strict or permissive discipline is more successful in handling this population and therefore different centers have different disciplinary policies."

The report observed, "There is no clear-cut policy on discipline. Experimentation without structure or control has led to confusion. OEO wanted to accomplish too much too quickly. We feel that this program should not have been launched as a full-fledged operation until . . . adequate guidelines had been established."

The study also criticized the methods of selecting the Rodman staff. It reported the following:

"Some staff members were hired without adequate investigation of the individual's background. Particularly neglected were inquiries into the levels of . . . skill in the particular field applied for. There also seemed to be little demand from SRA [Science Research Associates, the contractor operating the center] for experience in general as a prerequisite to hiring. SRA placed more emphasis on the applicant's enthusiasm for the social experiment involved in the Job Corps concept."

The report also decried haphazard screening procedures for the trainees which had the result that many were assigned to Rodman with neither capability nor inclination to benefit from the courses in operating IBM machines in which Rodman specialized—quite naturally, since SRA was a subsidiary of IBM. The Committee felt the poor screening was largely responsible for the low number of graduates and high number of transfers from Rodman. Of the 972 students enrolled at the Center from August 1965 to June 1966, only 28 graduated, while 111 were transferred to other centers. There is no indication that many of the others ended up operating business machines because 39 entered military service, 32 found jobs at home, 18 returned to school, nine left to get married, 42 were discharged for disciplinary reasons, four were discharged for medical reasons and 171 resigned for reasons not reported. At this time there were 518 at the center.

Even the transfers were a problem. Before Rodman could have a corpsman transferred to another center with subjects closer to his interests and abilities, it had to get permission from OEO. This was so slow in forthcoming that the citizens said it distressed the enrollees and created behavioral problems.

Such problems notwithstanding, the Committee found that in April 1966 OEO cut down on the screening and decided that aptitude tests "were no longer considered useful."

In addition, the Committee found that Rodman opened before the center was ready. It said that "physical facilities necessary for the operation of the center were inadequate when Rodman opened." It added that the strain was increased when too many enrollees were accepted too rapidly and that OEO "seemed unaware or unconcerned about these limitations."

The citizens of New Bedford, Massachusetts were unsuccessful when they asked OEO to move the Rodman Center from their community. Investigators from Representative Adam Clayton Powell's House Education and

Labor Committee looked into the situation at Rodman. The only faults they found were, "The cafeteria is grossly unsatisfactory and there is no gym for indoor recreation."

The Job Corps center in Casper, Wyoming run by the Bureau of Reclamation had its troubles too. Lee P. Banks was a resident recreation instructor there. On January 3, 1966 he was arrested for assaulting Robert Lee Towery, manager of the sporting goods department at the J. C. Penney Co. store in Casper. Mr. Towery ended up in a hospital for eight days with a fractured skull and other head wounds. He was unconscious for two days.

The center had hired Mr. Banks on the recommendation of the National Association for the Advancement of Colored People. In his application for employment, he admitted having been arrested in 1960 and serving sixteen months in prison. The center accepted his word that he was rehabilitated and put him to work after making only a quick check with his only local employer, the Episcopal Church, which said he was a good worker. His arrest record was not checked before he started work on October 30, 1965.

On December 7, 1965 the Federal Bureau of Investigation told the Civil Service Commission that Mr. Banks' police record included arrests for assault with intent to commit rape in 1954; assault and battery in 1955; rape in 1958; robbery with aggravated assault in 1959; larceny in 1960 and trying to obtain narcotics by fraud in 1961. He also had been arrested for investigation in February 1965.

The Civil Service Commission did not give this information to the Bureau of Reclamation until January 17, 1966, two weeks after Mr. Banks was arrested for assaulting Mr. Towery. Moreover, Mr. Banks continued to work at the camp after his arrest.

In his application for employment at the camp he had filled out a form which asked, "Have you ever been arrested, taken into custody, held for investigation or questioning, or charged by any law enforcement authority?" It required the listing of each arrest and warned that false or dishonest information would be punishable by fine or imprisonment under federal law.

On February 1, 1966, nearly a month after the Towery beating, the Civil Service Commission got around to asking him why he had not given all the information requested on his application form. Instead of replying, on February 28, 1966 Mr. Banks voluntarily resigned from his Job Corps position.

Incensed by the whole episode, Senator Milward W. Simpson, (R., Wyo.) asked why Mr. Banks had not been prosecuted for failing to disclose all of his police record in his application form. The Civil Service Commission replied that it did not submit the case to the Justice Department because "it has been our experience that persons who are separated and no longer federal employees are very rarely prosecuted." Commented Senator Simpson on the floor of the Senate, "As a lawyer I have yet to find in any law book or case history an example in which a person has escaped punishment for a federal offense by quitting his job."[16]

The extent to which sloppy checking of backgrounds resulted in the hiring of criminals probably will never be known. The case of Mr. Banks came to light only after he was arrested.

But disciplinary problems flared into the open even at the Job Corps Center for Women at Charleston, West Virginia which was maintained as a showcase because of its proximity to Washington. The Charleston center called police to help two girls who claimed to have been shoved from a window to a ledge outside the Job Corps hotel. On July 10, 1966 the *Charleston Daily Mail* reported, "Two policemen reported today they were reviled in the 'vulgarest, dirtiest, foulest' language and made targets of a barrage of beer and whiskey bottles when they answered a call at the Job Corps training center. . . ."

Inadequate screening also caused medical and emotional problems at Charleston, and OEO made matters even worse in April 1966 when it abandoned the requirement for even superficial medical examinations and used instead a "preliminary health questionnaire" which was designed by physicians to be administered by nonmedical personnel.

This meant that, before acceptance, Job Corps applicants had to answer questions based on what they knew, or were willing to tell about the state of their health. OEO also established a rule that the youngsters were to be given physical examinations at the centers within 48 hours after their arrival to determine if they had communicable diseases. The agency allowed 30 days for a complete physical.

Dr. Fred Cooley, the physician at the Charleston, West Virginia center, said the result was that some girls arrived with venereal diseases and other highly communicable ailments like scabies. Such maladies are difficult to diagnose without a complete physical, he explained. The consequence was that before having complete examinations at the center, the girls infected others.

Dr. Cooley also strongly felt that the girls should have been examined for pregnancy before being accepted in the Job Corps. He said this at least would have cut down on the twenty pregnancies during the first fifteen months of the center's operation. He pointed out, however, that it would be impossible to screen out all pregnant girls since one could become pregnant the day after passing an examination, and pregnancy cannot be detected accurately for six weeks.

Charleston Center Director Joseph Neely backed up Dr. Cooley and added that pregnancy examinations would have cut down on the expense of needless transportation to the centers of girls who would not be able to finish the courses, which, ironically, averaged nine months.

Mr. Neely went even farther and said OEO should not send girls who are mentally retarded or have severe emotional problems—and he received such girls at Charleston. Indeed, Mrs. Evelyn Kalinowski, a registered nurse employed at the center, suffered a broken shoulder while she was trying to deal with a hysterical student. The opinion of center officials was that the girl was so emotionally disturbed that she should not have been sent. She had to leave the Job Corps for this reason.

Another enrollee was a homosexual so "aggressive", center spokesmen said, that she upset the other girls. Eventually permission was obtained from OEO to discharge her for failure to attend classes.

Doing the best it could with a bad situation, Charleston improvised a screening program of its own. It kept the new girls together as a group for their first two weeks, with the idea of weeding out the troublemakers before they were able to affect the rest of the girls. Still, center officials felt their resources could have been better used if they had not been sent girls obviously incapable of benefiting from the Job Corps. Then, too, the officials were limited by the extent to which they could separate the newcomers from the other girls, since all had to share the same dining room and lobby.

At Charleston I also learned how OEO's haphazard assignments affected some of the girls. Center officials turned over their faculty lounge to me and brought in enrollees for me to interview.

A 21-year-old high school graduate from Boscobell, Wisconsin had the fair and well-scrubbed look of many Wisconsinites and an easy grace, but a brooding manner which seemed out of character with her appearance. This, I soon learned, was born out of disgust with the Job Corps which gave her a sense of futility because she didn't know where else to go.

When she enrolled, she stated she was doing so to learn

to become a library assistant. She said her request to be sent
to one of the five centers teaching such a course was turned
down, and she ended up at Charleston. Although that center had no classes in the subject, and no library worthy of
the name, it made a stab at teaching her on an individual
basis.

She told me she soon discovered she was wasting her
time on the course and that "most of what they taught me
here I had already learned in high school." Her request for
transfer to another center with regular classes in the subject
was turned down. At that point she gave up her hope of
obtaining a job as a library assistant to work her way
through the University of Wisconsin, following completion
of the Job Corps course.

At the suggestion of the Charleston center the girl started
studying typing and shorthand, with the idea of using those
skills to work her way through college. When interviewed,
she said she didn't particularly like the courses and might
change again.

An attractive Negro girl with sparkling eyes and a sharp
intellect was equally disappointed. She left her job as a
sales clerk at a department store in Jamestown, New York
in the belief that the Job Corps would train her to become
a practical nurse. After her arrival at Charleston, however,
she was told that so many had signed up for the course that
the center decided to lift the entry requirements and accept
only high school graduates. She had completed only the
eighth grade.

A young man I interviewed in the Adirondack Moun-
tains still isn't sure how he ended up in the Job Corps Conservation Center run by the Forest Service in Ripton, Ver-
mont. Here is his story, just as he told it to me as we sat on
the beach of a mountain lake.

"I had dropped out of high school after the second year
because I was bored to death. The tips on my job were

pretty good, and I was learning something about the hotel business. But then some guy on TV said, 'Join the Job Corps.' He made it sound really great, and I decided to try it.

"I ended up at the Conservation Center run by the Forest Service at Ripton. The cafeteria wasn't ready yet, and so we went to the Belmont Hotel at Middlebury [Vermont], about nine miles away, for breakfast and dinner. At breakfast, they gave us sandwiches to take back for lunch. The vocational shop and the warehouse weren't finished, and they hadn't even started to build the gym. There was nothing to do at the camp for fun except play records or look at TV. A lot of the time, the boys would just sit around with time on their hands.

"A couple of times they brought in some Poland Spring Job Corps girls for a dance, and ten minutes after the dance started, every guy would be out in the woods with some girl.

"I had completed tenth grade, and most of the boys couldn't read or write. The education was for people like them, and for me it was even more boring than high school.

"I didn't get any vocational training at all. They used me in the office because I was one of the few boys who could read and write. Mostly I was answering the phone and doing a little filing, nothing that required any special training.

"Quite a few of the boys smoked pot [marijuana] and nobody seemed to care. Nearly all of them drank, sometimes on the streets. Only about a third of us were white, and there were lots of racial fights. The fellows got bloody many times. Mostly they'd just bandage themselves up, and nobody would really do anything.

"There wasn't much the people running the camp could do. They knew that if they tried to crack down, the boys would gang up against them.

"They wanted to use me as an assistant leader, but that meant I would have had to report the boys when they weren't doing right and run the risk of getting my throat slit for reporting them.

"I figured I was better off as a bellhop. After ten days I just left for home without saying anything to anybody. I've been here for a couple of weeks now, and I haven't heard anything from anybody at the camp. My old job was filled, and so I'm working at a bar and grill. At least it isn't dangerous."

Officials in charge of the Women's Job Corps Center at Excelsior Springs, Missouri admitted to me that haphazard assignments of enrollees to centers made their task extremely difficult. They said they had absolutely no control over the selection of students and never knew what type OEO would send them. Taking a wild guess, they geared it to the level of first or second year high school dropouts. They found, however, that they had to vary their vocational menu to adapt it to the wide range in desires and aptitudes of the recruits they received.

The center was run by Training Corporation of America, a subsidiary of Westinghouse Air Brake, and besides offering training in electronic assembly, for which they were eminently qualified, they ended up giving courses in such subjects as flower-arranging and hairdressing.

From the House Education and Labor Committee, I managed to obtain a report resulting from a $200,000 investigation of the anti-poverty program by Chairman Adam Clayton Powell, a report never made public officially. (No one ever explained why.) It found that at conservation camps youths did not learn skills to help them obtain jobs when they returned home. The study reported that they spent most of their time on maintenance rather than "doing meaningful conservation work." The biggest problem permeating all of the camps, it said, was "the unhappiness of most of the enrollees at finding themselves out in the woods, away from civilization."

Here's what it said about the Los Pinos Center at Elsinore, California, run by the Forest Service:

"Because the area chosen is so remote, much of the time of the corpsmen is spent just keeping the camp intact. In fact, trying to keep the road open to the center is by far the most demanding job of all. The rest of the corpsmen's time is spent either shoring up the existing buildings so they won't wash down the mountain or building patios for the staff trailers."

The report said that at the Forest Service Fenner Canyon Conservation Center at Valerymo, California, disappointment at the remoteness of the place often led to resignation of the corpsmen. "Many of those that stay," it added, "are further disappointed in not being instructed in a specific skill."

At the end of 1966, St. Petersburg, Florida was the only town which had persuaded OEO to close a center. Residents had protested to OEO to no avail over rowdyism, drunkenness and soliciting by the girls on the street, all of which disturbed the peace of the quiet retirement community. To effect the closing required a refusal of the School Board to permit further use of its facilities, passage of a special ordinance precluding the use of a local hotel for a Job Corps center, intervention by the Governor of Florida, months of heated arguments between officials of the city and OEO, and a special trip to Washington by Mayor Herman Goldner and seven other city representatives.[17]

In Congressional testimony Sargent Shriver professed astonishment at the local "hostility" and said, "We were invited by the mayor and everybody who were knocking their blocks off to get us in there and later on they changed their minds."[18]

4

Life in the Job Corps

To get the real flavor of the Job Corps, it is necessary to visit a center. Take Charleston, West Virginia. The center is located in the heart of downtown in an ancient hotel once frequented by Mark Twain. It was rehabilitated for close to a quarter of a million dollars, and that didn't include furnishings.

Except for the location, life at the center might have been characterized as a modified country club existence. The girls had a six-and-a-half hour study day, with an hour and a half for lunch. The teachers did not give homework because they feared the students would consider this punishment or might dislike it to the degree that they would leave the Corps.

Of course studying could have been done voluntarily in the evenings, and I was told free tutoring was available. While I was there, however, I found no evidence that anyone was doing any studying, or even reading, in the evening. Moreover, the facilities were not conducive to such pursuits.

The library was minuscule and would have been crowded with even a dozen girls. The enrollment when I was there came to 257, compared with a capacity of 300. (I found only one girl in the library when I visited it.) Several duplicate volumes of Plato and Thoreau's *Walden* sat on the shelves and looked bookstore-new, although I was told they had been there for fifteen months. One official frankly admitted the books were not a happy choice for school dropouts.

The hotel rooms did not contain desks for each occupant. Each floor had a lounge, but the one I saw had only lounge chairs and a television set, no desks. Moreover, studying would have been impossible there since the only illumination in use in the crowded room came from the dim glow of the TV set.

Certainly anyone who required quiet for study would have had a hard time getting it at Charleston. The noise of screaming girls was continuous the whole time I was there; they weren't being bad, just noisy. I talked to one newcomer who said she hadn't slept in the three days she had been there. "The noise goes on all day and all night, and I think I am going to be sick if I don't get some sleep soon," she complained.

Although the center was in the heart of town, chauffered station wagons were kept for the trainees. Those interested used them to go to an outdoor private day camp for swimming, golf, tennis, basketball and picnics. The wagons also transported the athletic teams organized by the center.

A few minutes after I entered the center for the first time, I was followed by a group of screaming, running, jumping girls. I braced myself for a riot only to learn that the center had formed the only girls' intramural soccer teams in the state of West Virginia and that the winning team was showing its elation.

In addition to the organized sports, the enrollees also were offered the facilities of the nearby YWCA, including the gym and year-round swimming in the indoor pool. Moreover, the center itself afforded facilities for dancing, ping pong, talent shows and movies. It also had an arts and

crafts hobby center and a snack bar in addition to the
cafeteria. Movie theatres were within easy walking distance.

A special laundry room had automatic washers and dry-
ers for the convenience of the girls, but they were not required to take care of the linens for their rooms; maids
collected soiled ones and gave fresh ones once a week.
Maids also handled all cleaning work, except for the sleeping rooms. From what I could determine, caring for those
was optional. An evening inspection of the rooms on three
of the five sleeping floors revealed only one room with beds
made, and that had been done by a girl who scampered
ahead to prepare for my visit. Other rooms were in a general state of disarray. The youngsters told me they fixed
them up for the once-a-week inspections when rewards
were given for the best-kept rooms.

Since I had heard Charleston frequently hailed as the
best Job Corps center in the country, it seemed an ideal
place to see in practice what I had heard in theory. One of
the theories most often heard was that the Job Corps would
develop new teaching techniques which could be used by
public schools.

In the "classes" I observed, the teaching was being done
on an individual basis. While other students did their
"homework," the teacher would instruct one trainee at a
time. The "classes" had an average of five students.

"All educators have known for years that it is easier to
instruct on an individual basis," I said, "but what have you
developed here that can be used in the public schools?"
Several teachers, who themselves had been hired away from
such schools at more attractive salaries, had no answer.

A social studies teacher told me the new development
was that everything studied was related to the job the enrollee had in mind. I chose a student in this class at random
and asked her the subject of the book she was reading. The

answer was, "Tahiti." I then inquired about her chosen vocation and received the answer, "Electronics assembler." She didn't know of any connection between that and Tahiti.

In some cases it appeared that the center was attempting the impossible. One girl told me she expected to graduate as a secretary after studying for nine months. While her personality and appearance were attractive, her grammar was awful. I mentioned this deficiency to a center official and suggested it might hurt her chances for obtaining employment as a secretary. "Oh no, we'll work on her English, too," he explained. It seemed like a very big order, especially with no homework.

One official said, "She might not be able to get a job as secretary to a high corporate officer, but she might be happy working for a small firm, say an auto repair shop which does require some secretarial work."

I wondered, however, whether such a shop would have an expensive IBM electric typewriter like the one she had been taught to use. Use of mechanical typewriters was not taught, and they are far different from electric ones.

Adaptability to the kinds of jobs available was not taught in at least one course, practical nursing. After inspecting the simulated hospital room used for classes, I asked the instructor, Mary Morgan, if she also showed the girls how to cook and do other things they might find necessary in caring for a patient in a home. She said she told the trainees they would not have to bother taking jobs in homes because the demand for practical nurses was so great they could find employment in hospitals. She added that if they did accept a job in a home, they should expect the patient to hire a housekeeper to handle the cooking.

Much of the vocational training credited to the Charleston center actually was done outside. Girls studying to be hairdressers, for instance, did so at a commercial school, with the Job Corps paying their tuition. Girls studying to be "day care aides" obtained on-the-job training at a school for retarded children operated by a Charleston church.

When I left Charleston, the center was negotiating with a women's clothing store to give Job Corps girls on-the-job training as sales clerks.

Certainly Packard Bell, which operated the center, could have given on-the-job training in electronic assembly at its own factories.

If so much of the training was available elsewhere, why did the girls need the Job Corps? The standard answer was that it gave them basic education where public schools had failed and got them away from their poor home environments.

As noted, I failed to discover any innovations which would have been useful to public schools. The one pupil to one teacher ratio could have been used by the public schools, if they had had the virtually unlimited funds of the Job Corps.

Moreover, no one seemed sure that the life of relative ease at the center would make go-getters of school dropouts. Were virtually unlimited free recreation and chauffeured transportation preparing the girls to be productive citizens? The theory was that they were making the trainees happy and that this would give them a better frame of mind for tackling the future.

However, the girls still were associating with disadvantaged people, presumably, just as they did at home. I could not help but wonder if it really was benefiting the youngest (sixteen years old) to live and study with disadvantaged girls as old as twenty-two.

Even giving the center the benefit of the doubt and assuming that the environment was beneficial, how much could this nine-months stay counteract poor home environments? Nearly everyone I interviewed planned to return home after graduation.

Most of the enrollees were homesick and said West Virginia was too far from home for them to stay permanently. In any event, they could not have stayed at the center after graduation.

Reluctance to leave home permanently was the main reason Packard Bell hired only three center-trained electronic assemblers after operating Charleston for fifteen months. Explained one official, "The girls just wouldn't move all the way to California to work for us."

Girls with children at home partially supported by the Job Corps certainly were planning to return to the old environment. One enrollee from Kansas City, Kansas told me she was looking forward to resuming life with her three-year-old daughter after graduation.

"What does your husband think of your being in the Job Corps?", I asked.

"Actually," she replied, "it wasn't much of a marriage; I was married at thirteen. After I finish here, I am going back to the father of my child. I like him better than my husband, and so does my daughter."

When examining the life and problems at the Charleston center, it should be borne in mind that OEO officials were constantly touting it as the best in the country.

OEO's answer to its failure to win community acceptance for a Job Corps center anywhere in the environs of Washington, D.C. was to open one on the sly in the heart of the city. It wasn't even listed in OEO's official booklet of all Job Corps centers. While the entire Job Corps was really a mass experiment, the Capitol Center was specifically labeled "experimental," and it was indeed different from other centers.

Trainees lived in special sections of regular YWCA and YMCA dormitories. They bought their own food at restaurants out of a $4 daily food allowance. For the girls, part of this was in tickets for the YWCA cafeteria.

Westinghouse Electric Corporation operated the center for OEO. Officially the purpose was to arrange on-the-job training for graduates of other centers and to continue their basic education. The daily schedule called for four hours on the job, two hours of general education and one and a half hours of group guidance. When I visited it in February of 1967, the center was having difficulty both in obtaining enrollees and in finding training spots for those it had. With a capacity for 94 persons, it had only fifty.

Westinghouse told me that a secondary but important purpose of the center was to provide a steady source of Job Corpsmen for OEO headquarters. When the latter wanted clerical help for which it had not received funds from Congress, it had only to tell the center to send over Job Corps members for on-the-job training. When Mr. Shriver wanted to make a TV appearance with a Job Corpsman, all he had to do was phone the center. When he wanted to try out a new teaching method or material, the corpsmen were on tap to serve as guinea pigs.

Since the Job Corps paid the trainees, both Westinghouse and OEO thought that private companies would jump at the chance to obtain free help in labor-short Washington. This was not the case, however. After running the center for seven months, Westinghouse was able to find only three slots for trainees with private companies. It said the reason was that employers were fearful of violating minimum wage laws by hiring trainees with Job Corps pay which ranged from $30 to $100 per month and obviously was far short of the minimum wage of $1.40 per hour. In seeking federal training spots, the center steered clear of the Post Office Department, reasoning it was the only government agency with a strong union which might object to a training system which didn't pay the minimum wage. A sample list I was given showed that over half the trainees were working for OEO. The center director, Clifton Chadwick, told me that they worked chiefly as office boys, clerks and typists.

One corpsman, however, was assigned to on-the-job training in the office of Senator Robert Kennedy after the latter told the OEO he wanted to do his patriotic bit by helping to train a member of the Job Corps. At the start, the youth was full of enthusiasm over the prospect of working in such a glamorous spot. After three weeks, he reported that he could stand it no longer. His sole assignment had been to operate the Senator's Auto-Pen, a device which permitted anyone to sign the Senator's name with the appearance of an original signature.

The low enrollment meant that Director Chadwick spent much of his time traveling to other centers to recruit Job Corps graduates. When I chatted with him, he was planning such trips to Job Corps centers in Kansas City, Albuquerque and Los Angeles—at government expense, of course.

When I was at the center, they were trying a new system in basic education called "self-instruction." About fifteen students were studying independently, with a student from nearby George Washington University acting as the instructor, or really, the overseer. As each trainee entered the classroom he, or she, had to sign a contract which was an agreement to perform a certain amount of work.

The work was divided into compartments on written pages. Unlike books used in most conventional schools, the texts were written in extremely simple style with the idea that anyone who was literate could understand without help from a teacher. After reading a short passage, the student went to the next compartment which required him to answer questions regarding what he had read. The answers involved checking appropriate boxes or writing "yes" or "no". The instructor then checked the answers against a master form. If they were right, the student went to the next compartment. If they were wrong, he had to do it over. The student could not proceed to the next step until he had proved that he understood the preceding one.

After completing the number of compartments for which he had contracted, the student then was allowed to go to a small recreation room next door. There a motherly and pleasant Negro woman was making and serving excellent coffee, cake and cookies. The room had a pinball machine, a ping pong table and a limited assortment of table games. After a fifteen-minute recess here, the student was required to go back to the classroom, sign another contract, and proceed as before until he had completed his two hours a day of basic education. The idea of fulfilling the contract and obtaining the reward was to give a sense of accomplishment. The system had not been evaluated at the time I visited the center.

In one unfortunate instance, Mr. Shriver did not abide by the reaction of the enrollees to educational material he tried out on them. He asked them what they thought of an article on sex scheduled for publication in *The Corpsman*, a news magazine put out twice a month by OEO for Job Corps centers. After being told it was no good, he published it anyway and brought down a flood of criticism from Congress and the press for his lack of good taste and judgment.

"You probably spend a lot of time thinking about sex. Most people do," said *The Corpsman* in its issue of November 1, 1966. It then went on to describe in great detail the sex organs and the act of sexual intercourse. The article stated, "We are planning a series of articles in *The Corpsman* about sex; the developing of the reproductive systems in men and women, attitudes toward sex, dating and sex, venereal disease, marriage, planned parenthood and sex education." They never materialized except for one story in the November 15, 1966 issue which said OEO was including sex education as a part of Job Corps training.

5

Job Corps Jobs

After operating the Job Corps for two years, OEO had no reliable information on how well the program was succeeding in its goal—jobs for the graduates. In November 1966, official OEO figures showed that out of 13,253 graduates to date, 5,617 had obtained jobs. Even so, OEO was not able to supply facts to back up its job figures.

Officials of Federal Electric, the International Telephone and Telegraph subsidiary which ran Camp Kilmer in New Jersey, offered to supply me with statistics to prove the operation there was a success. These showed, they said, the number of graduates with jobs. When I asked for the names of the graduates and their employers, the official I was dealing with admitted he was unable to provide this. "If you can't supply any information to enable me to test the accuracy of your statistics, I am not interested in having them," I told him. I felt that without information on the kinds of jobs obtained and the length of time the graduates stayed on them, the figures would have been meaningless.

Undoubtedly the attitude of Federal Electric was influenced by the extreme reluctance of OEO to give out information on names of graduates and their employers.

Indeed, R. E. Kellogg, Vice President and General Manager of Training Corporation of America, Inc., the subsidiary of Westinghouse Air Brake which operated the Women's Job Corps center at Excelsior Springs, Missouri, informed me that the terms of TCA's contract with OEO prohibited the firm from giving me a list of the graduates and their jobs.

While in Charleston, West Virginia, I managed to obtain a list of the Women's Job Corps graduates and their jobs. The information on employers was so incomplete, however, that verification would have been impossible. When I asked for an improved document, it turned out that this had to be cleared with Washington. Indeed, I was not even able to obtain it without going to OEO headquarters at 1200 Nineteenth St., N.W., and conferring with five Job Corps officials.

Dr. Selma Lippeatt, the prim, tall, strawberry blond Director of the Programs Division for Women's Centers, said OEO felt it was important for me to have the material in the proper context and to understand its relation to the entire program. To help imbue me with this understanding, she summoned a quartet of OEO Job Corps officials who greeted me suspiciously and seated themselves in a semicircle in her spacious but spartan office at OEO headquarters.

Sister Francetta was a Catholic nun and Special Assistant to Dr. Benetta Washington, Director of Women's Centers. She looked like any other short, dark, graying middle-aged woman one might encounter on the streets of Washington, having permission from her order to wear lay clothes rather than the traditional nun's habit.

Margaret Mayes was the Project Manager for the Charleston Center. Some of the girls at the center who had met her during her frequent trips there secretly referred to her as their "mother hen." Her overly-protective manner made it apparent why she had earned the label.

Next to her sat Eric Purdon of the Office of Community Relations of the Job Corps. His engaging manner, combined with his tall, dark and handsome appearance, seemed admirably suited for such an office.

Finally, there was Ernest Gross, Job Corps Information Director, who said little and seemed bored with the whole thing.

I asked Dr. Lippeatt and her quartet what they wanted to tell me before giving me the list. Instead of giving the expected dissertation, however, they began asking me questions. They wanted to know what I planned to say in my book, and how I was going about obtaining my material.

Dr. Lippeatt wanted to know about my "collaborators." When I indicated I didn't know what she meant, she said, "Certainly you would not attempt to write on a subject of the dimensions of the Job Corps without at least 35 collaborators to feed you material. I know that when I wrote a book, my publisher insisted that I have such collaborators. Surely, you must have a similar requirement from your publisher."

Pressing me gently on the arm, Sister Francetta said, "What she means is that you have to have the people who can feed you input so that you can conceptionalize your material and bring it forth."

At that point the others joined in to make it clear that they were prepared to put me in touch with the right people to obtain the proper "conceptionalization." First of all, they explained, I had to see the Job Corps as a whole and must deal with statistics on the entire program rather than any one center. Since no one center was typical, I should not examine individual centers but rather should deal in generalities which they would provide about all centers.

"But," I interrupted, "I want to deal with people, not just a bunch of statistics."

"We will help you there, too," Dr. Lippeatt responded.

"We will furnish you the names and case histories of individuals which Mr. Gross will select and provide for you."

Finally, I got across the point that I would not submit to an inquisition on how I planned to write this book in order to obtain the information I had requested on the graduates and their jobs. I also made it clear that I had no intention of going along with their suggested modus operandi.

"Are you going to give me the information or not?" I asked.

Dr. Lippeatt said they were extremely reluctant to give out the list because someone might use it or sell it as a mailing list or might jeopardize the employment of the Job Corps graduates by contacting their employers.

"We understand you have hired a detective to pursue these girls," said Miss Mayes. I told Miss Mayes that I had no plans to hire a detective but that I would like to be able to do a spot check on the jobs to see if the figures were reliable.

At last, I obtained the list from Dr. Lippeatt—and it was not difficult to understand the aversion to parting with it. It showed that out of 189 graduates of Charleston, only 70 had jobs as of December 1, 1966. Others may well have found employment. The center just didn't know. It simply had established no workable system for checking up on what happened to the girls after they left the center. Moreover, it had not followed up on most of the girls who obtained jobs, to see if they performed satisfactory work.

What kinds of jobs were obtained at such great expense? The list revealed that 28 of them paid $1.50 an hour or less. Despite their Job Corps training, then, the girls with these jobs were paid at or below the rates for unskilled work.

As the pay levels indicated, many of the graduates were not working in the fields in which they were trained. A graduate electronics assembler, for instance, was working as a cook's helper at $1.25 an hour in Concord, New

Hampshire. Another electronics assembler was making $35 a week as a waitress in New Orleans. A graduate of the secretarial course was employed as a receptionist in Charleston at $1.25 an hour, and a girl who had passed the nurses' aide course was making 75 cents an hour as a waitress in Lubbock, Texas.

Only three graduates were making above $2 per hour. All were trained as electronics assemblers. One was making $2.71 as an electric bench assembler in Atlanta; another, $2.22 as a solderer in Broadbrook, Connecticut; and the other, $2.30 as a computer operator in South Kearney, New Jersey.

A tenth of the graduates with jobs were paid with federal anti-poverty funds. This included three employed by the Neighborhood Youth Corps in New Orleans, and one each by the Neighborhood Youth Corps in Knoxville, Tennessee; the Youth Opportunity Center in Detroit, Michigan; the Youth Opportunity Center in Cleveland, Ohio and the Women's Job Corps Center at Albuquerque, New Mexico.

Moreover, my spot check indicated that the list of employed graduates was not reliable.

One graduate in photography was listed as being employed at a photography shop. When I asked the manager if she still was employed there, here is the answer I received: "We were told that she was a trained photographer, but we discovered that she was not trained at all. The center didn't even have a photography course. [The official list of the courses at Charleston makes no mention of photography.]

"Nevertheless, we decided to keep her and train her. We treated her like a lady, really like royalty. We even gave her expensive clothes. But she made no effort to learn. In three months we were unable to do anything with her and discharged her at the end of that time."

Next I checked on nine graduates who, according to the

list, had been hired as electronic assemblers in a Midwestern plant of a well-known firm. The Charleston Center and some members of Congress alike had touted their employment of the youths as the center's greatest success story. The *Charleston Gazette* called it "vindication of the contention that idle, spiritless youths can, with persistence, education and a little luck, become productive members of society."

I learned, however, that the girls did not perform satisfactory work and all nine were no longer employed by the firm.

Here is how a corporate official explained the situation: "Because we were anxious to cooperate with the OEO program, we paid for the transportation of the girls to the plant and helped them find housing. Our plant manufactures relatively sophisticated avionics and electronic products and we, as do all companies in this field, have standards of proficiency which all new employees are required to meet after a suitable training and employment period. Normally, this is 50 working days. Because of our sincere desire to help these women adjust to their new working and living conditions, we extended their probation period an additional 30 days. None of them achieved the level of proficiency required of all our electronic assemblers. As a matter of interest, it is very unusual to have to terminate a new employee because of failure to meet these standards. In fact, the percentage of new employees terminated for this purpose is considerably below 5 per cent."

Next I contacted a research firm which had hired a Charleston graduate junior draftsman as a tracer. She was still in its employ, and when I asked if her work was satisfactory, I was told, "She is as good as any of the others I've hired from the Job Corps, and I've got about forty." He said he had yet to find a graduate junior draftsman who was capable of drafting. He had all of them working as tracers. One of his problems, he said, was that the tracers were required to sign their names to their work and many of them did not know how to do it.

Here is the rest of his story: "You should see the applications for work from the Job Corps graduates I didn't hire; I've got a stack ten feet high. They can't even write basic English and have no concept of how to properly apply for a job. Most of them can't even spell the name of this city. The majority have spent six months in the Job Corps and expect to go right into drafting. It just isn't possible. In six months you can't even give them basic education. I've hired the forty because the labor situation is so desperate, but based on my experience, I'd say only one in a hundred is any good."

Another Charleston graduate was on the list as being employed by a Baltimore book publisher as a keypunch operator at $57 a week. She kept the job for only two months.

The Capital Job Corps Center tried at every hospital in greater Washington to arrange for on-the-job training for girls who had graduated from Job Corps courses as practical nurses and nurses' aides. There would have been no cost to the hospitals; the pay would have come from the Job Corps. Yet a center official told me, "We have been unable to persuade a single hospital here or in nearby Virginia and Maryland to accept a single graduate as anything higher than a bedpan emptier, and our graduates won't do that."

Amazed and shocked, I replied, "I can't understand it. There is a severe shortage of help in Washington hospitals, and many of them are strapped for funds. Why won't they accept your graduates at no cost?"

Here is the reply I received: "There is not a nursing or nurses' aide course taught in any Job Corps center anywhere in the entire country which meets the minimum requirements of any hospital in the whole Washington area."

At mid-1966, OEO gave the Senate Labor and Public Welfare Committee a list of companies which had supplied "profitable employment" to Job Corpsmen from the Breckinridge and Atterbury centers.[1] Illinois Senator Everett Dirksen, Minority Leader, decided on a random check and phoned four of the employers.

The first one said the corpsman in question "really did not know anything about the subject that he was supposed to have been trained in." The company offered to train him in the skill that he supposedly had learned in the Job Corps, but he left after two weeks.

The second employer said the corpsman he hired showed little interest in the job requiring the skill he had studied in the Job Corps and left after two weeks.

Here is how the Senator reported his conversations with the two other employers:

"The employer described the trainee as 'irresponsible,' and made the observation that in spite of the fact that he came 'highly recommended,' it was obvious that 'his training did not do any good'; that he was sadly disappointed in the Job Corps trainee, particularly since he came so highly recommended. The Job Corps trainee stayed for two and a half weeks and is now 'drifting around town, doing odd jobs' . . .

"The fourth employer indicated that it was the policy of his company, one of the larger companies in the country, to cooperate with the Job Corps training centers in attempting to provide employment for Job Corps graduates. This particular Job Corps trainee was employed in the spring of the year. . . . He worked less than one week, before quitting."[2]

An investigation by the *Tulsa World* had similar results. A letter to the newspaper from OEO in Washington suggested the former might find an interesting human interest story in the progress made by four Job Corps trainees from Tulsa. *World* reporter Jim Henderson followed up all four.

He found that two were fired for "loafing" on the job and two simply walked off their jobs after the first few weeks.

In January 1966, OEO published a study of the first 30 graduates of the Job Corps one year later. It boasted that one "is currently employed at the University Club in Baltimore as a general office assistant."

The *Baltimore Sun* checked up and found that the youth actually was working at the Club as a porter and janitor at a salary of $40 a week. Before his Job Corps training, he was employed at a supermarket at $43 a week. He had studied cooking at the Ouachita Job Corps center near Hot Springs, Arkansas.[3]

I asked Job Corps headquarters for the names of companies in the Washington area which had hired Job Corps graduates. I was given three names. One had hired three Job Corpsmen at its automotive repair center at Falls Church, Virginia. All three "had the basic fundamentals of auto repair and that was it; they were not skilled workers," a firm spokesman reported. One did not have a driver's license, and that made it impossible for him to drive, which was part of his job.

All were started at the rate of $1.50 an hour. One decided that auto repair was not for him and enlisted in the Navy. Another became homesick and went back to southern Virginia. The third boy was being trained on the job and was performing satisfactorily.

The second company said it hired six Job Corpsmen as drafting trainees but had to discharge them when it closed its Washington engineering office (after losing its contract with OEO for performing engineering services in connection with Job Corps centers).

The third company didn't know what I was talking about when I mentioned its employment of Job Corpsmen.

OEO might have had better luck in locating its graduates if it had carried out original plans to help them obtain jobs. In the first two years, the program was conducted on such a crash basis, however, that all thought of this went by the wayside. But this was not made known to those who handled the publicity campaign.

Take the case of John Miller, a Washington area builder. He was facing a severe labor shortage when he heard a television plea to hire Job Corpsmen. This seemed like the answer to his problem. Even if they were unskilled, he was willing to train them, meantime paying $2.15 an hour.

Mr. Miller made four phone calls to the Job Corps without success. He also phoned the headquarters of OEO and got a run-around. Many phone calls later, the United Planning Organization—the local anti-poverty organization supported with OEO money—sent him ten men who were not Job Corpsmen. Half of them quit before the day was out because the work was too hard.

In its May 27, 1966 issue, *Modern Grocer* magazine reported it had received a phone call from Job Corps headquarters in Washington asking for help in placing Job Corpsmen trained in supermarket work. As requested, the magazine carried a story saying that these men were available. Indeed, it went even further and made phone calls to key people in the grocery industry, referring them to the Job Corps to obtain workers.

Modern Grocer reported the "results":

"We sat back then, waiting to see doors swing wide open and Job Corps graduates pour through. The doors did open. Key people in the stores phoned in, wrote; there were even personal calls. With what results? To date not a single candidate for a job has been supplied by the Job Corps. Calls to the New York office, letters, have turned up zero. . .

"We think this matter of jobs and of stores needing people badly, who are not available, directly affects our entire economy, and we ask, 'What's with the Job Corps? Who's kidding whom with the people's money?' "[4]

I talked with a girl from Silver Spring, Maryland who

had graduated from the Charleston Center as a cosmetician, having studied the subject there for one year. A month after graduation she had no idea how to go about obtaining employment in her chosen field. She had passed the West Virginia examination for cosmeticians. Upon returning home, however, she learned, to her surprise, that this did not entitle her to practice in the state of Maryland. "I don't know what to do to take the state exam; nobody at the Charleston Center said anything about it," she told me. The girl had made repeated phone calls to the Job Corps in Washington but had received nothing more than a promise that the proper person would call her.

With a little more initiative, the girl obviously could have found out herself how to go about taking the state exam. Thus she was partly to blame for her plight. On the other hand, perhaps OEO should not have expected such know-how and initiative from an underprivileged girl. In any event, the case highlighted the lack of follow-up procedures. In addition, the question remained whether her training in West Virginia would enable her to pass the Maryland exam.

When I talked with the girl she had been unemployed for one month, the time since her graduation. Though frustrated in her attempt to practice her new vocation, she was unwilling to go back to her old one of house-cleaning.

The Job Corps did accomplish something worthwhile, however. It focused public attention on the faults of the public schools and the neglect of vocational education and training. It was the Job Corps centers which discovered that substantial numbers of youngsters who had gone as far as the fifth and sixth grades of grammar school were functionally illiterate.

The Job Corps undoubtedly helped to inspire a special study by the U.S. Chamber of Commerce titled *The Disadvantaged Poor: Education and Employment*. It criticized the schools for often putting their failures in vocational-technical courses and failing to recognize "the important part craftsmen and technicians play in this technological age." Moreover, it said, "In some places courses are still centered around woodworking and mechanical drawing at a time when the economy needs—and compensates well—mechanics, computer operators, electrical appliance repairmen, welders, tool and die makers, carpenters, lathe operators and a host of other highly respectable skills."

Also, the Chamber charged that over half the states discourage vocational training by withholding unemployment compensation from unemployed workers undergoing such training. "The system," it concluded, "should encourage, not discourage, workers to seek new jobs and to acquire job training and upgrade labor skills."

The Chamber also lashed out at labor unions for restricting apprentice training, particularly for Negroes. "Union political pressure on state and local licensing agencies can give control over entrance to trades such as the plumbers and electricians," it said.

The report described the situation in St. Louis as typical of that in cities across the nation. "According to the Justice Department," it said, "the St. Louis Building and Construction Trades Council, affiliated with the AFL-CIO, controls most of the employment opportunities in the building trades. Yet, four AFL-CIO locals within the Council, with combined membership of more than 5,000, had only three Negro members as recently as early 1966."

By February 6, 1967 Representative Ogden R. Reid (R., N.Y.) reintroduced a bill which had been passed by the House but not the Senate in the previous session. It was aimed at strengthening the Fair Employment Practices Commission, particularly to bring about equality in apprenticeship training. He suggested that unemployment among Negroes might be relatively high because only 2 to 3% of apprentices were Negroes.[5]

Meantime, at the suggestion of the Administration, Congress reduced the enrollment goal of the Job Corps from 100,000 to 45,000. Shortly after that, Secretary of Defense Robert S. McNamara announced that the Defense Department would accept 40,000 men for military service who couldn't pass the written entrance tests.

Was this a decision to have the Army rather than the Job Corps play an increasingly large role in helping educationally deficient young men? At least one Congressman thought so. Representative William H. Ayres (R., Ohio) charged on the floor of the House that this showed, "The President and the Secretary of Defense already recognize the expensive futility of the existing Job Corps. . . ."

Not so, retorted Mr. McNamara. He said the Job Corps could take care of those youths "whose educational deficiencies are so severe that we could not reasonably count on bringing them up to an acceptable level of performance even with our present training procedures." He didn't say how he expected the Job Corps to do the job with an average enrollment of nine months. Unwittingly, what Mr. McNamara had revealed was that neither the armed services nor the Job Corps had the solution to the problem of these boys.

6

The Cost of the Job Corps

Whatever the results of the Job Corps, there was little doubt that it was expensive. A study by the House Republican Poverty Subcommittee revealed that over one-third of the staff at five urban Job Corps centers received salary increases of over 20% when they went to work for the Job Corps. The centers were Custer at Kalamazoo, Michigan; Breckinridge, at Morganfield, Kentucky; Kilmer at Edison, New Jersey; Rodman at New Bedford, Massachusetts, and Atterbury at Edinburg, Indiana.

For example, at Kilmer the Manager Administrator went from a job paying $2,704 to a post paying $15,392. Kilmer's Manager went from a $5,800 to a $15,017 salary, and its Senior Contract Administrator from a $9,200 to a $14,186 salary. Rodman's Director of Curriculum went from $10,300 to $18,000 per annum, and Atterbury's Chief of Security went from $5,004 to $12,000.[1]

A Congressional investigation in late 1965 showed that Atterbury had 500 staff members and only 300 corpsmen. And Senator Strom Thurmond (R., S.C.) revealed that in November 1965, the enrollees at Camp Breckinridge outnumbered the staff by only the narrow margin of 358 to 350. Moreover, he said, "The Director of the Breckinridge Camp was fired because his wife and the wives of 51 other middle-management staff employees were on the camp's payroll."

In some instances OEO ran up extraordinary costs in order to open centers quickly. The decision was made to pour substantial sums into rehabilitation and conversion of properties which were only under short-term leases. Here are the reasons a top OEO official gave me for this:

1. Speed. "This was faster than new construction."

2. Appropriations. "It is hard to buy with limited funds because that involves a large initial outlay. Renting enabled us to stretch our money out over more centers over a longer period rather than to use up our initial appropriations in just purchasing a few centers."

3. Size. "We did not know the proper size for a center and still don't know (after two years) and hated to get tied down with some of the wrong size because we feared there would be no ready market for the sale of such centers."

4. Community acceptance. "We could not reasonably predict reception in a community and felt we had to be ready to leave."

OEO employed Consolidated American Services, Inc. to conduct feasibility studies of potential Job Corps centers. Fred MacDonald worked on the surveys for Con Am. In affidavits filed with the House Education and Labor Committee he declared that some buildings were rehabilitated at costs varying from $10 to $35 per square foot when new construction could have been furnished at approximately $7.50 a square foot. And, in addition, OEO was paying rent for the buildings and acquiring no equity.

This led to almost incredible confusion and controversy involving the Charleston Center. William Belcher, employed by Con Am as an engineering consultant, turned in an unfavorable report on the feasibility of using the Kanawha Hotel as a center. It was, he said, in need of complete and expensive renovation, was in violation of city building codes in several areas, had unsuitable kitchen facilities, inadequate space generally and no parking facilities, as required by the city.

After receiving his recommendations, OEO instructed him to return to Charleston, conduct a second survey of the hotel and turn in a more favorable report. When he gave an unfavorable report a second time, Con Am discharged him.[2]

Subsequently Dan Miller resigned as chief engineer for Con Am's poverty contract and charged that the selection of the Kanawha Hotel was "politically motivated."[3] In addition, Representative Quie revealed that the hotel was owned by the Kanawha Hotel Corporation, whose President was Angus Peyton, West Virginia Democratic Commissioner of Commerce and unsuccessful candidate for the State Senate in 1964.

Packard Bell won the contract for operating the Charleston Center in the Kanawha Hotel on the basis of an estimate that rehabilitation costs would come to $100,000. By March 1966, Representative Quie said, the rehabilitation cost was $225,000.[4] Bernard L. Boutin, who was OEO Deputy Director at the time, said the correct figure was $187,000.

Over nine months later, however, Milton Fogelman, Chief Contracting Officer for OEO, told me that total rehabilitation costs at Charleston had not yet been determined. Packard Bell informed me in November 1966 that so far they had paid $228,000, against that estimate of $100,000.

With OEO agreeing to foot the bill for all reasonable costs, the firm had contracted with the George Higginbotham Company of Charleston to rehabilitate the hotel. Mr. Higginbotham, however, failed to complete his work and to pay his subcontractors. As a result Packard Bell sued him on January 20, 1966 for $100,000 for breach of contract. The following month Higginbotham countersued on grounds of breach of contract for the same amount.

Meantime, Packard Bell said that Higginbotham failed to pay his subcontractors and that the subcontractors obtained liens on the building. So that it could keep its crash schedule for opening the center, Packard Bell paid $28,928.69 to the lien holders and hired a new general contractor to complete the work.

At the end of 1966, Packard Bell was hoping it would win its suit against Higginbotham and that if it did not, OEO would pay for the loss as part of the reimbursable costs.

Whatever the exact cost for rehabilitating the Kanawha it looked high for a property which was leased for only two years at $94,800 a year and, according to Representative Quie, had been appraised by reliable Charleston real estate brokers at $250,000 prior to renovation.

Representative John M. Slack, Jr. (D., W.Va.) declared that the hotel really was a bargain for OEO because it occupied extremely valuable land. "The city is enclosed by hills, and the limited amount of flatland has always been disproportionately valuable," he said.[5]

When I asked Mr. Fogelman why he approved establishment of a center on such high cost land, he said it was because it was in depressed Appalachia.

Feasibility studies by Con Am also showed that Job Corps centers should not have been established at Camp Atterbury and Camp Rodman because expenses were likely to be excessive. Here too, the aforementioned Dan Miller said that the selections were "politically motivated."[6]

Donald Garner, a Con Am project engineer and construction cost estimator, submitted a report recommending abandonment of the Rodman site because it was unserviceable and would be too expensive to rehabilitate. Many buildings were rotted, he found, and should have been condemned. OEO went ahead with Rodman anyway and ended up with rehabilitation costs of $1.7 million, against an original estimate of $800,000.[7]

At Poland Spring, Maine, rehabilitation costs came to $1.2 million, exactly twice the original estimate, and at Excelsior Springs, Missouri, they exceeded the estimate of $400,000 by $100,000.

At Camp Atterbury in Indiana, the original rehabilitation estimate was $500,000 and actual costs soared to $3.7 million. Moreover, that did not include over $2 million for equipment.[8] When Congressional investigators visited the camp in September 1965, they were told that higher labor costs than expected were one of the reasons the rehabilitation figure ran over the estimate. This seemed understandable to them when they found that four mechanics took one-and-a-half days at $9 an hour, each, to repair a steam trap when a new trap could have been purchased and installed for $24.

Rehabilitation also apparently left something to be desired at Camp Gary in Texas, despite its cost of $5.7 million.[9] A Con Am engineer advised his firm that the lighting system there was a potential hazard because no preventive maintenance had been in effect for twenty years. His warning was largely ignored until President Johnson was presiding at the dedication of the camp. At that time, the lighting system failed.

For most conservation camps, new construction was necessary since appropriate facilities did not abound in the middle of national forests, national parks and similar locations. Building such camps was not cheap despite the fact that most of them accommodated a maximum of one or two hundred boys. Construction of the Mountain Home camp in Idaho, for instance, ran close to a million dollars ($965,000) despite the fact that it had maximum capacity for only 200 boys. The Castle Valley camp at Price, Utah was even more expensive on an enrollee basis since it had construction costs of $781,000 for a maximum capacity of 112 youths. Nevertheless, the government said that the Castle Valley cost was typical.[10]

Transportation costs, too, ran up Job Corps expenses. OEO purposely sent the enrollees far from home to get them away from what it considered poor environments, and this resulted in federally-financed plane trips for the corpsmen, costing taxpayers an estimated $11.7 million in fiscal 1967.[11]

OEO rules to the contrary, one enrollee from Rhinelander, Wisconsin managed to be assigned to the Job Corps Center at Clam Lake, only 90 miles away from his home. Nevertheless, OEO made a transportation project out of getting him there.

Here, in the words of Representative Quie, is what happened: "Before reaching his destination, the enrollee's travels spanned two days and more than 400 miles. He had to be put up for the night and fed two meals, changed planes three times, took a bus ride and ultimately a car ride; all paid for with federal funds.

"The trip ... could have been much quicker and cheaper ($35) by taxicab ... The final touch of irony was that a free ride could have been secured ... with a Forest Service Radio Operator who travels daily from Rhinelander to Park Falls, Wisconsin, which is very near Clam Lake."[12] (The camp was operated for the OEO by the Forest Service.)

At some centers transportation costs for the youths reached fantastic figures. In 1966 they were running $1 million a year at Camp Gary in Texas, and just short of that at Camp Parks at Pleasanton, California.[13]

Price was no object in sending the youths home for Christmas to bolster their morale. OEO paid for plane trips for 13,000 corpsmen to go home for Christmas in 1965. Representative Thomas Pelly (R., Wash.) said this cost $1.9 million and pointed out that, "Servicemen on leave from Viet Nam or military posts get no federal money for transportation in the U.S.; they pay their own way."

While the airlines offered tickets to military men at half-price on a "seats available" basis, Congressmen complained that many soldiers that Christmas were "bumped" by Job Corpsmen with full-fare tickets.[14]

Despite this criticism, OEO spent $1 million to send 8,596 corpsmen home for the Christmas of 1966, and servicemen continued to be bumped.[15]

But the free round-trip plane travel by the Job Corpsmen was not limited to the holiday season. In addition to receiving his initial free transportation to a center, each was given a free plane trip home once a year for an average distance estimated at 1,275 miles.[16]

At last, toward the end of 1966, Congress clamped down —somewhat. It passed an amendment to the Economic Opportunity Act specifying that an enrollee must be assigned to the center nearest his residence provided it meets his needs.

Transportation was not all that was free, however. So were education, training, food, housing, clothing, recreation and medical and dental care. In addition, enrollees received a monthly "living allowance" of $30 a month which could be increased up to a maximum of $20 a month extra "for outstanding achievement in academic work or community service." When they left the Job Corps, they were given an additional $50 for each month they had remained. While in the Corps, they could have $25 of this paid monthly to a dependent, parent or other relative. Thus, while Sargent Shriver told Congress that a Job Corps enrollee got $30 a month compared to $94 for an Army private, the pay for the former actually could go to $100.[17]

OEO's handling of the free clothing aroused the ire of Representative Paul A. Fino (R., N.Y.). He discovered that at a time when the Army had a uniform shortage, and the Job Corps had only 17,000 members, OEO spent $370,000 for 30,000 brass-buttoned jackets for Job Corpsmen. Here is what he said on the floor of the House:

"Why spend $370,000 getting them special blazers? I know another type of outfit they could wear. It has brass buttons too. I firmly believe we ought to draft our nation's punks and hoods instead of coddling and paying them in the Job Corps. Why should juvenile virtue be rewarded with military service in the Vietnamese nightmare, while a record of delinquency exempts punks from the Army and puts them in line for Job Corps coddlings?"[18]

While the extravagance was apparent, at the end of two years, nobody was sure what the Job Corps was costing per youth. This is what the Minority of the House Education and Labor Committee had to say:

"The cost of this single anti-poverty program is appalling. Costs everywhere are exceeding estimates. The combination of high property rentals, excessive salaries and underestimated site rehabilitation costs has resulted in a cost per enrollee that has been variously estimated as $9,210 to $13,000 per year... When costs are evaluated on the basis of cost per graduate, the results are even more astounding."[19]

Even figured for enrollees, costs exceeded $13,000 at some centers. According to Senator Strom Thurmond, they came to $22,000 at Camp Atterbury,[20] and Representatives Fino and Goodell found the costs per graduate came to $39,205 at St. Petersburg, Florida.[21]

The main reason costs were so uncertain was that in the first two years OEO had not settled any contracts for operating the Job Corps centers. How much of the unforseen costs OEO would allow still was up in the air.

The center at St. Petersburg presented a case in point. At the end of 1966, OEO had terminated the contract of the Pinellas County School Board for operating it—indeed the center itself was terminated—but no settlement was in sight. Allowable costs were so much in dispute that the General Accounting Office was conducting a full-fledged investigation, and OEO officials were talking about referring the controversy to the Contract Disputes Board they had set up within their agency to handle such cases. One of the chief issues in dispute was how much OEO should spend to put the property back into shape to operate as a hotel.

The Charleston Center also had some potential unknown costs. At the end of 1966, the center had a suit pending by Marjorie Wasserburger, the former Chief of Basic Education at the center. On February 25, 1966 she had sued for $225,000, charging breach of contract in dismissing her. By the year's end, there was no way of knowing the outcome of the case, or whether OEO would consider it as an allowable cost if the center, operated by Packard Bell, lost the case.

Enough was known of Job Corps costs, however, to make comparison possible. According to Representative Quie, residential vocational schools had average costs of $2,600 per student per year.[22]

James R. Clemens is a former president of the Williamson Free School of Mechanical Trades, a residential vocational school at Media, Pennsylvania. In a letter to Senator Hugh Scott (R., Pa.), Mr. Clemens said his school could educate and teach a skill to a youth for $2,300 a year.

By 1966, members of Congress were beginning to feel the ire of taxpayers over Job Corps costs. Representative Edith Green (D., Ore.), an early advocate of the Corps, told this to the House on September 28:

"I had a letter the other day from a woman in my district

who said, 'How can I possibly pay taxes to support people
in the Job Corps centers at $13,000 a year?' She said, 'Our
total income is $6,000 a year, and we have three children.
We had hoped that we would be able to send our three
children to college. Instead of that you are passing a program in the Congress of the United States which says that
I am to pay taxes to support one person at $13,000 a
year.' "[23]

7

The Congress
and Changes
in the Job Corps

By late 1966 it was becoming so obvious that OEO was making a fiasco of the noble-sounding Job Corps program that Congress no longer could be complacent. In amendments to the Economic Opportunity Act that year it attempted to deal with the Job Corps problems of scandals, discipline, high costs and ignorance of results; and it even got into enrollment figures. It was obvious at the outset, however, that the Congress was not going to solve all the problems. Indeed, it appeared that it was creating several new ones.

The new legislation specifically provided that directors of Job Corps centers must have full authority to take appropriate disciplinary measures against enrollees, including dismissal. Thus, the aforementioned Charles H. Stoddard belatedly won his point, though he had long since departed from the Bureau of Land Management.

I talked with many center directors, however, who said

that in the case of a purely voluntary program and with dropout rates already high, they were generally afraid to enforce strict discipline and looked upon it as a last resort.

Congress did not go so far as to say that the centers should not enroll youths with criminal records. It merely provided that in accepting youths for the Job Corps, OEO should not violate parole or probationary procedures of a state.

The 1966 amendments also ordered OEO to try to find out what happened to Job Corps graduates at regular six- and nineteen-month intervals "to the maximum extent feasible." Subsequently the *Washington Post* declared, "Everyone in the Poverty War knows this is impossible."[1]

OEO had already tried to check up on the Job Corpsmen it had apparently lost irretrievably. In July 1966 it sent questionnaires to 1,474 of the 6,500 Job Corpsmen with "known job placements" in an effort to determine if they were still employed. Even though it promised a dollar for each reply, it received only 465 answers.[2]

At the end of 1966, OEO officials were talking about tracing the corpsmen through their Social Security numbers, presumably a thought which took two years to occur to them.

In desperation, OEO hired pollster Louis Harris to find out what had happened to the graduates on the basis of a 5% sample, with the hope that he would be able to find that many. He was just starting to try as this was being written.

The Congress, in its amendments, limited operating costs on the average to $7,500 per enrollee, annually. However, this appeared more restrictive than it actually was. It did not include capital costs which took in the fantastically high rehabilitation expenses. Also it applied only to centers which were in operation for nine months or more, thus eliminating "start-up" costs.

Still, it was obvious that some individual centers would have a difficult time getting in line with the mandatory average figure. At Huntington, West Virginia, for instance, operating costs per enrollee were at an average annual rate of $24,000 during the first six months of operation.[3]

Having originally envisioned an enlistment of 100,000 youths, Congress limited the capacity of Job Corps centers to 45,000 enrollees in 1967. There seemed little danger of exceeding the limitation, or, indeed, even coming within shooting distance of it. Costs were running so high that OEO did not have the money for expanding capacity that much, despite the fact that President Johnson asked Congress for $295 million for the Job Corps for fiscal year 1968, compared with an appropriation of $211 million for the previous year.

At the time, OEO said this would enable it to expand capacity at Job Corps centers to accommodate 41,000 youths, and this compared with spaces then available for about 35,000. What it didn't mention publicly, however, was that it then had thousands of empty beds. No one seemed sure of the exact number. A joint Labor Department-OEO press release issued November 20, 1966 said enrollment was "over 25,000." With capacity of 35,000 that would mean 10,000 vacancies, give a thousand or so to account for that modifier, "over." But the next day OEO announced that enrollment totaled 29,126. Thus, vacancies stood somewhere between 5,874 and 10,000, and OEO was plunging ahead to add new capacity when it couldn't fill what it had.

Against the planned capacity figure of 41,000, President Johnson told Congress he was figuring on an enrollment figure of 38,000. This indicated that somehow he was expecting the Job Corps to reduce the number of empty beds to 3,000 while adding 6,000 beds.

Prospects for reaching that goal appeared exceedingly

dim, especially in view of the fact that enrollment actually decreased following a massive recruitment drive for 20,000 youths by OEO and the Labor Department. When the agencies jointly announced the drive on November 20, 1966, enrollment was 29,126, according to official OEO figures. At the end of the drive, January 3, 1967, again according to OEO official figures, enrollment stood at 28,966. This was clear evidence that the Job Corps couldn't even hold its own in the face of massive recruitment efforts. (Nobody seemed sure what had become of the original avalanche of Job Corps applications; they were considered too old to be worth pursuing.)

Prior to the release of the official figures on January 3, I asked Ernest Gross, Information Director for the Job Corps, if it had met the goal of 20,000 new enrollees by the end of 1966. He replied, "Of course not; we didn't have a goal of 20,000 by the end of 1966."

Reminded that a Joint Labor Department-OEO press release stated that this was the case, Mr. Gross replied, "That must have been talking about the fiscal year."

The following is quoted directly from the official announcement:

"The recruitment drive, to be conducted by the U.S. Employment Service and the Job Corps, is the largest concerted Corps enrollment effort to date. Its goal is 14,000 youths by the end of November and 20,000 by December 31."

The Legislature further complicated matters for OEO by specifying that by July 1, 1967 not less than 23% of the Job Corps enrollees must be women. Originally, the House had stated that at least 10,000 women should be in residence and receiving training in Job Corps centers by July 1, 1967. After the bill went to conference, the 23% specification emerged.

Since OEO had nothing more than an enrollment goal

for July 1, it had trouble figuring out how to comply with the 23% mandate.

Representative Edith Green (D., Ore.), who had sponsored the legislation to put women in the Job Corps, told me that the figure of 45,000 should be considered a goal and that OEO should base the 23% on that and recruit more women. However, David Squire, Deputy Director of the Job Corps, told me that OEO didn't have enough money to enroll 45,000.

Fearing that it had neither time nor money to increase capacity and enrollment to meet the 23% requirement by July 1, OEO launched some desperate expedients. On January 5, 1967 it announced that at Tongue Point, Oregon it would convert the center to accommodate women instead of men.

This was right in Representative Green's own backyard, and it infuriated her. The location, she said, was not suitable for a center for either boys or girls because it was too isolated. "There is no place for on-the-job training and there are no jobs in the area," she explained. She added that there were no recreational facilities except for the ocean which is warm enough for swimming only three months a year.

The legislator also pointed out that the center was too expensive, with operating costs running at $13,000 per boy. She added that while it had a capacity of 1,250, the highest enrollment it ever reached was 880. It was down to 500 by January 1967.

I was unable to obtain from OEO any estimate on the cost of converting Tongue Point. I asked several officials if they had done a feasibility study before making the conversion decision. Some said they had, and some said they hadn't. The former said they did not feel the figures were firm enough to make public.

At any rate, I learned that the operation involved ripping out automotive training equipment and installing stoves and other facilities for domestic training. It also meant replacing long lines of urinals with more feminine facilities with private enclosures.

In January 1967, OEO also announced that to comply with the 23% mandate it would cut back on the number of trainees at Camp Kilmer at Edison, New Jersey by 700. This seemed strange, however, since enrollment at the time was 1,400 and had never reached the capacity of 2,300. Some members of Congress felt that the action was an effort to blame the under-use of capacity on them rather than on OEO's inability to attract youths to Kilmer.

Interesting to note is the fact that at the time it announced a cutback in male trainees at Kilmer, OEO signed a contract with Litton Industries to increase male enrollment by 200 in 1967 at Camp Parks at Pleasanton, California.

Another 1966 Congressional change in the Job Corps was the specification that trainees be assigned to centers near their homes. This reversed the OEO practice of sending them far away on the theory that they needed to be removed from the poor influence of their homes and families.

Several center directors told me the banned practice was not only expensive; it didn't work. Homesickness had been a paramount problem for all of them. Trainees left the Corps in droves because of it and those who stuck it out often left their after-graduation jobs because of it.

One center director declared, "We could do a lot more about helping corpsmen find employment, if they came from near the center. In most cases, if a fellow is a thousand miles from home, he wants to go back there after graduation. But we know about jobs available in the local community. Also, the local folks often resent it when the government helps outsiders to get the local jobs. That's particularly true when the government picks a poverty pocket for the location of a center."

In 1966, the House voted to require the OEO to establish qualifications for contractors operating centers as assurance that they possessed the capacity and educational resources to carry out their obligations. The measure did not get through the Senate, however.

In party-line votes, the House turned down several amendements proposed by the Republicans. One would have established procedures for evaluation of enrollees to identify those with criminal records. Another called for the discharge of anyone convicted of a felony. Still another would have precluded the government from paying legal costs for arrested Job Corpsmen when local communities were accustomed to providing such service without cost to persons unable to pay. Said one Republican, "We don't do this for our soldiers and sailors, why should we do it for the Job Corpsmen?"

On January 24, 1967, OEO issued an official statement apparently attempting to show that the proposed budget for the Job Corps then pending in Congress was lower than the comparable figure for the previous year. It said that an appropriation request for $295 million for the Job Corps should be compared with $320 million for the previous year. To be certain of my ground, I checked with Joseph Laitin, Assistant to the Director of the Budget Bureau, and found that, as I suspected, the figures were not comparable. The $295 million should have been compared with $211 million for the previous year.

In budgeting, federal agencies have one set of figures for new obligational authority. That is the permission they seek from Congress to obligate themselves to make expenditures. Then they must keep books, of course, on the actual expenditures they make. But OEO had lumped together $211 million of obligational authority and $109 million in expenditures in one year and compared the resulting figure with obligational authority only, exclusive of expenditures.

In January 1967 Louis Harris came out with his first Job Corps study. It covered dropouts rather than graduates, as specified by Congress, and was titled "A Study of Job Corps Non-Graduate Terminations."

The following month OEO trumpeted, "Enrollment in Job Corps can improve the employment potential of a youth and the value of the program is appreciated even by those who left before completing their training. This is a finding by Louis Harris and Associates which conducted a survey of young men and women who left Job Corps before completing training. An 11% sampling of 10,858 young men and women who resigned or were discharged was made in the study."

Noting that the OEO press release said the Job Corps "can improve the employment potential" (and not that it results in more jobs), I began the first of a long series of attempts to obtain a copy of the study from OEO. Half a year later, Herbert J. Kramer, OEO Assistant Director for Public Affairs, permitted me to borrow copies of the Louis Harris studies for OEO. The covers and every page were labeled "confidential" in bold type. After reading them, it was not difficult to understand why. They showed a reduction in employment for youngsters after Job Corps training.

The dropout report showed that 56% of the sample were working before the Job Corps, whereas only 54% were doing so after leaving it.

"Almost one in five feel they are worse off now than before they went into the Job Corps," said the study.

It pointed out that of those unemployed after their stint in the Job Corps, 59% either had been working or going to school before entering the Corps.

For those who were able to find jobs afterwards, the median hourly rate was $1.23, an increase of eight cents over the pre-Job Corps rate, not even enough to keep up with the minimum wage. But only 2% found employment through the Job Corps. Of those looking for work, only 5% were being helped through the Corps. The study also said that 42% didn't get the training promised, and 16% either didn't know what they had been trained for or had not received any training by the time they left.

Louis Harris also did a survey for OEO titled "A Study of August 1966 Terminations from the Job Corps." Dated March 1967, it was based on a sample of 868 out of 3,073 names supplied by OEO and was also labeled "confidential."

Even though this covered graduates as well as dropouts, it showed that 57% were working after leaving the Job Corps, whereas 58% were doing so beforehand.

The median length of time for holding a job was 2.4 months. (This was not even the length of the three-month probationary period commonly offered by employers.) Only 6% kept their jobs more than six months. In addition, less than half of those with jobs were working at what they were trained for in the Corps.

The survey found that 61% of the graduates were working pre-Job Corps and 66% afterwards. For those in the sample who found jobs upon leaving the Corps, the median hourly pay was $1.32 an hour, 15 cents an hour better than before their expensive training.

8

Industry
and
the Job Corps

Congress and the poor were not the only ones fooled by the Job Corps. Private enterprise was, too, as some of its prominent members learned after plunging into the operation of Job Corps centers.

In the beginning, company representatives nearly fell over each other in their scramble for OEO contracts. The attraction was two words, long dear to the hearts of those who do business with Uncle Sam—cost plus. But this time there was a new wrinkle. The bewhiskered gentleman would bear the cost of investment in plant. Said one company president, "That made Sargent Shriver look better to us than Santa Claus."

In the case of, say, defense contractors, the companies usually already have the plants in which to perform the work, facilities in which they have tied up their capital. As a rule, they figure on amortizing their investment in twenty years.

Those who knocked on OEO's door, however, were told they could forget about tying up their capital. The government would provide free facilities in the form of unused military camps and veterans' hospitals. When these were not available, it would pay the rent for hotels and other commercial facilities. Rehabilitation obviously would be necessary, and OEO would consider this an allowable cost.

One corporate policymaker told me, "To make any profit at all without tying up large amounts of capital is miraculous. This is better than we could do by putting our money in a bank or savings and loan."

The companies were engaged to teach the Job Corps enrollees a vocational skill and improve their basic education. Neither OEO nor Congress set any minimum requirements for educational and training capability on the part of the contractors. Time after time, OEO policymakers told me, "They are the experts in this field; we aren't." But they hired companies engaged in the manufacture of items like electronic equipment and business machines to teach subjects like basic education, culinary arts, landscaping, beauty culture, flower-arranging and nursing.

Moreover, OEO set no minimum standards either for the courses taught or for graduation. When queried about this, officials gave the same response, "The contractors are the experts; we aren't."

What happened as a result was that OEO paid fantastically high sums for the education and training of Job Corpsmen to contractors who had not established their qualifications and who were not required to give any minimum performance in return. Thus a graduation certificate from the Job Corps could mean anything—or nothing. Potential employers didn't know what to expect.

Most companies initially were given two-year contracts for operating the centers. Among those who received contracts were Westinghouse Electric Corporation, Westinghouse Air Brake, General Precision Equipment Company, Thiokol Chemical Corporation, U.S. Industries, Inc., Federal Electric Corporation, RCA, Litton Industries, IBM, Burroughs Corporation, Packard Bell Electronic Corporation, Philco Corporation, Avco Corporation, General Electric Company, and Xerox Corporation. Their fees were set at a maximum of 4.7% based on the estimated cost of carrying out the contracts.

Many of them saw the Job Corps as an opportunity to get in on the ground floor of the expanding educational and training market which they saw as second only to defense as a potential. One company officer pointed out that the Department of Health, Education and Welfare was talking about spending $35 billion in the next ten years, just for education, and expected underdeveloped countries to look to the U.S. for help in the education and training sorely needed for carrying out their development plans.

All in all, at first glance, it looked as if the companies couldn't lose. In the light of actual experience with the Job Corps, however, some of them were having second thoughts. Indeed, several were alarmed. Sure and quick profits began to look farther and farther away. Unforeseen costs cropped up right and left, and it seemed likely some of these might have to come out of profits.

Moreover, public relations went from bad to worse. While the Job Corps did, indeed, identify the companies with the field of education, it was often in a bad sense.

For instance, the *Chicago Tribune* quoted the American Federation of Teachers as saying that the center at Excelsior Springs, Missouri, run by Westinghouse Air Brake, was a complete failure. In addition, teachers at the center went on strike from June 1, 1966 to June 16, 1966 in a dispute over their proper duties. Also, a group of local citizens obtained a warrant against the center director for conducting a public nuisance.[1]

In its first four months of operation, the Huntington Center in West Virginia, run by Xerox, had four different directors.[2] And in August 1966 nine of the fifteen members of the resident leader staff resigned because of a dispute over changes in regulations.[3]

The aforementioned citizens' report of the Rodman Camp made it more than obvious that they were not happy with Science Research Associates, the IBM subsidiary in charge of Rodman.

As is obvious from this account, scandal did not spare the centers run by commercial contractors. That fact alone made their Job Corps ventures look like losing propositions. Most of them customarily spent substantial sums to promote good public relations. In many cases, the amounts were in excess of the profits they originally expected to reap from the Job Corps. Thus, for questionable monetary profits, they were nullifying many of the effects of their public relations expenditures.

While the contracts guaranteed a maximum fee of 4.7% plus costs, the fee was based on the original cost estimate, and contractors admitted they had very little to go on in making the estimate. One flaw in the contracts was that they were unclear over which unforseen costs would be borne by OEO.

The turnover at OEO headquarters was so high that having an understanding with any individual there often meant very little; he might not be there the next day.

In the words of one official of the General Accounting Office (GAO), "There is a lot of hazard in these cost-plus contracts." He explained that OEO paid contractors monthly but that all such disbursements were subject to recall after a final OEO audit. Contractors also could be required to refund money to OEO after a GAO review and a final determination by the Comptroller General of the U.S.

Both on Capitol Hill and at the GAO, predictions were made that the cost accounting would go on for years, just as it has for some defense contractors with cost-plus arrangements with the Pentagon. At the end of 1966 the GAO already was beginning to question some rehabilitation costs, and they involved a good deal of money, as noted in chapter six.

In addition, there seemed to be inequitable treatment for contractors who used government facilities for the centers. Since such facilities were furnished free, they could not be included in the cost estimate on which the fee was based. When a contractor rented a commercial facility, however, the rent could be counted as part of the cost on which the fee was based.

In numerous instances, contractors paid for unforeseen costs out of their profits. Unable to acquire a qualified center director at the OEO maximum of $20,000 a year, IBM hired one for $25,000 for its Rodman Center and dipped into its own till to make up the difference.[4]

Avco had such difficulty in attracting teachers for its Poland Spring Center that it paid for extensive relocation costs which OEO refused to allow in full.

At Charleston, West Virginia, Packard Bell received OEO approval to run up additional costs of $200,000 just in employing extra "resident advisers." These were women who lived in the dormitories with Job Corps girls to give advice and guidance and try to keep order. If the GAO disallowed just this one item of cost, it would be more than enough to wipe out Packard Bell's total profit on the two-year Charleston contract. But there were other costs beyond Packard Bell's original estimate, both potential and actual. The potential ones included the aforementioned court suits. Among the actual ones was the cost of hiring off-duty policemen to maintain order in the center lobby and the area surrounding the building.

Understandably, some of the firms invited to bid for Job Corps centers began to take a harder look at OEO ground rules. After engaging in preliminary negotiations for a center, Raytheon Company, for one, decided the ground rules made success impossible and that it would not proceed without substantial changes. By the end of 1966 they were not forthcoming.

Firms also began to make sure of community acceptance before signing up to operate Job Corps centers. That is why OEO was unable to carry out its aim of establishing a regular center in the vicinity of Washington. Contractors investigating potential sites could not find a single one which had community acceptance.

One of the persons I talked with was Joseph Alexander, Fairfax County supervisor in nearby Virginia, who told me the citizens in his district were opposed 100% to OEO's idea of locating a Job Corps center in their neighborhood.

9

The Beginning
of Community Action

While community action was the boldest and most important part of the War on Poverty, defining it is extremely difficult; the Economic Opportunity Act did this so broadly that it meant virtually anything the OEO Director wanted it to mean. Verbose and vague, the Act said a community action program (CAP) was one which mobilized community resources for an attack on poverty, one "which provides services, assistance, and other activities of sufficient scope and size to give promise of progress toward elimination of poverty or a cause or causes of poverty through developing employment opportunities, improving human performance, motivation and productivity, or bettering the conditions under which people live, learn and work."

One of the chief selling points for community action was that it would involve the poor in helping themselves, instead of merely giving them handouts. Congress bought this idea. Acting on what Sargent Shriver said was his suggestion, it wrote into the Act a provision calling for "maximum feasible participation" of the residents of the areas involved in community action.[1] Later it became apparent that nobody knew what this meant. Interpretations were as numerous as the aims of the interpreters.

What specific CAP's held the most promise? How much money should a specific one get? How should the poor be mobilized for this participation? All these questions were for the OEO Director to determine. As a result of his decisions, taxpayers' money supported some highly questionable activities, including the organization of boycotts and militant demonstrations, one of which culminated in an attack upon a police station. Federal anti-poverty money also went to pay exorbitant salaries to community action employees, some with criminal, leftist, and even Communist backgrounds. Too, it paid for expensive fiascos in attempts to elect representatives of the poor. In addition it fostered the creation of cooperatives in competition with private enterprise (to be discussed in a later chapter).

The OEO Director's interpretations of community action also led to Head Start programs; the Economic Opportunity Act did not even mention Head Start or any kindergarten program. As will be shown in later chapters, Head Start had questionable results for the children involved and resulted in attempts by so-called representatives of the poor to take over control of public schools. In addition, at the time this is being written, fraud and other alleged crimes in connection with Head Start programs are the subject of several investigations, including one by the U.S. Department of Justice.

What Mr. Shriver's real intentions were remains an unanswered question. I found no one who was convinced that he wanted the community action centers to become the basis for leftist influence through a nationwide network of Communist-style cadres of the poor, even though it seemed increasingly that this is what they were becoming. Some saw Mr. Shriver as a "do-gooder" who didn't realize the trouble he was inviting. Others considered him an extremely ambitious man who would do business with the devil himself. Still others saw him as an outstanding salesman who lacked the administrative ability for the job he had undertaken.

However, anyone who took the time to study the genesis of community action could not have failed to recognize its dangerous potential. Unlike the Job Corps, community action did not start on a massive scale at once; it had a pilot project, Mobilization for Youth.[2]

The theoretical basis for MFY was published in 1960 in a book titled *Delinquency and Opportunity*, by Richard A. Cloward and Lloyd E. Ohlin, both of the New York School of Social Work of Columbia University.[3]

Wide-scale juvenile delinquency results from the lack of opportunities for lower-class youths, the authors maintained, particularly where this is connected with race or nationality. Young people who attribute their lack of success to lack of opportunity, rather than to lack of ability, are at odds with the established social order. The resulting tension can be relieved, the authors reasoned, "if the alienated person can gain the support of others who are in the same position and who share the view that their misfortunes are due to an unjust system of social arrangements."

Messrs. Cloward and Ohlin decried a breakdown in the cohesion and organization of some slum communities and warned of increasing violence without it. Their conclusion was that "the major effort of those who wish to eliminate delinquency should be directed to the reorganization of slum communities." The authors left no doubt they advocate organizing those in rebellion against the established social order.

At mid-1966 Mr. Cloward spearheaded a plan circulated widely among civil rights organizations and militant antipoverty groups. According to the North American Newspaper Alliance, the plan was "to persuade millions of Americans to get on the relief rolls—to bankrupt the welfare agencies. The purpose is to provoke a financial crisis that would force Congress to enact a guaranteed annual income for all Americans."[4]

Nobody seems to know whether President Kennedy personally read *Delinquency and Opportunity*. Richard Boone, who served on the President's Committee on Juvenile Delinquency, told me, however, that the President was much impressed with the theory of the book.

In 1962, some years after the book was published, President Kennedy began funding Mobilization for Youth to the tune of $7 million as a three-year social experiment on the Lower East Side of New York. An additional $4.2 million came from the City of New York and $1.8 million from the Ford Foundation.[5]

During its pilot project stage, MFY had in microcosm most of the troubles which later developed in community action programs across the country. Communists and other subversives on the MFY payroll preached revolution, organized rent strikes and aided school boycotts.[6] And, just as in the case of the CAP's which succeeded MFY, this did not deter the federal government from pouring in money.

An FBI investigation showed that Communists were working for MFY in July 1964 when President Johnson gave the organization another federal grant of $1.5 million.[7]

Even earlier, on January 27, 1964, the principals of four New York City school districts wired the Superintendent of Schools and the President of the Board of Education urging an investigation of MFY. They expressed alarm over "full-time agitators and organizers for extremist groups."[8]

By August, the *New York Times* reported that the FBI investigation showed two MFY employees were currently members of the Communist Party, three others were "hard-core leftists" and 32 others had "former links to Communists or alleged Communist-front groups."[9]

Here are other startling facts about MFY brought out in a report issued in December 1964, by the New York (State) Senate Committee on Affairs of the City of New York.

The roster of MFY employees included the following:

Archie Shepp: Employed in the MFY "Coffee House Program" and a member of the Lower Manhattan Youth Club of the Communist Party while so employed. Recommended for MFY job by Carole Pina.

Carole Pina: Paid $100 a week to work 20 hours a week as a student researcher for MFY. "MFY officials were unable to locate Miss Pina at the time this Committee was unsuccessfully attempting to subpoena her." While on MFY payroll went to Cuba. Castro government paid for trip. Group in which she traveled issued a statement in support of the Viet Cong in South Vietnam.

Esther Gollobin: Member of the MFY Board of Directors, member of the New York County Committee of the Communist Party and a Party organizer for the Lower East Side Section.

Constance Bart: An MFY administrative secretary. Kings County Educational Director of the Communist Party. "Acted in an official capacity" at meetings of the Flatbush Club of the Communist Party in Brooklyn. Married to Phillip Bart, Organizational Secretary of the Communist Party.

Calvin Hicks: Group worker in MFY Youth in Action Program. Member of the Lower Manhattan Youth Club of the Communist Party. Executive Secretary of Monroe Defense Committee established to defend Robert F. Williams. The latter allegedly kidnapped two people and organized armed violence in Monroe, North Carolina. The report observed that Mr. Williams had fled to Communist Cuba to escape the kidnapping charge.

(In his book, *The New Left*, Phillip Abbot Luce, a former leader of the pro-Chinese Progressive Labor Party, identified Mr. Williams as the "Chairman in Exile" of the Revolutionary Action Movement. The latter, he said, "is preparing to launch a guerrilla warfare operation." He quoted Mr. Williams as saying in Hanoi in November 1964, "As a representative of the Revolutionary Action Movement, I am here to give support to the Vietnamese people in their struggle against U.S. imperialist aggression."

(Said the *New York Times*, "From Cuba Mr. Williams supplies members of the movement with treatises on how to make Molotov cocktails and to conduct guerrilla warfare. Robert Williams is an implacable advocate of violence, revolution and Communism.")

Because of his advocacy of violence, the National Association for the Advancement of Colored People removed Mr. Williams as Chairman of its Monroe Chapter.

Marc Schleifer: Part-time consultant to MFY. Editor of book by Robert Williams, *Negroes with Guns*. Book defended program of armed violence. Published by Marzani & Munsell. Mr. Marzani identified as member of Communist Party by undercover agent of New York City Police Department.

Leroy McRae: MFY community organizer. Active member of Socialist Workers Party, an organization on the Attorney General's subversive list. National Organizational Secretary of the Young Socialist Alliance, the Socialist Workers Party's Youth Organization.

Marvin Markman, representative of the Youth Division of the Communist Party, told a meeting of the New York County Coordinating Committee of the Communist Party that party members should become active in all possible levels of MFY because it would provide a good mass base for Party operations in the area.

Grace Cade and Pedro Otero, MFY employees, were co-chairmen of a rally on the Lower East Side to promote a

1964 rent strike. Mr. Otero, along with MFY workers Calvin Hicks and Leroy McRae, served on a publicity committee for the rent strike. In addition, MFY paid for 10,000 rent strike handbills and put its phone number on them.

Featured speaker at the rent strike rally was Jesse Gray, a former Communist Party organizer for Harlem. After the Harlem race riot in the summer of 1964, Mr. Gray "issued a public call for 'a hundred skilled black revolutionaries who are ready to die' to correct . . . 'police brutality'."

MFY also played a role in the New York school boycott of 1964. Its employees aided community organizations which conducted the boycott and made MFY facilities and equipment available to them.

The New York Senate Committee report included the following statement by Florence S. Becker, Assistant Superintendent of Schools for New York City:

"The trouble between MFY and the school principals began last summer when it suddenly became painfully apparent that massive attacks were being launched against the schools and school personnel by groups organized and led by some staff members of MFY. The destructive, vicious, false charges were different from the city-wide attacks, in that the leaders, supposedly our friends, were professionals engaged in a program supported by public funds. . . . Suddenly the schools—not only the school system, but also the local schools, their principals and teachers as individuals—were singled out as an enemy of the community, the reason for all the ills of the minority groups."

In a joint declaration published in the New York (State) Senate Committee report, principals of four New York City schools in MFY's area declared:

"At various times we heard the following from Mr. [George A.] Brager (Director of the MFY Action Program):

" 'Principals are inflexible.

" 'It is unfortunate that you are being hurt but MFY is not responsible for the actions of the groups.

" 'This is a revolution! Someone has to get hurt.' "

So much for the New York Senate Committee report and the inspiration for community action.

In starting the War on Poverty, Congress not only failed to study the genesis of community action in Mobilization for Youth, it also ignored the portent of the proviso for "maximum feasible participation" in community action by the residents of the areas involved. Nothing in the Congressional debate indicates that in adopting the OEO suggestion Congress foresaw that it would be used as a device for creating new and sometimes dangerous political power groups.

After a study for OEO of the procedures for selecting representatives of the poor to obtain their "maximum feasible participation," here is what the American Arbitration Association concluded:

"The concept [maximum feasible participation] is historic, yet a search for the full rationale behind it, for a record of the protracted hours of argument, probing and debate that would be expected to lead to such a revolutionary notion, is quite in vain. The phrase, and the thought, seem to have no legislative history. Scholars and critics of the Act have noted the extraordinary broad grant of discretionary powers that were left to the administering agency by the Act, and one of these certainly was the Maximum Feasible Participation language."[10]

The minimal Congressional opposition that existed was centered on charges that the whole idea was ridiculous. This was true even after the proviso for "maximum feasible participation" had been on the books for a year. Just before Congress passed a Republican amendment in 1966 calling for one-third participation of the poor, Representative

Ogden R. Reid (R., N. Y.) declared, "I have no objection
to the poor being involved in this. But on a practical basis,
an amendment of this kind, it seems to me, would be just as
logical as passing a law saying that one third of all the de-
feated candidates for Congress ought to be seated in the
House, or every time a business starts up, there ought to be
at least as one third of the board of directors people who
have gone bankrupt."[11]

Prior to passage of the amendment, OEO held several
elections to select representatives of the poor to take part in
running community action programs. They were costly
failures.

In the Watts area of Los Angeles, OEO set up 154 poll-
ing places, chartered 25 buses to take people to the polls,
paid for the printing of 100,000 leaflets and ran up total
expenses of $61,000. (In addition, 600 volunteers rang
doorbells to get out the vote.) Of the 400,000 considered
eligible to vote, only 2,659 did so. That came to less than
1%, at a cost of $22.94 a vote.[12]

In Boston 2.4% voted at a cost per vote of $10.58. In
Cleveland a 4.2% turnout cost $1.07 a vote. In Kansas City,
a 5% turnout cost $1.89 a vote.[13]

Following these fiascos, OEO paid the American
Arbitration Association $26,447 to make a study to de-
termine what went wrong. The AAA found little that was
right. There were no uniform qualifications for voters
city-by-city. The minimum voting age ranged from 15 to
21, depending upon the city. Some cities allowed anyone
living in a poverty area to vote, while others required voters
to be impoverished. Moreover, standards of poverty varied.
For some cities, it was less than $3,000 per annum while in
others it was as high as $4,500 per annum. In all cases
studied, little proof of poverty was required.

The AAA study said the poor could see no advantage in
voting in elections because the War on Poverty had been

oversold, and they could not see that it was doing them any good. It also found that the candidates had no reputation for concern with the problems the elections purported to address. Moreover, the study explained that the poor did not connect the elections with any political machine and thus did not see that there were any political favors to be dispensed to voters. Also, many potential voters objected to being stigmatized as poor to qualify to cast their ballots. It concluded, "The poor are suspicious of these elections as an effort by the establishment to reach its arm into their community for who knows what sinister or cynical purpose."[14]

Small wonder that the OEO made the study available to me only after being prodded for two weeks.

Finally, however, Mr. Shriver conceded to Congress, "These elections perhaps are not proving to be as effective a weapon as we thought. . . . We are disappointed in them."[15]

Still OEO had the responsibility for seeing that one third of the members of community action boards were representatives of the poor, not necessarily the poor themselves. Finally, in desperation, OEO declared, "Any selection process which insures maximum feasible involvement of the poor is potentially acceptable. However, OEO urges communities to meet the initial requirements of the amendments in the simplest and least time-consuming manner even though, subsequently, it may be found that a change in the selection process is desirable to increase the degree of participation of low income groups and individuals."

The agency warned, however, that boards which failed to have one-third representation of the poor also would fail to receive OEO money. To use a charitable word, OEO was flexible in carrying out the Congressional requirement. It granted funds to Atlanta which had almost no poor on its board, while the mayor of Los Angeles accused Mr.

Shriver of cutting off funds to his city in an attempt to force it to give more voice to the poor in planning.[16] Still no one was sure whether the poor or their representatives, whoever they were, should form policy or simply take part in program operations.

A Congressional expert on the War on Poverty told me, "The apathy of the poor indicates how easy it is to get control of the community action programs. I think Congress meant to induce people to help themselves, but it is not being interpreted that way."

Indeed, Representative John H. Buchanan (R., Ala.) identified Henry Winston as "a Communist spokesman" and quoted him as saying the following:

"Today, the Economic Opportunity Act contains a section which calls for 'maximum feasible participation' of the poor themselves in the fight against poverty. It has already become the basis for organizing struggles in the slums and ghetto communities, and it offers the point of departure for helping to rally the rank-and-file millions into a powerful mass movement . . ."[17]

The problems engendered by the phrase "maximum feasible participation" became dramatically clear during a forum on the subject held as part of the meeting of the Citizens' Crusade against Poverty in Washington in April 1966, which later became a near-riot. Presiding at the discussion was Bayard Rustin, Director of the A. Philip Randolph Institute, who led the 1963 civil rights march on Washington.

While Mr. Shriver had claimed that he originated the phrase, an OEO official told the discussion group, "The words are broad enough for the American people to build meaning into them."

Though several Southern anti-poverty workers complained that they weren't participating enough, a woman from Cleveland maintained that her participation was too much for her. "I've been to seven conferences in the past month and have accomplished nothing. I have received no pay for this participation. This is not right because I have worn out my shoe leather and paid for transportation. No poor person wants to work on an anti-poverty board for less than he is getting under welfare," she declared.

This suggestion came from an anti-poverty worker from New York: "We're going to have to shape President Johnson up and tell him we know how to run our own program. We don't need an election, and we don't need to ask the poor what they need."

Mr. Rustin wrapped up the discussion by concluding that participation of the poor had been a failure so far. Poor people, he said, should be paid to serve on community action boards.

"Although the poor know the right thing to be done, they lack the skill to deal with government double talk in laying out plans," Mr. Rustin suggested. This, however, brought cries from the audience of, "No! No, man! Just give us the money. Don't give us plans. Money is what we want."

Subsequently OEO agreed to pay out-of-pocket expenses of volunteers who served on community action boards. It also decided it was necessary to train them to carry out their new responsibilities. On March 30, 1966 Melvin Moguloff, Regional Director of the OEO in San Francisco, told how this should be done when he addressed the Conference on Training for Community Action at Howard University in Washington. Community action workers, he said, should be trained to know all the resources available to help the poor and to intervene to redress imbalances.

"We are now in the realm of building and exercising units of political influence, so that these units may contribute to change in the policy of those agencies whose resources are critical to the needs of poor people," Mr.

Moguloff declared. He added the following: "In whatever new roles are to be established, we must support the following functions:

"... Educating clients to understand that they are a valuable resource to agencies—that if they do not choose to play the role of client, the producing system will collapse. This is exactly the gambit used in the school boycotts —schools after all need pupils, as welfare departments need poor people. ...

"Educating clients to stop expecting to be punished in their treatment by agencies. The formation of client protective groups may be a critical device in this direction."

10

Community Action Across the Country

The known extent to which OEO gave money to questionable persons, organizations and activities in the name of community action is enough to stagger the imagination. The full extent will probably never be known because OEO lavishly parcelled out money to literally thousands of local agencies. It failed to adequately study the petitioning organizations, their employees, or what they planned to do. Moreover, to keep track of the funds granted often proved impossible. With dozens of OEO-funded agencies sometimes functioning in a single city under one umbrella agency, close administration went by the wayside.

When the inevitable scandals resulted, the course OEO pursued depended upon which side brought the most pressure. In some cases it continued to fund agencies found to be misappropriating federal money and/or dominated by leftists. In other cases it even gave new grants to groups in the middle of Justice Department investigations of them for possible misappropriation of funds.

After some members of Congress began to fume about Communists and criminals being on Community Action

Program (CAP) payrolls, OEO issued a directive saying that subversives and persons convicted for crimes of moral turpitude should not be hired. It didn't say anything about getting rid of those already on the payroll; it just said not to hire any more of them.[1]

This remark was prompted from Edwin H. Seeger, Counsel for the United Planning Organization, the top anti-poverty agency for the District of Columbia: "OEO presumably is aware of the fact that absolute compliance with the provisions of the directive is unattainable, inasmuch as no funds are available for background investigations."

James Kelleher, who served as OEO Deputy Director for Public Affairs, told me that OEO turned down the idea of having the FBI do a security check on CAP directors and their immediate subordinates. When OEO concluded that there was no Negro leadership in the deep South except the militants, OEO told the CAP people not to be militant on government time or use government facilities, according to Mr. Kelleher.

The situation prompted these remarks from Senator Robert C. Byrd (D., W.Va.):

"The purpose of the CAP's is being subverted by extremists and activists, and federal funds are being used to support activities not in the least related to constructive anti-poverty efforts. . . . Picketing, demonstrations, rent strikes and sit-ins are not activities which will provide poor people with the education, training, or jobs they need. It may be fun for activists to engage in this type of program, but it seems to me of little benefit to the poor. Such activities are designed to fight city hall and not to fight poverty. Groups indulging in this type of action certainly should not be receiving federal money."[2]

Since no one person could study in depth all that occurred under the CAP's, it is possible to take only a cursory glance at cases brought to light across the country and then study others in detail in separate chapters.

Anne Braden was one of the incorporators of the West End Community Council, Inc., a CAP in Louisville, Kentucky which received a $28,000 anti-poverty grant. Mrs. Braden was identified under oath as a member of the Communist Party.[3] She and her husband, Carl, were listed on a "Call for Strike" flyer as sponsors of a national student strike which the Communist newspaper, *The Worker*, said "will include demands to bring the GI's home, to end the draft and to abolish complicity by universities and colleges with the war effort."[4]

Fulton Lewis III reported that the Council was active in housing demonstrations early in April 1967 which resulted in violence. He added that Mrs. Braden was the unpaid publicity director for the Council and was very active in the role.[5]

During hearings of the Louisiana State Joint Legislative Committee on Un-American Activities in March 1967, Committee Counsel Jack N. Rogers testified that Mrs. Braden "is currently, along with her husband, Carl Braden, managing the Southern Conference Educational Fund, a cited Communist front. She and her husband both cooperate in the publishing of the *Southern Patriot* . . . which has been cited by the United States Congress as a subversive newspaper."

Mr. Rogers also testified that Virginia Y. Collins, a community worker in the Louisiana War on Poverty, was a member of the Board of SCEF and a special assistant to James Dombrowski, Director of the SCEF. Her paid anti-poverty job was with the Social Welfare Planning Council of New Orleans which received federal anti-poverty funds.

Champ Baker, Director of the Louisiana OEO, told the same hearing that OEO in Washington, D.C. sent two young men from the Columbia University Law School to evaluate the anti-poverty program in Louisiana. One of them, Everett Crawford, told Mr. Baker that he didn't think Louisiana was "noisy enough" and suggested the need for more racial turmoil like that experienced in Bogalusa.

The *Chicago Tribune* reported that Richard Criley served on the Lawndale, Illinois, War on Poverty Advisory Committee and that he had been working "with identified Communists and Socialists to organize a political group on the West Side which will support only candidates who oppose American policies in Viet Nam." The newspaper added that Mr. Criley led demonstrations against the House Un-American Activities Committee when it held hearings in Chicago in May 1965 and that Miss Lola Belle Holmes, an FBI informant, testified at the hearings that Mr. Criley was a Communist.[6]

Mr. Criley was removed from the poverty committee only after Alderman Edward T. Scholl asserted that transcripts of hearings before the U.S. Senate Judiciary Committee showed his Communist affiliation dated back to the 1930's.[7]

In the fall of 1966, James J. Flynn, mayor of Perth Amboy, New Jersey, charged anti-poverty workers with contributing to riots there. He specifically accused the local anti-poverty boss, Milton Zatinsky, with trying to "foment and incite unrest, agitation and disorder."

Raphael O. Lewis was Executive Director of Community Action for Youth, Inc., a CAP in Cleveland, another riot-torn area. This is what he said in a paper for presentation to the Conference on Training for Community Action in Urban Ghettos, at Howard University in Washington, D.C. in the spring of 1966: "The notion is that social change frequently requires prior rehearsal of actions which will not itself provide solution to problems. It is necessary for these rehearsals to proceed, no matter how painful or bloody the results may be, in order to set the stage for the next sequence of circumstances which can provide solutions to the problems at hand."

Though Saul Alinsky, a self-styled professional radical and organizer of the poor, called the War on Poverty a "prize piece of political pornography,"[8] he too was on a CAP payroll. Here is what *Counterattack* said about him:

"The Community Action Training Center opened by Syracuse University appeared largely patterned upon Alinsky ideas. . . . The University placed Alinsky under contract to organize the poor at federal expense so that they could force greater concessions from the community.

"For this Alinsky was paid $10,000 a year, also from federal funds furnished the center. To earn this, Alinsky made 48 appearances at the center during 1965 'to rub the sores of discontent' in Syracuse. . .

"They [the students] were trained in the art of sit-ins, demonstrations and marches against the community from which they expected to exact tribute on behalf of its indolents and laggards."[9]

It is not known whether demonstrators at Syracuse City Hall were trained by Mr. Alinsky. In any event, when they were arrested, CAP funds were used to pay their bail.[10]

In March 1967, Wendy Goepel, an employee of the OEO in Washington, was in Lowndes County, Alabama helping to prepare an application for the county to be the first in the nation to have a rural anti-poverty medical program. This was under a 1966 amendment to the Economic Opportunity Act which stated, "The [OEO] Director is authorized to make grants to, or to contract with, public or private non-profit agencies in order to provide assistance necessary for the development and implementation of comprehensive health services programs focused upon the needs of persons residing in urban or rural areas having high concentrations of poverty and a marked inadequacy of health services."

The following is from a report of the Alabama Legislative Commission to Preserve the Peace, a branch of the Alabama state legislature, dated March 21, 1967 and titled *OEO Personnel and Operation in Lowndes County:*

"The U.S. Office of Economic Opportunity has announced it is assigning to Lowndes County, Alabama, Miss Wendy Goepel. Her duties, as announced, will be to coordinate a pilot 'medicaid' program, which will be used as a pattern for similar programs throughout the U.S. between now and 1975. . . .

"Wendy Goepel, a 27-year-old Stanford University graduate, has established a background of 10 years of pro-Communist activity, which includes:

"1. Attended Communist World Youth Festival at Helsinki, Finland.

"2. Member of DuBois Club . . . identified by FBI Director J. Edgar Hoover as a youth project of the Communist Party, USA.

"3. Miss Goepel served as a lieutenant and strike organizer for Cesar Chavez, National Farm Workers Association. Chavez was trained as revolutionary by Saul Alinsky, who bills himself as a 'professional radical' dedicated to radical change in our society.

"The background of N.F.W.A. is radical in the extreme. It was organized to stage the so-called Grape Workers strike in Delano, California in 1965 and was aided in that effort by a host of known Communists, including Bettina Aptheker, Berkeley riot leader and daughter of Communist Party theoretician, Herbert Aptheker (Miss Aptheker has publicly announced she is a member of the Communist Party); Robert Treuhaft, West Coast Communist attorney and his wife, Communist writer Jessica Mitford Treuhaft (now a contributing editor to *Ramparts* magazine); Holland Roberts, Communist educator who is currently organizing tours of the U.S.S.R.; Mickey Lima, Communist Party chairman of Northern California, and a score of other pro-Communist professors, ministers, lawyers and newspaper editors (including Sam Kushner, of the West Coast Communist Party organ *People's World*).

"The N.F.W.A. has spread through Texas, Wisconsin and other Eastern farm states, and is currently operating in Florida, Mississippi and the Black Belt of Alabama, including Lowndes County.

"The addition of Miss Goepel, with her background in the N.F.W.A., would lend emphasis to the current 'colonizing' of radical groups in the Black Belt, while in the pay of OEO. . . .

"We here raise the question not only of why Miss Goepel and others of her persuasion should be sent to Lowndes County, Alabama, BUT WHY ANY PERSON WITH THE CLEAR COMMUNIST RECORD OF MISS GOEPEL SHOULD BE IN THE PAY OF THE UNITED STATES GOVERNMENT?' "

OEO also gave money to the striking grape workers mentioned in the above-quoted report. The *Washington Star* said the following after OEO announced a $267,887 grant:

"The timing appears to have been an incredible blunder by the OEO. It embarrassed the strikers, outraged the landowners and ignited an ever-widening circle of opposition from within the city and state . . . At the request of the recipients themselves, the government held up the funds, pending the settlement of the strike. The strike leader, who is also the man chosen to head the anti-poverty program when the strike ends, says he asked the government not to make the grant during the labor dispute, but nothing came of the request . . . Although the money was approved as a community action program it came under provisions of the Economic Opportunity Act relating to migrant workers. It did not require the approval of any local or state agency . . . At the center of all the turmoil stands one man, Cesar Chavez, the director and founder of the National Farm

Workers Association and the person who will head the poverty program for the migrant workers."[11]

The Chavez organization also was connected with a grant OEO was going to make until California Governor Ronald Reagan vetoed it. OEO attempted to renew a $109,520 grant sought by the California Self-Help Corporation of Del Ray.

Governor Reagan thus announced his veto:

"There is no reason why the taxpayers should be forced to pay for a program in which people are trained in methods of striking and demonstrating . . . The center has loaned its personnel to the United Farm Workers Organization Committee and its predecessor, the National Farm Workers Association in Delano, for extensive periods to help in unionizing farm workers."

The governor explained that the Self-Help Corporation operated the California Center for Community Development and that "leaders of the center have publicly stated that they have sought to encourage farm workers to organize, strike and boycott.

Nation's Business found the following when it looked into the CAP in California:

John Ross was a member of an anti-poverty advisory board in San Francisco. He also was a member of the Progressive Labor Party which the FBI called a Communist group with allegiance to Red China.

Howard Harawitz, a member of similar board in Berkeley, was a former member of the W.E.B. DuBois Club which FBI Director J. Edgar Hoover called "Communist spawned." In addition, Attorney General Nicholas de B. Katzenbach petitioned the Subversive Activities Control Board to declare the clubs subversive.

William Callison was a CAP community organizer in Richmond and a former member of the left-wing May 2 movement.[12]

Representative Florence P. Dwyer (R., N.J.) revealed that $246,836 of anti-poverty money went to the California Self-Help Service Corps, a CAP located twelve miles north of Gilroy. It used an abandoned and condemned grammar school. Mrs. Dwyer said instruction included lectures from officials of the Student Nonviolent Coordinating Committee and that a poster on a wall of a classroom said, "We're going to tear this country up; then we're going to build it back, brick by brick until it is a fit place for human beings." The executive director of this CAP was formerly an organizer for the Congress of Racial Equality in the Watts area of Los Angeles.[13]

A study made for the National Association of Housing and Redevelopment Officials showed that over a period of two years, community action groups financed by OEO organized a series of disruptive protests and demonstrations against public housing authorities around the country. Said the report, "Local authorities in approximately 20 cities found themselves the targets of civil rights or tenant organizations charging the public landlords with failure to do their job and going so far, on some occasions, as to compare them with the slumlords they were presumed to displace." The report did not identify the 20 cities.[14]

In Cleveland, a group receiving OEO money piled rats and trash on the steps of City Hall to dramatize the conditions under which slum dwellers live.[15]

These developments failed to shake the cool of Vice President Hubert H. Humphrey, however. He told a New Orleans audience that if he lived in a rat-infested slum, "there is enough of a spark in me to lead a pretty good revolt."

But the growing and seemingly endless list of examples of use of community action funds for questionable persons and activities upset others. Representative Charles E. Goodell (R., N.Y.) expressed outrage when he discovered that in Durham, North Carolina nine anti-poverty workers used anti-poverty vehicles to transport people to Democratic precinct meetings.[16]

Representative Robert L. F. Sikes (D., Fla.) didn't like it either when he learned that five CAP workers from Akron got $16 per diem, plus transportation and hotel expenses, to lobby in Washington for the Greater Summit County Community Action Council, a CAP agency.[17]

The government was lavish in spending CAP money in other ways, too, especially on salaries. In New Haven, Connecticut, the executive director of the CAP (Community Progress, Inc.) received $25,000 a year, compared with a salary of $18,000 for the mayor of New Haven.[18]

Most of the top administrative personnel received substantial pay increases when they went to work for the St. Louis CAP, the Human Development Corporation, according to Representative Durward G. Hall (R., Mo.). He said General Manager Samuel Bernstein went from $18,500 to $24,000, Stephanie B. Stevens from $9,111 to $16,000, Curtis Gatlin from $9,900 to $16,000, Jacquelyn A. Walton from $7,500 to $12,000, Harold Antoine from $9,000 to $12,000 and Donald Checket from $9,500 to $12,000. Moreover, many of them had further boosts after a short time on their new jobs.

Social, Educational Research & Development, Inc. received a $105,247 anti-poverty contract to train workers in community action, as well as to acquire work experience and adult basic education (to be discussed later). According to Representative Albert H. Quie (R., Minn.), it was a one-man corporation run by John W. McCollum, a $90-a-day OEO consultant. Said Rep. Quie, "SERD not only failed miserably in its assigned task of training poverty officials, but it is reported that guest speakers, who received their regular pay in federal tax dollars, were paid honorariums of $75 a day plus expenses."

OEO goofed again when it announced a grant of $43,511

for a CAP to serve St. Charles, Lincoln, Warren and Montgomery counties in Missouri, according to the Republican Poverty Memo of July 26, 1966. The donation was based on an OEO assumption that these counties had 120,000 needy persons. A Congressman from the area, however, pointed out that the total population of the area came to only 105,000. OEO then investigated further and discovered there were only about 5,000 needy families in the area.

In Boston, the executive director of Action for Boston Community Development received $27,500 a year while running a program which, late in 1965, was the subject of nation-wide publicity concerning political corruption, misuse of funds and fiscal irresponsibility.[19]

By March 1966, OEO, the FBI and the Labor Department all had launched investigations of ABCD, sparked by complaints from youths that they received federal income-tax forms showing more income than they actually received and by the inability of ABCD to locate some 200 persons listed as employees.[20] In the course of 1967, however, no findings of any of the investigations had been revealed.

In Newark, New Jersey, the CAP director received $24,000 a year, only $1,000 less than the mayor of Newark and more than the salaries of the members of the city council.

In Los Angeles, an official in the city school system received $75 a day in CAP money for 28 days while he was being paid full time and overtime from the Los Angeles city school funds.[21]

Federal auditors found that when Paul Barker was the CAP director in Indianapolis, Indiana he violated federal regulations in receiving an anti-poverty salary while he was on the payroll of another government agency.[22]

According to President Johnson's 1967 budget, 1,032 CAP workers were to be paid $10,000 a year or more from federal funds.[23]

But New York obviously qualified for the prize for having the biggest mess in community action, even though relatively little information was available, compared with all that was going on in the big city's 80 agencies involved. Up to January 15, 1967, community action in New York City had cost OEO $125 million. OEO made a grant of $260,490 to evaluate the anti-poverty program in the city and see how it could be improved. The evaluation never was made, and the money was returned intact.[24]

To my knowledge, the only audit of a New York CAP ever made public was the one by the city's comptroller, Mario Procaccino, on Haryou-ACT—although half a dozen investigations had been launched regarding that one organization. It was an amalgamation of Harlem Youth Opportunities Unlimited and Associated Community Teams. Under Haryou-ACT came more than 100 community groups.

Of the $13,393,430 in anti-poverty funds which Haryou-ACT received between July 1, 1964 and June 30, 1966, Comptroller Procaccino found that over half went for salaries. Here are a few of his findings regarding the spending of the exorbitant sum of $7.3 million for salaries:

". . . Certain persons were hired for positions for which they did not possess the required qualifications. . . . Some employees were overpaid. However, no refunds were forthcoming . . . Employees working in one program were charged to another program. The fact that the programs may not have been funded by the same government agency was not considered . . . Some hourly employees were paid for a full week even though the time records indicated that the individual did not work a full week . . . The time clock and time cards were not under the visual control of anyone."

(According to the *New Amsterdam News*, 37 persons on the payroll made more than $10,000 a year.)

In addition to the millions for salaries, Mr. Procaccino

found an additional expenditure of $281,206 for "consultant fees." A number of the so-called "specialists" hired as consultants, however, were merely "routine clerical employees." Some of them, he said, had served for long periods of time at fees in excess of the maximum allowed under OEO regulations.

Here are a few other startling findings by the Comptroller:

While the balance in the Haryou-ACT treasury was $38,943 on June 30, 1966, accounts payable were at least $600,000, although the exact amount "could not be determined." Unpaid bills were not centrally filed.

Expenditures of $569,066 were impossible to identify clearly with any program. No accountability for petty cash advances was established. Haryou-ACT withheld $199,732 in payroll taxes from salaries, but instead of giving the money to the federal government and New York State, used it to continue programs.

There was no control over personal phone calls, with the result that phone bills came to $101,530. Payments to restaurants for $15,617 were charged to meetings and conferences.

The Board of Directors and the Executive Board gave little or no recognition to the administrative aspect of the program. The Executive Director was not aware of what his subordinates' duties were.

The $25,000-a-year Executive Director Livingston L. Wingate was given a leave of absence to reconstruct the books during the period of the investigation and shortly thereafter was reinstated without any public announcement that the accounts were in order. According to Mr. Procaccino's account, they definitely were not.

The Minority Views in the House Education and Labor Committee 1966 Poverty Report contained some startling revelations about Haryou-ACT, too. It said the latter leased

six cars and two station wagons from a small travel agency
at $90 a week, plus gas, for each car. "The travel agency,
however, reportedly rented the cars from the Hertz U-
Drive-It firm for $65 a week . . . In addition . . . a member
of the travel agency which leased the cars to Haryou-ACT
was reported placed on the Haryou payroll at $175 a week
as a 'consultant.' "

While Haryou-ACT announced a grandiose program
for vest-pocket parks in Harlem, "only three were completed, and no one seems to know how much money was
spent or why only three parks were completed."[25]

Some $40,000 worth of toys from a well-known manu-
facturer never were used and were stored in a warehouse
for more than a year with the agency paying high storage
fees for them.[26]

LeRoi Jones's Black Arts Theater obtained $115,000 in
Haryou-ACT funds before being cut off by OEO.[27] Mr.
Jones once wrote, "The force we want is of 20 million
spooks [Negroes] storming American cities with furious
cries and unstoppable weapons. We want actual explosions
and actual brutality."[28] When fifty New York policemen
raided his theater, they discovered a rifle range, an arsenal
of deadly weapons, a pipe bomb, sharpened meathooks,
pistols, knives, clubs and a cache of ammunition.[29]

It was impossible to tell what went on at New York's
Mobilization for Youth, mentioned earlier as the inspiration
for community action. Despite repeated attempts over a
period of many weeks, I was unable to obtain the names of
the people on its payroll even though I quoted section 202
(a) (5) of the Economic Opportunity Act which stated
that any organization, public or private, which accepts
OEO funds must make public upon request "current lists
of names of employees of the agency, including enrollees
in programs under the Economic Opportunity Act, to-

gether with their job descriptions and their rates of compensation." Thus I could not tell if MFY still had Communists on its payroll, as the report of the New York State Senate Committee indicated it did at the time of its investigation in December 1964.

However, MFY did break into public print on March 25, 1967 when the *New York Post* reported that the organization defended ten persons who were arrested for staging a protest in January in St. Patrick's Cathedral against the war in Vietnam. The *Post* said demonstrators unfurled an antiwar poster in the Cathedral in the middle of the Sunday morning mass. Val Coleman, MFY Public Relations Director, maintained his agency had taken the case because the defendants were indigent and unable to afford lawyers' fees. Said the *Post*, "But according to police files, all 10 in the group are over 21, most are college-educated and all but one employed. Disputing these records, Blaustein [Arthur Blaustein, Director of Public Affairs for OEO in New York] said that a preliminary check revealed the demonstrators had met federal standards of poverty."

Youth-in-Action, New York's CAP for the Bedford-Stuyvesant section of Brooklyn, also engaged in a questionable activity when it launched a 30-car voter registration motorcade led by James H. Meredith in the summer of 1966. Meredith said over an amplifier, "If you don't come out and register, Youth-in-Action will have to come and get you out."[30]

Then there was the case of the Reverend Willie M. Johnson. The Bronx minister faced a 145-count indictment which alleged he had stolen $7,760 in anti-poverty funds and had tried to steal $15,199 more. It said he had presented false bills and vouchers and demanded kickbacks from staff members.[31] When Justice Joseph A. Sarafite attempted to hear the case on March 21, 1967, supporters of the minister disrupted the courtroom by shouting in his defense, and the judge postponed the hearing. No one was arrested for that demonstration.[32]

A $15,000-a-year New York CAP Director was arrested for disorderly conduct in another instance, however. Lloyd A. Johnson, Director of the Brownsville-East New York Community Progress Center, according to the *New York Times*, was "proud of his arrest on June 24 [1966] for disorderly conduct while trying to see Governor Rockefeller at his office in Manhattan. He was with a group seeking the Governor's help in moving an anti-poverty bill that was stuck in a state Senate committee." Commented the *Times*, "He does not think the center should originate civil and social protests, but he expects it to lend vocal and consultative support to such efforts as boycotts, demonstrations, sit-ins, voter registration drives and attempts to curb slum profiteering. . . ." Mr. Johnson was responsible for administering an anti-poverty budget of more than $1 million a year.[33]

New York anti-poverty funds also financed a Chicago trip by four CAP workers to organize a Puerto Rican protest march. They were Ted Valez of the East Harlem Tenants' Council and three staff assistants.[34]

Perhaps the most ridiculous use of anti-poverty funds occurred when New York's Economic Opportunity Committee put up 50 slum-dwellers at the luxurious Astor Hotel. The Committee sent them there during a cold spell in January 1966 when their Harlem apartments were without adequate heat.[35] A month later, ten of them were still there, enjoying wall-to-wall carpeting, color television, and a daily allowance for eating in restaurants.[36]

By 1967, New York Mayor John Lindsay supplanted the Economic Opportunity Committee with the Human Resources Administration (HRA) which was supposed to create some order out of the chaotic War on Poverty in

New York. Incredible as it may seem, when I asked the
HRA if it funded a particular organization as a CAP, nobody knew. I was referred repeatedly to Sally Coler and
was told she was drawing up an organization chart and that
she was the only one who would know. Finally I learned
that Miss Coler no longer worked for the HRA and that
nobody else had taken up her duties.

Since New York could not even keep track of its own
CAP's, it is not surprising that neither Congress nor OEO
could begin to cope with the whole vast nation-wide program which was growing daily in many directions. Indeed,
in one day, April 10, 1967, OEO put out 79 separate announcements of expenditures in the War on Poverty, most
of which involved CAP's and were singularly uninforma-
tive. Sargent Shriver consistently and successfully ignored
requests for information.

On the floor of the House on April 17, 1967 Representative Albert H. Quie (R., Minn.), who was the co-chairman
of the Republican Ad Hoc Anti-Poverty Subcommittee,
said he had been trying unsuccessfully for eighteen months
to get information from Mr. Shriver, and could not even
get him to acknowledge his letters in less than a month.
Finally Representative Quie evoked a response when he
wired Mr. Shriver, "Unless you advise me to the contrary,
staff investigators, House Education and Labor Committee,
will be at your office, nine a.m. Monday, April 17, 1967 to
commence four-week investigation at OEO headquarters."[37]

This evoked a quick reply. Mr. Shriver told Representative Quie, among other things, that he could not have any
of the audits of CAP's he requested. Even though some
went back as far as 1965, he said, "most of the audits on
which you requested reports have not as yet been brought
to final resolution." Some members of Congress, including
Representative Quie and Minnesota Republican Repre-

sentative Charles E. Goodell, had the feeling that OEO purposely was holding up the release of such reports so that when they were made public they would be too old to be pertinent to current conditions.

11

United Planning Organization

A prime example of a CAP lay right in Washington, D.C.'s own backyard—the United Planning Organization (UPO). It started out as what its name implied, a planning and coordinating group. Soon, however, it degenerated into a massive and overpaid organizing effort which resulted in picketing, boycotts, marches, a sleep-in and even an attack upon a police station.

UPO's $25,000-a-year director was James G. Banks, who had been recommended for the job by Charles A. Horsky, President Johnson's adviser for D.C. affairs. To take the post, Mr. Banks left D.C.'s Redevelopment Land Agency (RLA) which had made a spectacular mess of urban renewal. RLA was denounced both by the General Accounting Office and the people who saw their homes and businesses displaced by the federal bulldozer. Both said RLA failed in the job of relocation.[1] Mr. Banks was in charge of relocation.

While UPO's 54-man Board of Trustees was supposed to set policy, several members of the Board told me that Mr. Banks really did this. For instance, on October 26,

1966, Mr. Banks wrote a memorandum to the Executive Board informing it that "This year the United Planning Organization and its contracting agencies will concentrate heavily on community organization activities." The Board had never made any policy determination on this, or indeed, even discussed the matter.

In at least one instance, it had little opportunity for profound policy considerations. Here's the story one of the Trustees told me: On short notice, during December 1964, the Trustees were summoned to an 8 a.m. meeting on a Friday after word was relayed from the White House that President Johnson wanted to announce the program for which UPO would seek OEO funds. Since the program document was quite thick, they obviously did not have time to study it and still approve it in time for a Saturday announcement. When Mr. Banks assured them that the D.C. Commissioners had approved it, however, the Trustees went ahead and okayed the program. Later some of them checked and found that the D.C. Commissioners had not approved it.

Mark Sullivan, Jr., another Trustee, had served since the beginning of the War on Poverty. The following is excerpted from his letter of resignation dated November 18, 1966:

"I was pleased to accept membership on the Board . . . in the belief that an expert, careful planning program could do more, by developing correlated programs, than could be done by individual agencies on their own. . . . My disillusionment with UPO's intention of doing the job and doing it right commenced very early. It is now complete. . . .

"UPO has done nothing in the way of educational planning . . . It has merely acted as a conduit for federal funds. . . .

"It has not begun to prepare any comprehensive plan for

job-training . . . It has no inventory of job vacancies and no program for training people to fill these vacancies. . . .

"Instead it has become an operating group that does little planning and conducts its operations inefficiently and at great administrative cost. As a consequence, funds designed to help the poor instead subsidize a vast and growing bureaucracy. . . ."

UPO salaries paid in 1966 bear out the last statement. At that time UPO had eleven employees making $15,000 and over, 23 making between $12,500 and $14,999 and 38 making between $10,000 and $12,499.[2]

That same year Congress passed an amendment to the Economic Opportunity Act specifying that OEO must not finance CAP salaries in excess of $15,000. This did not make it mandatory for UPO to cut its salary scale, however, because it had money from outside OEO which it could use to augment the salaries.

At the time Mr. Sullivan resigned, UPO had received grants totaling $25 million, of which $3,361,000 came from the Ford Foundation.[3]

Naturally interested in how the Foundation's money was being spent, a Ford Foundation panel conducted a review of UPO and came up with findings similar to those of Mr. Sullivan. In a report issued May 18, 1966, the panel said, "Programs in the crucial areas of education, employment and housing seem to have made little progress."

The panel said this about UPO training: "The panel was never able to get a clear picture of how neighborhood workers were trained, other than what appeared to be a belated effort to train en masse those already selected. UPO itself seems to recognize the inadequacy of training, but has formulated no ongoing program to accommodate this necessity."

(In the fall of 1966 while they were mulling over a proposed UPO grant application to OEO, the D.C. Commissioners asked the OEO for guidelines defining the role of anti-poverty workers paid with OEO funds. OEO replied that it did not have such guidelines.)[4]

The review also found that treasury and accounting functions were not separated and that "without a proper segregation of these functions, there can be no control of cash receipts or expenditures."

UPO was too much even for Adam Clayton Powell's House Education and Labor Committee. Here's what the Committee said on March 1, 1966, in a report I obtained from the House Education and Labor Committee which was never officially made public: "Even though UPO received its first funds in November of 1964, there is little evidence that any of its programs has made any significant contribution toward even beginning to lift people out of poverty. . . Since it became a community action agency, UPO has been in a constant state of administrative confusion, expansion, revision, reorganization and 'crash' programming activity. . . It is one of the tragedies of our time that here in the Nation's Capital, in the very shadow of the House and Senate, and the White House itself where the whole concept of a massive effort against poverty originated, the Anti-Poverty Program should be one of the weakest in the nation."

Considering UPO's hiring practices, this should not have been surprising. Representative William H. Ayres (R., Ohio) lashed out at the organization for hiring hardened criminals as youth counselors. "Has Mr. Banks informed Washington parents that their children are being counseled by an $8,650 employee whose professional qualifications include desertion from the Armed Forces in time of war, soliciting for prostitution, grand larceny and forgery?" he asked.

Representative Ayres revealed that another UPO youth counselor had a criminal record dating back to 1952, which included eleven arrests for crimes ranging from larceny to passing bad checks. He said a UPO neighborhood development worker had been arrested for a sex crime, larceny and bail violation.

Mr. Banks defended his hiring policies by stating that a large proportion of poor people have police records. The Congressman called this "a contemptible slander on the poor" and said Mr. Banks should not hire persons with long records of serious crimes involving moral turpitude.

Also on the UPO payroll were members of the Student Nonviolent Coordinating Committee (SNCC), the militant black power group headed by Stokely Carmichael. They included Dick Jones, a SNCC organizer employed at a UPO community action center; Herbert Kelsey, a SNCC organizer and a UPO housing coordinator, and Michael Searles, a SNCC member employed at a community action center.[5]

Without naming him, the Ford Foundation panel said the director of a UPO center in Southeast Washington was "an experienced professional, educated in law and experienced in SNCC."

Lonnie King, Jr., one of the founders of SNCC, was an Executive Director for Change, Inc., a community action agency funded by UPO.[6] At the same time he held his UPO job, he also was president of the D.C. Young Democrats. His dual job-holding went unchallenged until he came up for re-election, and a rival candidate suggested that he was using UPO as a base for furthering his political goals.[7] Only then did OEO get busy and request his suspension pending an investigation.

Even though UPO facilities had been used for putting out a Young Democrat newsletter and the publication listed a UPO phone number, the Board of Change found that no regulations had been violated. It reinstated Mr. King.[8] Change president, Ruth Webster, who made the reinstatement announcement, evidently was not opposed to extracurricular activities. A month later, in April 1967, she attended a rally of striking housekeeping employees of Suburban Hospital in Bethesda, Maryland and promised to take members of her group to another rally of the strikers a week later.[9]

Mr. King stayed reinstated for only about a month, however. Daniel Ingram, Director of Public Relations for UPO, told me that while his agency felt that employees of delegate agencies were free to engage in political activities, it decided that "taking into consideration all the factors in Mr. King's case" and foreseeing the possibility that a center director's community organizing and political activities might be confused in the public mind, it asked Mr. King to choose between politics and his UPO job. He chose politics and resigned. During the period of his reinstatement, Mr. King was one of those who went to the 13th precinct police station in D.C. to protest police brutality when Marion Barry, former SNCC director in Washington, and Lester McKinnie, then Washington SNCC director, were arrested for disorderly conduct.[10]

The preceding August, a UPO worker was involved in a riot at the 11th precinct police station in D.C. According to the *Washington Star*, William M. Michaels, a community organizer for UPO at Southeast Neighborhood House (a community action center), transported demonstrators "to and from the police station."[11]

Negro teen-agers went on a two-hour rampage throwing rocks, firecrackers and bottles at the station and hurling bricks at cars and buses.[12] Subsequently W. Crosby Roper, Chairman of the Board of Southeast Neighborhood House, said that demonstrations and picketing were endorsed as "a legitimate community action program."[13] A grand jury investigated the violence but refused to indict anyone.

Other militants worked for UPO, too. William N.

Hobbs was an Administrative Assistant in UPO's Public Information Office at a salary of $7,770. He also was Co-Chairman of the Action Coordinating Committee to End Segregation in the Suburbs (ACCESS).

For several days in September 1966, ACCESS picketers, led by Mr. Hobbs, demonstrated at the Buckingham Apartments in Arlington, Virginia, to protest alleged racial discrimination. When Arlington police asked the group to walk in areas where they would not prevent persons from entering and leaving various other shops and businesses in the area, Mr. Hobbs pointed his finger at a police officer and said, "We intend to disrupt the Arlington business and the community as much as we can . . . and the Police Department will protect us."[14]

The following months ACCESS conducted a three-day march into Northern Virginia to protest the quality there of Negro housing. Charles Jones, who shared the co-chairmanship of ACCESS with Mr. Hobbs, spoke at a rally during the march and praised his "old friend," Stokely Carmichael, for his efforts on behalf of black people all over the world.[15]

At the same rally, Lacey Street, director of an anti-poverty center in Gum Springs, Fairfax County, Virginia, branded as "Uncle Toms" a group of middle-class Gum Springs residents who opposed the march.[16]

In November 1966, ACCESS pickets supported a rent strike against David Lazarus, owner of apartment buildings in the Cardoza Heights area of Washington. Mr. Hobbs told reporters the picketing was to point up "the fact that when the suburbs are segregated, it removes the option for Negroes of moving out of the slums in the city."[17]

The preceding August, one hundred persons pitched tents and camped on the site of the old Sibley Hospital in Washington in an attempt to force immediate action on construction of low-income housing. They were under the supervision of the Urban League's Neighborhood Advisory Council, a UPO agency.[18]

It was in August, too, that the D.C. Coalition of Conscience led a sleep-in of two hundred at the Anacostia-Bolling military complex in Southeast Washington in a demand for conversion of the 900-acre installation into a low- and medium-income housing development. Among those who participated were members of Southeast Neighborhood House and Rebels with a Cause, both funded by UPO, as well as residents of the Barry Farm public housing project organized by UPO.[19]

At one of its council meetings, UPO even went so far as to appeal for volunteers to picket a merchant who had opposed voting rights for D.C. residents.[20]

After the headquarters of the D.C. Welfare Department had been picketed for a week, Welfare Director Donald Brewer said, "I resent this outburst that appears to be sponsored by the United Planning Organization."[21]

This failed to deter either the UPO or the pickets, however. At mid-June 1966, the *Washington Post* reported, "Two groups of Washington citizens organized largely by the UPO stepped up their efforts to revise public welfare rules yesterday by picketing the house of Sen. Robert C. Byrd (D., W.Va.) . . . Starting about 7:30 a.m. a group from the Barry Farm public housing project in Anacostia, most of whom are welfare recipients, marched and sang in front of Byrd's house . . . Two UPO workers were present. One, Phil Perkins, a neighborhood organizer in the Barry Farms area, joined the marching line at 8 o'clock to lead the singing."[22]

When he headed the Washington branch of SNCC, Marion Barry was an invited speaker at a UPO meeting where he declared, "We have to run D.C. Transit out of business and let the government take it over. Otherwise . . . [they] will continually try to raise the fares."[23]

UPO also was militant about getting money for itself. The aforementioned Ford Foundation panel reported that a group organized by UPO in Southeast Washington "were proud of their successful sit-in carried out . . . inside the national offices of the OEO. As a result . . . OEO authorized UPO to use lapsed grant funds to hire more neighborhood workers."

Beginning early in December 1966, UPO sparked a campaign for more money. Mr. Banks told a UPO planning session on December 3, "Simply because we are testing established conditions, we are going to have a hard time."[24] The previously mentioned Dick Jones of UPO and SNCC led about thirty persons out of the meeting when the discussion turned to how to operate with less money.[25]

Then, on December 18, 1966, UPO was prominently represented in a crowd of about 1,000 persons who gathered in Lafayette Park across the street from the White House to press for more money for CAP's. Pete Green, a UPO neighborhood worker, occupied the speaker's platform with James Farmer, former director of CORE, and Etta Horn, of the Welfare Alliance organized at UPO Neighborhood Center #3.[26]

Mr. Farmer said Congress cut back on money for the CAP's because "they are afraid of the poor organizing." He called for a massive anti-poverty march on Washington "that will make all previous marches seem like child's play."[27]

Miss Horn said Congress was "sick—if not sick physically, sick mentally." She declared "Congress wants to send the poor people back to slavery, and they don't give a damn how they do it."[28]

The following month UPO workers were on the other side of the street, picketing the White House itself and demanding money for UPO.[29]

At least one UPO agency, however, had more money

than it knew what to do with. The Metropolitan Citizens
Advisory Council, made up of representatives from the ten
UPO community action centers, spent about $110 for a
buffet dinner for its members March 29, 1967 to use some
of the nearly $1,000 in unspent federal anti-poverty funds
appropriated for its operating expenses. The money not
spent by the end of June 1967 had to be returned to the
OEO. Council Chairman Thomas Payne told members
that he would explore possibilities of future box suppers
at UPO headquarters or meetings with meals in restaurants
or other eating places.[30]

UPO's handling of its portable swimming pool program
gave a measure of its managerial ability. During the summer of 1966, it was in charge of a $111,000 program for
leasing seventeen portable pools as a quick means of keeping Washington cooled off so that it wouldn't have the
much-threatened "long hot summer."

The D.C. Department of Recreation contributed $34,000
for lifeguards and watchmen, and the Labor Department
$13,000 for National Youth Corps members to serve as
pool helpers to do such chores as cleaning the pools. OEO
put up the remainder and channeled it through UPO as
the manager of the program.

The opening of the first pool was spectacular. The plywood sides of the above-ground structure collapsed, and
20,000 gallons of water gushed into the street. Fortunately,
no one was in the pool at the time.[31] UPO paid for an additional $5,000 in engineering services so that the other
pools would not collapse, too. However, the plywood sides
continued to warp and buckle and let the water drain out.

Moreover, vandalism was an insurmountable problem.
According to D.C. Recreation Superintendent Joseph H.
Cole, vandals cut the thin plastic sides and let the water out,
tampered with the electrical systems and the rigged-up
showers, pulled out the rubber matting and dumped everything from baby carriages to beer cans in the pools.[32]

Half of the pools were in operation for only two weeks or less and none for longer than a month. Indeed, the pool at Stuart Junior High School was open only two days "due to vandalism and poor management," according to Mr. Cole. He added that "Many of the pools were closed during their dates of operation because of vandalism . . . improper filtration and warping of the plywood frames."[33]

James Tompkins, Swimming Pool Director for the D.C. Recreation Department, told me that seven of the pools were too far gone from vandalism to be used. In addition, Mr. Tompkins said there were too many health problems which UPO had not foreseen. All the pools lacked adequate filtering systems. Moreover, the seven were set up either at schools or recreation centers, and none had sufficient shower and toilet facilities. In some cases, they had to rig up hoses for makeshift showers, and this displeased the Health Department which said the swimmers should take warm showers before entering the pools. (With inadequate filters, this seemed doubly important.)

UPO affairs reached the height of ridiculousness, however, when the agency announced that it would put on a baby show May 20, 1967, featuring the babies of unwed mothers. Ruby Jones of UPO said the purpose would be to give the girls a chance to show pride in their babies.[34]

12

Community Action and Co-operatives

One of the many facets of community action was a well-planned scheme to use federal anti-poverty funds to foster the creation of co-operatives in competition with private enterprise.

Over 20,000 consumer aides operating under CAP's spread the gospel of co-operatives all over the country. Harping on the theme that "The Poor Pay More," they "educated" consumers to believe that merchants were cheating them and that supermarkets were getting more than a fair profit. As an answer they promoted co-ops and/or buying clubs to evolve into co-ops.

In addition, OEO paid special experts to travel to centers of budding co-op activity to help with the technicalities. They helped already established groups as well as new ones, if the former were willing to expand to accommodate new members classified as impoverished by OEO.

Then too, OEO made sizeable grants for the establishment of credit unions, aided in promotional work by the Bureau of Federal Credit Unions and CUNA International (formerly the Credit Union National Association). The idea was that credit unions, essentially co-ops themselves, would "spin off" other types of co-ops.

Washington officialdom indirectly did its bit, too, to break down America's traditional antipathy to co-op food outlets. The latter have never been very popular in this country, unlike in Europe, because of the great efficiency of American supermarkets. But Secretary of Agriculture Orville L. Freeman said that somewhere between the food producer and the consumer someone was getting more than a fair share of profits, and the Federal Trade Commission, with great fanfare, launched an investigation to determine the villain in rising food prices. The National Commission on Food Marketing issued its own studies which dwelled on supermarket profits, and the Bureau of Labor Statistics emphasized the reluctance of supermarkets to go into poor neighborhoods in a study titled "Prices in Poor Neighborhoods."

Since supermarkets often were among the first stores looted and burned during riots, it appeared that the anti-supermarket propaganda succeeded only too well.

The OEO launched its promotional effort for co-ops in 1965 at a closed conference for Community Action workers it held jointly with the President's Committee on Consumer Interests.

The keynote address was delivered by David Caplovitz, author of the book *The Poor Pay More* (which a study by the Bureau of Labor Statistics later refuted). "I have been asked to characterize the marketplace in low-income communities," said Mr. Caplovitz. "This can be done in almost a single phrase. It is a commercial jungle in which exploitation and fraud are the norm rather than the exception."

Dr. Sanford Kravitz, then Chief of Research and Program Development for the Community Action Program, said the answer was to form consumer co-ops, credit unions and buying groups.

A year later the clan gathered again at OEO headquarters. That time the keynote speaker was Theodore Fleming, Program Associate of the American Baptist Home Mission of New York City. "Disorders must be understood as pent-up resentment against deprivation of the rights of the poor to participate in the urban consumption process," he told the assembly of co-op leaders and community action workers. He added, "The co-operative movement must become a power instrument with which the poor can implement programs to improve their lives. It must call for total reconstruction of all the public and private institutions in society that prevent the poor from participating in the Americanization process." Co-op members, he said, should be trained to take part in the functions of government. The curriculum should be "action-oriented" and should include field trips to all seats of power.

The conference moderator, Kiernan Stenson, Deputy Director of Action Housing in Pittsburgh, warned, however, "Don't try too hard to involve activist groups in co-ops; don't drain off their energy and reduce their effectiveness in an area which needs their vitality."

Marta Valle, representing New York's top anti-poverty, OEO-funded agency, the Human Resources Administration, told the conferees, "In New York City, we haven't begun to explore the potential [for co-ops]. . . . We hope to be able to spin off local co-ops to go into business to provide what local business may be needed."

Gladys Aponte, Director of Consumer Education for Youth in Action in New York City, was a featured speaker. "When you see the fraud tactics used in the ghetto, you will never believe it," she declared. She said her consumer education emphasized what happens when people default in payments, garnisheeing and the like.

"We hope," she revealed, "to establish buying clubs to

develop into little co-op stores. Then we hope, with help
from OEO, to establish the little stores into a few large
co-ops."

At the time she spoke, Mrs. Aponte had already launched
her co-op program. Its first manifestation was a little co-op
grocery store which opened in October 1966 in the Bedford-Stuyvesant section of Brooklyn. OEO announced:
"The consumer aides have started their own grocery co-
operative headed by a man who started out as a consumer
aide student."

From the Youth-in-Action community action center on
Sumner Avenue, supported by OEO, 22 full-time, OEO-
paid consumer aides fanned out over the neighborhood,
knocked on doors and told people that if they didn't want
to be victimized by unscrupulous merchants, they should
join a food buying club which would enable them to purchase groceries at wholesale prices.

The aides recruited 43 club members and called at the
home of each once a week to take food orders. After obtaining the orders from wholesalers, they had the club
members pick up their groceries in the store which Youth-
in-Action managed to obtain rent-free for two and a half
months. Meantime, the aides helped the club members conduct benefits to raise money for the store.

Officials of CUNA International told me they were
working with Mrs. Aponte to establish a number of co-
operative stores in the Bedford-Stuyvesant area. The technique, they explained, would be first to set up buying clubs.
As soon as the members had saved enough money through
credit unions, they then could turn the buying clubs into
full-fledged co-op stores. When I talked with Mrs. Aponte,
her consumer aides had petitions from 2,500 in the area
who wanted credit unions.

OEO had hired Gerald King of CUNA International on

a year-round basis to travel across the country and help set up credit unions. In addition, it made grants to 50 credit unions in 27 states to pay for staff and facilities.

Said a special report by CUNA International: "Some of us may feel it would be better to start with two or three volunteers in each group and let them build a credit union slowly and solidly, a dollar at a time. But the anti-poverty program wants the benefits of a credit union launched in full operation—perhaps even capitalized—ready to meet immediate needs which cannot wait. It is the most dazzling social opportunity in our history."

Typical of the OEO grants to credit unions was $40,398 to the National Association of Colored People's credit union in Sacramento, California and $150,000 to the Unity Credit Society in the Watts area of Los Angeles.

In addition, OEO made a grant of $125,000 for experts from the Bureau of Federal Credit Unions to conduct four-week training sessions for representatives of anti-poverty groups. They taught financial counseling, opening and operating credit unions and a one-week course in bookkeeping. The so-called "Moneywise" projects were held in Boston, New York, Los Angeles, Chicago, Washington and New Orleans.

Subsequently, OEO announced that it had given $200,320 to low-income residents of the Pilsen area of Chicago "to test the concept that members of a poor community can create and operate successfully their own institutions. Specifically, the Pilsen Neighbor's Community Council will sponsor a consumer education and action program that combines the activities of a credit union, a buying cooperative and a housing corporation."

Out in San Francisco the local community action agency known as the Bay Area Neighborhood Development Foundation (BAND), did its bit to promote co-ops. Supported both by Bay area co-ops and $603,501 from OEO, BAND had 50 consumer aides. It distributed a leaflet which declared, "Most people don't think a supermarket is a dangerous place. But actually it is. Only smart shoppers escape without getting hurt."

The Articles of Incorporation of BAND included the following purposes:

"To conduct basic educational research in the field of urban consumer education, directed toward encouraging the formation of consumer cooperatives.

"To provide specific information about the formation and operation of consumer cooperatives to individuals and groups interested in the formation of such cooperatives."

Members of the Board of Directors of Associated Cooperatives, an organization of local consumer co-ops, were the sole voting members of BAND, and they selected the BAND board.

BAND declared, "We hope to develop in each area an independent organization of consumers. After discussion and study, this may lead to some kind of self-help activity like a community credit union." Then, of course, the "spin off" of other types of co-ops could begin.

But, as noted, OEO was interested in established co-ops, too. A prime example was the case of Greenbelt Consumer Services, Inc., a co-op operating twelve supermarkets, six pharmacies, six auto service centers, three furniture stores, a bakery and related services in Washington, D.C., Maryland and Virginia.

An OEO-supported community action center was the locale for the opening of a campaign May 28, 1966, by anti-poverty and civil rights workers to take over the management of GCS. It already had annual sales of over $32 million, but the insurgent group wanted to increase this vastly by branching out in Negro ghettos. It also wanted to emphasize social service.

Timothy L. Jenkins proposed five candidates, including

himself, for the co-op's nine-man board. He was Deputy to the Commissioner of the U.S. Equal Employment Opportunity Commission and, according to literature distributed by his sponsors, "has held responsible positions in such groups as . . . the Federal Programs Section of the Student Nonviolent Coordinating Committee."

Also on the slate with Mr. Jenkins were Steven Lowenstein, Deputy Special Assistant to OEO Director Sargent Shriver, and Alan McSurely, Director of the Suburban Programs Division of the United Planning Organization and an OEO community organizer.

On August 31, 1967, the *Washington Star* reported that Mr. McSurely and his wife, Margaret, were arrested and charged with possessing seditious materials, including Communist literature and films. The paper identified them as former UPO employees and "now field workers for the Southern Conference Educational Fund." As noted in an earlier chapter, the Louisiana State Joint Legislative Committee on Un-American Activities called the SCEF "a cited Communist front."

Subsequently, a panel of three federal judges turned the McSurleys free. The judges ruled that Kentucky's sedition law is unconstitutional and that sedition is strictly a matter for federal prosecution.

In 1966 Mr. McSurely and the other candidates attributed their defeat to the inability to obtain the membership list of the co-op.

Afterwards, James Scott, a friend of Mr. McSurely and Director of the federally supported Fairfax, Virginia antipoverty program, said that, as part of the program, he wanted to have poor people from outlying areas become members of Greenbelt's co-op grocery store in Falls Church, Virginia and have the community action program provide bus transportation to the store for them at least once a week.

This idea was reminiscent of one for Greenbelt's store in Piney Branch, Maryland, reported by the *Washington Post*. The idea, apparently, was to bus new co-op members to the market and eventually have them take it over. L. D. Pratt presented the idea to Greenbelt last November, accompanied by Ralph Featherstone. Mr. Pratt, said the *Post*, is a "silent partner in the leadership of the Free D.C. Movement." That was the group which conducted boycotts of Washington stores and buses in January 1966. The announced purpose was to bring down fares and force merchants to support voting rights for D.C. residents. Mr. Featherstone worked in the local office of SNCC.

Meantime Greenbelt's present management wanted to establish new co-ops in poverty neighborhoods, Paul G. Nelson, Assistant General Manager, told me, despite the fact that many of the people in such neighborhoods didn't even know what a co-op was.

Happily for GCS, OEO donated money to inform the local impoverished citizens on the advantages to them of co-ops. Specifically, it approved a grant of $383,672 to the UPO for "Consumer Information and Education" which included heavy stress on co-ops.

By December 1966, Pauline Myers, a UPO consumer specialist, had set up a fifteen-member board to form the Shaw Area Community Cooperatives in Washington. The idea was to sell shares to 500 families in the area and then contract for group health insurance, buy food and develop low-cost cooperative housing.[1]

That same month Grafton F. Francis, a neighborhood counselor for Baltimore's Community Action Agency, revealed that he had recruited 75 families from public housing projects to join a buying co-op which he hoped would evolve into a regular co-op grocery store.[2]

In April 1967, the *Washington Post* said anti-poverty workers were members of a group trying to establish a

Negro co-op grocery store in the Hough area of Cleve-land[3] which had recently been torn by race riots.

As word of OEO's program came to light, little by little, it took private businessmen by surprise because, while promoting it frantically locally, the agency soft-pedaled it nationally. Negro leaders, however, were jumping on the bandwagon with alacrity.

Floyd McKissick, National Chairman of CORE, announced he wanted his organization to build a chain of 50 co-op supermarkets in North Carolina and had asked OEO to spend $250,000 for one such market to demonstrate its feasibility.

Martin Luther King told a Grenada, Mississippi audience that his Southern Christian Leadership Conference planned to build supermarket co-ops all over the South. And Stokely Carmichael said on television that he wanted co-ops for all Negro ghettos. By March 1967, the Poor People's Corporation, a co-op started and headed by Jesse Morris, a field secretary for SNCC, had 110 employees. It manufactured 46 items ranging from dolls to quilts in 11 co-op "factories" in Mississippi and already had retail outlets in New York, Detroit and Jackson.[4]

13

Rural Co-Operatives

Thanks to the activities of the Agriculture Department in spreading the word over the years, a vast co-op informational campaign was not needed for the program to get started in agricultural areas. As a result, the rural portion of OEO's program is farther along than the one in the cities.

OEO made loans to rural co-ops, with the Agriculture Department's Farmers Home Administration handling the administration. They parcelled out $5.9 million for 391 co-op loans in 1966 and planned an additional 400 of them in 1967 for $5 million. OEO officials said the Economic Opportunity Act gave them virtually unlimited authority to do anything in regard to co-ops except set up communal farms. They took wide advantage of this and in some notable instances in Alabama and Louisiana gave OEO money to co-ops run by known leftist racial agitators.

Prior to the War on Poverty, the FHA had lacked authority to make co-op loans (grant authority was completely new) for two decades. The depression of the 1930's resulted in the creation of the Farm Security Administration and the Farm Credit Administration with its Banks for Cooperatives. By 1946, however, FSA had evolved into FHA, and FCA had become a separate and independent agency. Thus, since that time, the Agriculture Department had been giving no more than technical assistance to co-ops.

One of the featured speakers at the OEO co-op conference in 1966 mentioned in the preceding chapter was Father Albert McKnight, a Roman Catholic priest. He was there in his capacity as a leader of OEO-funded co-op activities in Louisiana.

Here is the story of Father McKnight's involvement revealed during hearings in March 1967 by the Joint Legislative Committee on Un-American Activities for the State of Louisiana:

He was on the board of Acadiana Neuf, Inc., the community action agency which got about $3 million in antipoverty money from Washington in just one year. Acadiana Neuf had the responsibility for deciding how to parcel out the money to delegate agencies in Louisiana. One of these was Southern Consumers Educational Foundation (SCEF). Father McKnight was Treasurer of this and also was on its board. Thus he was acting in an official capacity as both donor and recipient. In the latter role he was supposed to account to Acadiana Neuf for the spending of money.

Where do co-operatives come into the picture? Father McKnight was president of Southern Consumers' Co-operative which received money from SCEF. So did a credit union in Vermilion Parish, and he was on the board of that.

Just how much SCEF money went to co-operatives and how it was spent is a little hazy. Regarding SCEF, the accounting firm of Peat, Marwick and Mitchell said, "Due to the lack of internal control on the disbursement of funds, we are unable to express an opinion as to the propriety of expenditures represented by the financial statement of Acadiana Neuf, Inc."

It is known that $48,000 of federal anti-poverty funds went to the Sweet Potato Alert Program, an educational effort to spread the gospel of co-operatives. One of the three field captains who carried on this educational program was John Zippert.

This is how Mr. Zippert has been identified by both the Louisiana Joint Committee and the Alabama Legislative Commission to Preserve the Peace, a branch of the Alabama State Legislature:

He was a CORE field worker and had a 2A draft deferment on the basis that his work with CORE was essential to the national health, safety and interest.

In 1965 he participated in a teach-in at City College, New York, to protest American efforts in Vietnam. Others who took part were Herbert Aptheker, whom the Alabama Commission called a "Communist party functionary"; Allen Krebs, "admitted Marxist"; and Robert Keisler, President of the college's W.E.B. DuBois Club (which, as noted in an earlier chapter, was identified by FBI Director J. Edgar Hoover as a youth project of the Communist Party, USA).

Mr. Zippert also was a member of the American Youth Festival Committee's Policy Committee set up to recruit young people to the Communist-dominated World Youth Festival in Algeria in 1965 (later cancelled because of the overthrow of the Ben Bella regime). Discussing Mr. Zippert's activities in connection with orientation for co-operatives, Richard B. Millspaugh, a member of the board of Acadiana Neuf, commented to the Louisiana Joint Committee, "Knowing Mr. Zippert's activities, I wasn't satisfied that he was the proper person to give orientation to anybody."

Nevertheless, Mr. Zippert, according to the Committee, was instrumental in organizing the Grand Marie Vegetable Producers' Cooperative at Sunset, Louisiana, which evolved from the Sweet Potato Alert. The Committee revealed that Grand Marie got $68,000 from the Farmers' Home Administration.

Here is what happened to some of it, according to testimony of Committee Counsel Jack Rogers: "We offer into the record photostatic copies of four checks, the first one of which is drawn on the account of the Grand Marie Vegetable Producers Cooperative, Inc. for $5,000 to the CORE Scholarship, Education Defense Fund, Inc. It is marked in the upper left-hand corner 'crates.' The second check from the same account is payable to Mr. John Zippert in the amount of $1,750. It is marked in the upper left-hand corner '$240 repair, $1,510 labor.' It is dated August 2, 1966. This is the same date as the one to CORE. The next check is also payable to John Zippert on the same account, dated August 25, in the amount of $18.83, marked 'telephone' in the upper left-hand corner. The last one is also dated August 2, 1966, payable to John Zippert on the same account in the amount of $154.30, marked in the upper left-hand corner 'legal fees, inst., rep., o., s.' whatever this means. . . . The checks are all counter-signed by the Farmers Home Administration, Crowley, La."

Mr. Zippert also was one of the organizers of the Southwest Alabama Farmers Cooperative Association of Selma, Alabama, according to the Alabama Legislative Commission to Preserve the Peace (ALCPP). On May 11, 1967, OEO announced a grant of $400,000 to that co-op, thus removing any doubts about its objecting to supporting co-ops run by black activists.

Shirley Mesher put the program together and was officially listed as the "coordinator." According to the ALCPP, Miss Mesher worked as a coordinator, too, for SNCC and had the black panther emblem painted on the door and windows of her office on Franklin Street in Selma. She was a marshal for Martin Luther King in the Selma-to-Montgomery civil rights march in March 1965 by his Southern Christian Leadership Conference. She "associated closely with James Bevel" who led the anti-Vietnam demonstration in New York City in the spring of 1967.

Other organizers included Edward Brown of the Citizens Crusade Against Poverty (discussed in a later chapter) and three members of the leftist National Sharecroppers Fund, Jac Wasserman, James Mays and Michael Kenny.

OEO funded the co-op against the advice of Joseph Bradford, who opposed the action as the agency's regional representative and shortly thereafter was promoted to head OEO's Rural Task Force. In an official memorandum to OEO, dated January 18, 1967, Dr. Bradford declared, "OEO can hardly blindly afford to commit money and manpower to an endeavor which is doomed to fail. . . . Education and financing pose acute problems in this situation. Both are excessively limited, but essential for the clientele. They have practically no history in co-operative production and marketing; failure can be easily built into the effort."

In addition, the entire Alabama delegation in the U.S. Congress pleaded with OEO not to fund the co-op, as did the following men from Alabama, who traveled to Washington and personally asked OEO not to give money to the co-op: W. H. Knight, Probate Judge, Hale County; Goldsy Tucker, County Commissioner, Hale County; Crowell Pate, Jr., Mayor, Lowndesboro; Bill Dannely, Probate Judge, Wilcox County; Frank Thomas, Commissioner, Marengo County; B. A. Reynolds, Probate Judge, Dallas; Joe T. Smitherman, Mayor, Selma; Leight Peques, Mayor, Marion; Joe Knight, Community Action Agency, Selma; Dave Nettles, Probate Judge, Monroe County; L. B. Whitfield, III, Whitfield Pickle Co., Montgomery; J. G. Alfred, Whitfield Pickle Co. and Ed Strickland, Staff Director, Alabama Legislative Commission to Preserve the Peace.

After OEO made the grant anyway, the Alabama legislature passed a joint resolution which urged the agency to rescind it. The resolution said the co-op "was organized at the instigation and under the direction of civil rights worker Shirley Mesher, a prime participant in the Black Panther movement in this area . . . and . . . in reality funds will be spent to finance the lawless Black Panther movement designed to overthrow the government of this country and particularly the governments of southern states." It charged the grant was "for the specific purpose of promoting Black Power in Alabama, and not for raising the economic level of low income farm families who could be more effectively aided by other means."

The biggest co-op loan made through the Farmers' Home Administration was $700,000 for thirty years to the 1,100-member Southeastern Farmers Grain Association, Inc., a grain-marketing co-op in Warsaw, N.C. The money was to be used for construction of a 500,000-bushel grain elevator. A bank for co-operatives had offered to lend 60% of the construction costs, but FHA didn't want a second mortgage and didn't think the co-op should bear the costs of obtaining two loans.

How FHA checked the income of all 1,100 members is a mystery. Its regulations, however said that 66% of the members had to have "low income," as must 51% of those served. According to FHA, income was low when it was insufficient to provide the basic needs for a minimum level of living, pay necessary farm and other operating expenses and meet required payments on the farm and other essential income-producing property.

Most of the FHA loans were relatively small, however. It approved a $55,000 loan for thirty years to the Southhaven Farmers' Association Market, De Soto County, Mississippi, for a co-op store to sell fresh fruits and vegetables. Other loans included $25,000 for a co-op retail farm supply store by the Farmers' Service Corporation of Jennings County, Indiana, and $26,000 for a landing and marketing facility at Port Norris, New Jersey for 27 oystermen who formed the New Jersey Tongers Cooperative Association.

In Menominee County, Wisconsin, anti-poverty community organizers decided that residents there had to go too much out of their way to shop. The result was that a group they organized applied for a loan of $175,000 to open a co-op general merchandise store. It had tentative approval at this writing, pending a local determination that such a store would primarily serve low-income people.

The Gilbert Creek Community Action Group, organized with OEO funds, already had a co-op food store in operation at Baisden, West Virginia. Said the OEO, "The people along Gilbert Creek decided they were tired of 'owing their souls to the company store'".

14

Head Start

As noted in the first chapter, Head Start was launched as a part of community action in an attempt to sell the War on Poverty. It not only had the sure-fire attraction of something for nothing, but also the ages-old appeal of ostensibly helping poor little children. How could it go wrong? OEO demonstrated this in a multitude of ways.

From the start, the concept was not clear. OEO itself admitted that Head Start programs came "in all sizes and shapes" and depended upon local decisions. The agency required only that the programs "show promise of making a meaningful contribution to the elimination of poverty." At this writing, OEO still had not made clear what constituted a "promise" or a "meaningful contribution." What gradually became obvious, however, was that the government was using the appeal of Head Start as a wedge for greater federal control of public education at all levels.

In financing groups to run Head Start programs, OEO, in several instances, deliberately went outside the public school systems which OEO officials called "the establishment." This occured most notably where "the establishment" vigorously opposed federal control of education. The object, OEO contended, was to give the poor direct participation in the program. One result was the funding of leftist groups.

With only vague criteria as a guide and a great rush to spring into action on a vast scale, it should not have been surprising that administration of Head Start was chaotic. Representative Paul A. Fino (R., N.Y.) called it "the most expensive baby-sitting program in our history."

After plunging into Head Start, OEO decided to try to figure out what it had done. By May 1967, it had spent $8.5 million budgeted for that purpose even though some agency officials admitted privately that evaluation was impossible, and one told me that it was as experimental as the program. So far none of the evaluators had revealed any evidence that Head Start was helping poor youngsters or lifting anybody out of poverty. Nevertheless, OEO constantly touted Head Start as its most successful program.

Examples abound of the administrative chaos. Public school officials of North Tonawanda, New York told OEO in August 1965 that they wanted to begin a year-round Head Start program in October. It took them until late November, however, even to obtain the application forms which covered 31 pages. After finally obtaining $20,345 from OEO for a program limited to the summer of 1966, North Tonawanda School Superintendent Maurice Friot declared, "After we had been put through a long struggle and been subjected to a minute examination with respect to our proposal, it was maddening . . . to have our people attend the training session and find there were people there who had been funded who had not made arrangements for transportation . . . teachers . . . teacher's aides . . . [and] who did not know where they were going to house their programs."[1]

After spending over a year tangled up in OEO's red tape, public school officials of Waterloo, Iowa withdrew their application for a year-round Head Start program.[2]

School officials of Laramie County, Wyoming also decided it wasn't worth it and gave up after they had spent

$1,500 in staff time, phone calls and other expenses and several months in "a maze of bureaucratic involvement" in an attempt to obtain OEO approval of a year-round Head Start program.[3]

After school officials at Port Huron, Michigan filed a mountain of reports with OEO in applying for a Head Start program, the agency informed them they had made so many errors that they would have to resubmit their reports. But when School Superintendent Gerald S. DeGrow phoned OEO in Washington, he learned that the inexperienced OEO staff had created a hopeless mess in processing Head Start forms which came in from all over the country. To get new reports to give the staff another chance, OEO had notified all school districts to file new ones.[4]

In April 1966, Mrs. Randolph Guggenheimer resigned as co-chairman of New York City's Head Start program, charging it was in a state of chaos. Mayor John Lindsay said her charge was "entirely valid," and Mrs. Anne M. Roberts, Executive Director of the Economic Opportunity Committee (then the top city anti-poverty office) declared, "Certainly there has been chaos in mounting such a vast new program."[5]

In Fairfax County, Virginia, OEO approved a program and then made two-thirds of the children enrolled ineligible by lowering the income limits.

This was not the case, however, in Montgomery County, Maryland, which adjoins the District of Columbia. Members of Congress were asked to enroll their children in the program there, with the explanation that some of the top figures in the Johnson Administration were enrolling their youngsters. The explanation was that the program wanted some children who came from "advantaged families" in the hope that some of their culture might rub off on the children for whom Head Start was intended.[6]

In 1966, OEO took the Head Start program in East Feliciana Parish, Louisiana away from the Louisiana Education Association, an all-Negro association of Louisiana school teachers which had conducted Head Start the previous year. The ground for the action was not that the association was incompetent, but rather that it was operating a segregated program in contravention of OEO rules. OEO then turned Head Start over to the leftist Southern Consumers Education Foundation which operated a program so segregated that it conducted classes in Negro homes and transported the pupils in private automobiles owned by Negroes.[7]

The five Head Start programs operated by SCEF had never been audited, Roland M. Hebert, former executive director of Acadiana Neuf told the Louisiana Joint Legislative Committee on Un-American Activities in March 1967. As noted in chapter 12, SCEF was a delegate agency for the community action agency, Acadiana Neuf.

Serving on the Acadiana Neuf board was Marion White, an attorney and a close friend of the aforementioned John Zippert. According to Committee Counsel Jack Rogers, Mr. White told an Acadiana Neuf board meeting, "We are not only going to take over Acadiana Neuf, but the school board and the police jury too."

Free physical examinations for the youngsters were an aspect of Head Start much-lauded by OEO. After reading in the *Congressional Record* of September 27, 1966 that some doctors rushed the tots through the exams so fast that they were able to collect $100 an hour, I asked Dr. Robert E. Cooke about the medical program. He is Director of the Pediatrics Department of Johns Hopkins Hospital in Baltimore and had organized the planning group for Head Start.

This was Dr. Cooke's reply: "The medical program was

very spotty, with some areas, such as Baltimore, putting on an excellent medical program, with follow-through for defects discovered. A number of other places, however, had rather inadequate medical programs, and very cursory examinations were done with no follow-up of defects discovered."

To my knowledge, by May 1967 the only evaluation of Head Start to be made public was the one done for OEO by Max Wolff, Senior Research Sociologist at the Center for Urban Education, New York City, and Annie Stein, Staff Assistant at the Center. The work was done under contract with the Ferkauf Graduate School of Yeshiva University, New York City.

Studying children who went from Head Start classes to four public kindergartens in Manhattan, they said that they made out better than non-Head Starters only for the first few months. Then their initial advantages disappeared. Moreover, the report said that in racially-mixed schools, the Head Starters did not have even initial advantages over other kindergarten pupils.

"The teachers themselves were a more decisive factor than participation in Head Start . . . Head Start children scored higher if they had good teachers, but lower . . . if they had poor teachers," the researchers concluded.

"We can easily predict that even the finest pre-school experience for deprived and segregated children will wash out and disappear as these children pass through the grades," they volunteered.

Sargent Shriver seized upon this immediately. "Our urban public schools are critically inadequate to meet the needs of the children of poverty. This seems like a harsh judgment, but it is borne out by a recent follow-up study of Head Start children," he declared, not mentioning that the study was limited to four New York schools. "The disappointment and discouragement of the slum school classroom caused many of them to fall further behind than children who had not had the Head Start experience. The readiness and receptivity they had gained had been crushed by the broken promises of first grade," lamented Mr. Shriver.

Then, like Michael Harrington and others before him, Mr. Shriver leaped to a grand conclusion: "What is needed is a projection of Head Start into the primary grades which we might call Operation Keep Moving." (OEO's budget request for fiscal 1968, still pending in Congress, in May 1967 asked for $135 million for a "new program . . . in the primary grades to sustain the gains made in pre-school programs under project Head Start.") This, he said, would limit class sizes to fifteen children, use teachers' aides and volunteer sub-professionals in the classroom, establish tutorial assistance (making use of members of the Neighborhood Youth Corps and VISTA), provide books, films, television and educational toys, "maximize" parental involvement and initiate a new training program for child development specialists.

Mr. Shriver said further, "If school systems will pick up the challenge and keep moving, one year at a time, the results will inevitably be a revolution in education systems from pre-school through pre-college. I feel sure that if the pressure to effect this change is great enough, funds will be available from the federal and state governments to make this revolution possible."

Here, as Mr. Shriver seemed to acknowledge, was a revolutionary proposal for federal control of education, and he wanted to go even farther. From Operation Keep Moving, he said he wanted to go to Upward Bound (the OEO program already in operation to prepare high school students for college), to "college work-study."

After careful scrutiny of the Wolff-Stein report, I could find nothing to justify Mr. Shriver's drastic conclusions.

Head Start children adjusted more easily to school at first, but after some months the others adjusted, too, and caught up, it found. There was no indictment of the school system, just a finding that Head Start was of no lasting benefit and that good teachers were what made good schools.

Still the hoopla for Head Start continued. The Public Relations Society of America launched pilot projects in New York, Atlanta, Cleveland and Los Angeles to promote Head Start. In charge of the operation was Holmes Brown, who had handled the first Head Start publicity. He said that in a year-round, gratis program, chapter members would prepare news releases, television spot promotions and even advertising. "Public relations has got to get a community all steamed up," he declared.[8]

By the end of 1966, Education Commissioner Harold Howe, II chimed in. He called for wholesale application of Head Start standards in the primary grades and, like Mr. Shriver, plugged for limiting classes to fifteen pupils. Such application, he said, would cost $1200 per student per year, two to three times what public schools were then spending.[9]

At least one voice of the poor was heard, however. Eugene Hill from the Center for Community Action Services in Albuquerque, New Mexico told the Ribicoff Subcommittee of the Senate Government Operations Committee, "If a man is unemployed, a child day-care nursery doesn't solve his problem . . . You prescribe an aspirin for my cancer and give it to my child."[10]

OEO plunged ahead with more formal evaluations of Head Start. According to Pauline Tate, OEO Information Specialist for Head Start, the agency spent $2 million for evaluation in 1965 and $2.9 million in 1966. In addition, it had budgeted $6 million for it in 1967 and another $6 million for 1968.

Midway in the spending of those millions, Edmund W.

Gordon, part-time OEO Research Director for Head Start, commented that most of the research so far had been "proving the obvious." And the Planning Research Corporation noted that most of the evaluation had been done by persons with a self-interest in Head Start.[11]

15

The Child Development Group of Mississippi

The shocking saga of the Child Development Group of Mississippi glaringly demonstrated the extent to which a Head Start program could become involved in political activities. I pointed this out in an article published in *Barron's National Business and Financial Weekly* September 26, 1966 and reprinted in the *Congressional Record* the following day. In view of the facts the article brought to light, the events which took place subsequently are almost unbelievable. They can best be appreciated by reading the story exactly as it appeared in *Barron's*, reprinted here by permission of *Barron's*. It read as follows:

Head Start for What?
The Story of the Child Development Group of Mississippi

By Shirley Scheibla

"No part of the [anti-poverty] funds appropriated by this paragraph shall be available for any grant until the

[Office of Economic Opportunity] Director has determined that the grantee is qualified to administer the funds and programs involved in the proposed grant."

1966 Anti-Poverty Program Appropriation Bill

Washington—Like thousands of others throughout the U.S., a group of poor little children in Shubuta, Miss. have been attending Head Start classes under federal auspices to prepare them for entering elementary school. They must have gotten a liberal education. For classes were held next door to, and run from the home of a militant civil rights leader, Mrs. Allie Jones, chairman of the operation. Other groups used the home, too, including one woman in residence there accused of transporting persons for the purpose of prostitution. Civil rights meetings were held and, according to signed affidavits, breaches of peace occurred, and murder was attempted on the premises.

The Shubuta classes are just one example of scandalous Head Start operations, run with federal grants of $7 million, by the Child Development Group of Mississippi (CDGM), an unincorporated organization controlled by leftist militant civil rights workers, representing chiefly the Student Nonviolent Coordinating Committee, the Congress of Racial Equality and others.

Inciting to Riot

SNCC, the Negro group which launched the cry, "black power," is led by Stokely Carmichael, who was recently arrested in Atlanta on charges of inciting to riot. Mr. Carmichael also has urged Negroes to refuse to serve in Vietnam. The National Director of CORE is Floyd McKissick, who declared on a television program last month: "Nonviolence is a thing of the past. Most black people will not agree to be non-violent."

Investigations just completed by the Senate Appropriations Committee, the General Accounting Office, the Office of Economic Opportunity and Sen. John C. Stennis (D., Miss.) reveal that funds given to CDGM have been used to finance civil rights violence. Investigators have irrefutable evidence that those responsible for the Head Start program have paid money directly to SNCC, and that Head Start school rooms, kitchens, grounds and automobiles have been placed at the disposal of civil rights activities.

With its entire $7 million grant already spent, the Child Development group has made a request for $21 million to finance year-round operations. However, owing to the investigation, the Office of Economic Opportunity has been asked to withhold further funds from CDGM. In the face of overwhelming evidence, the agency is expected momentarily to comply.

Check to SNCC

Here is the almost incredible story. On May 18, 1965, OEO announced a grant of $1.4 million to Mary Holmes Junior College, West Point, Miss., for a Head Start program. In less than two weeks, the college gave at least one check for $200 to SNCC. (A photostat of the cancelled check is in the files of Sen. Stennis.)

The college then contracted with CDGM to carry out the whole program. Paul J. Cotter, investigator for the Senate Appropriations Committee, later testified that the college was "used merely as a conduit for the federal Head Start grant . . . to avoid the possibilities of a governor's veto." (Section 209 of the Economic Opportunity Act says a governor may not veto an OEO grant "to any institution of higher education.")

Sargent Shriver, who heads the War on Poverty, insisted that there was nothing unusual about funding a college to operate a Head Start program; OEO, he said, does so in many states. Mr. Shriver, however, failed to add that for the other Head Start programs, the National University Extension Association arranges one-week orientation courses for teachers. Mr. Shriver made an exception for CDGM and allowed it to give its own orientation courses. He also permitted the agency to select and train non-professional teachers from among the poor (in line, says OEO, with the Economic Opportunity Act, which stresses maximum feasible participation of the poor in the War on Poverty).

The Group's Head Start program is unique in other respects, too. It doesn't come under the direction of local community action programs. Moreover Senator Stennis has discovered that most of its Head Start areas are identical with SNCC's organizing targets.

Militant Arm

CDGM began its statewide operations from its headquarters at Mount Beulah, a former Negro college at Edwards, Miss., which also happens to be the conference headquarters of the Delta Ministry, the militant Mississippi arm of the National Council of Churches. Perhaps the most outstanding member of the Delta Ministry is its associate director, the Reverend Warren McKenna. Herbert Philbrick, who was a Communist for the FBI, declared in Congressional testimony: "When I was an active member of the Communist Party, I knew McKenna well as one of the leading collaborationists of and apologists for the Soviet Union. At one time we spoke together from the same platform at a Communist-sponsored youth rally."

Rev. McKenna also has been listed as a faculty member of the Samuel Adams School in Boston, the principal Communist Party training unit in New England. In 1957 in defiance of the U.S. State Department, he led a group of 41 young Americans into Red China. While there, he had his picture taken with Premier Chou En-lai.

Dr. A. D. Beittel, Chairman of the Board of CDGM, is also a member of the Board of Directors of the Delta Ministry.

The Reverend Arthur Thomas is a director of both the Delta Ministry and CDGM. Also on the CDGM board is Miss Thelma Barnes of the Greenville office of the Delta Ministry.

Of the 30 people who organized CDGM, 21 had militant civil rights backgrounds. Here are a few examples: Louis Grant, a field coordinator for CDGM, was a field organizer for SNCC and also a member of CORE in New York City. He was arrested on June 14, 1965, in connection with civil rights demonstrations in Jackson, Miss.

Frank Smith, Coordinator of the CDGM Community Staff, also was arrested in Jackson on the same date for the same reason. He is a member of both SNCC and CORE.

Launched CORE Chapter

Miss Jeanne Herron, Program Coordinator for CDGM, launched the CORE chapter in Philadelphia. John Harris, CDGM Field Coordinator, was a chapter chairman for SNCC and handled voter registration demonstrations.

R. Hunter Morey, a member of the CDGM central staff, has a business card which identifies him as a representative of both SNCC and CDGM. In effect, he is the Mississippi director for SNCC.

So much for who's who in CDGM. Shortly after its inception, it was in so much trouble that the General Accounting Office, the Senate Appropriations Committee and OEO itself started to investigate. They charged that $1,129 of federal money was used to pay expenses, fines and bail of Head Start employees. When Jeanne Herron and Robert Dodge demonstrated on the U.S. Capitol grounds on August 9, 1965, against U.S. involvement in Vietnam, they were employed by CDGM headquarters.

Mr. Shriver finally got the CDGM to refund $373 to OEO. In the other cases, he said the Group wasn't using federal money and that he could not control what Head Start employees did off duty.

The books of CDGM proved to be in chaotic condition, once Congressional investigators obtained them. On this score they told the Committee: "CDGM books and records were removed surreptitiously from the Mount Beulah headquarters and taken to New York City by the accountants. It took three days to get the books back to Mississippi."

In all, the investigators questioned expenditures of $400,-000. Here's what Senator Stennis told the Appropriations Committee: "Checks on federal funds [were] . . . issued to individuals in the amount of $100 each and charged to petty cash without supporting vouchers. Some of these checks were issued to individuals who had been arrested in connection with marching protests in Jackson. Checks were issued to individual members of the central staff . . . for many hundreds of dollars without supporting the receipts . . . Thousands of dollars had been spent for supplies and equipment, much of which is placed in churches and other private buildings without adequate inventory or other records, and recovery of this property is improbable if not impossible."

Fee Overstated

Here are some excerpts from OEO's own Audit Findings and Recommendations: "The $30,710 fee paid to the Delta Ministry at Mount Beulah for feeding and housing CDGM employees during the week of teacher orientation . . . appears to be overstated by approximately $21,000 . . . We found documentary support for only 657 of the 831 persons who supposedly attended the conference . . .

"We found no evidence to support CDGM's non-federal share contribution of $180,568. (Federal law requires grantees to provide at least 10% of the cost of Head Start projects.) The approved budget indicates that the non-federal share will consist of volunteers' services, donated equipment and facilities . . .

"Three thousand chairs . . . were purchased at a cost of about $6,500, although the grant conditions prohibit project funds from being expended for the purchase of furniture . . . CDGM rents a fleet of about 12 automobiles. However, . . . no procedures or controls were in existence to restrict the use of such vehicles to official business."

Like the Committee investigators, OEO also questioned outlays totaling $400,000. Its officials indicated they thought the matter should be cleared up before granting further funds.

Greenville "Squat-In"

Shortly thereafter, demonstrators broke into a locked empty building at the U.S. Air Force Base at Greenville, Miss., for a 29-hour "squat-in." Their leader was the aforementioned Rev. Thomas. At least three Mississippi newspapers quoted him as saying that one of the major purposes of the "squat-in" was to jar loose funds from OEO for the financing of CDGM.

After the demonstrators refused to obey the U.S. Attorney General's order to leave, the Air Force brought in air policemen from four states to remove them. They had to carry out Rev. Thomas.

Here's what the *Delta Democrat-Times* reported on February 2, 1966: "Rev. Art Thomas . . . observed that most news stories he had seen made a point of saying that the demonstrators kicked, screamed, cursed and bit the airmen who were under orders to remove them from the building. Rev. Thomas said the demonstrators had considerable provocation for the cursing and abuse they heaped upon the airmen."

On the same date, the *Commercial Appeal* quoted Suffragan Episcopal Bishop Paul Moore, National Chairman of the Delta Ministry, as saying that the decision to carry out the Greenville operation "was made during a conference last week-end at Mt. Beulah."

Reuther Speaks Out

A few days later Walter Reuther spoke out. (Besides heading the United Auto Workers, he is Chairman of the Citizens Crusade Against Poverty, which achieved notoriety a couple of months later when it booed Sargent Shriver out of its meeting and staged a near-riot.) Said Mr. Reuther, "The poor of Mississippi need their faith in the federal government restored by immediate and vigorous federal action . . . Current delay in funding the pre-school program sponsored by the CDGM has produced great frustration and lack of faith in the intentions of the federal government. Poor children should not be made to pay the price of administrative delay." (Minutes of a CDGM board meeting on June 5, 1965, indicate that the CCAP had donated $4,000 to the Group.)

When the Greenville operation failed to produce fresh federal funds for CDGM, the latter tried another tactic. It sent 48 of its Head Start students to Washington for three days. Accompanied by 25 teachers and parents and two nurses, they sang for members of Congress, toured the White House and presented a gift to Mrs. Lady Bird Johnson.

Meanwhile, CDGM was negotiating with OEO. The latter managed to get a refund of $4,223. While OEO auditors recommended that an additional $12,338 be recovered, at last report it had not been.

"Merely Forgiven"

Negotiations continued, and OEO finally got the items in question down to $31,726. This, however, prompted Senator Stennis to remark, "The unauthorized and questioned expenditures of $400,000 were neither recovered nor explained; they were merely forgiven."

At OEO's suggestion, CDGM agreed to put $35,000 in escrow, an amount they both deemed adequate to cover the questioned items. Subsequently, OEO gave the Group a grant of $5.6 million for 1966.

Abuses, on a grander scale, continued. For three days in June 1966, about 200 participants in the so-called James Meredith march in Mississippi camped at and used the facilities of the Belzoni Head Start center. On June 24, the Reverend James F. McRee, Chairman of the Board of CDGM, fed several hundred Meredith marchers at the Canton Asbury Head Start center.

Asked why black power signs were displayed in its Head Start classrooms, CDGM declared, "Some buildings used by CDGM during the day serve as community centers which host a number of different activities during the evening . . . It would in no way reflect on CDGM for black power signs to be displayed in such a building in connection with the other organizations in the community it serves."

Still without any public explanation is why CDGM wrote checks to "employees" who did not live in Mississippi. For instance, one for $101.29 and dated August 12, 1966, was made out to Willie Watley, whose reported address at the time was Chicago.

Threaten Boycott

On July 22, 1966, a school day, the aforementioned Mrs. Allie Jones and three paid Head Start teachers visited at least two stores in Shubuta, Miss., during school hours to make demands not connected with Head Start classes. At both places the women presented a paper headed SHUBUTA HEAD-START COMMITTEE which said, "We, the members of the Community Planning and Improvement Committee . . . make these demands . . ." They included colored employes in all business concerns, more jobs, new factories and Negroes added to law enforcement agencies. They threatened to boycott Shubuta merchants unless the demands were met within one week. They carried out this threat, and on August 6 and 20 demonstrated in front of Shubuta stores.

Complaint affidavits signed by Shubuta citizens before the Mayor's Court of Shubuta testify that the following events took place at Mrs. Jones' home:

April 7, 1966—John D. Smith, son-in-law of Mrs. Jones, disturbed the peace in the home. Joe Staten, another son-in-law of Mrs. Jones, made threats with a shotgun in the yard of the home.

September 5, 1966—Rachel Smith (wife of John D. Smith and daughter of Mrs. Jones) "did unlawfully assault and attempt to take the life of John D. Smith with a 30-30 rifle."

September 5, 1966—Minnie Lee House, who makes her headquarters at the Jones home, unlawfully transported persons for the purpose of prostitution.

As for the physical condition of the Jones home, the local bank appraises it at $1,000 maximum.

Here's what Committee investigators found regarding other CDGM Head Start centers: "Several centers were little more than four room shacks with bath, accommodating 60 to 80 children with a staff of 10 or more. They were over-crowded and in soiled condition."

For its centers, CDGM paid rents ranging from $140 to $400 a month, "While their owners went out and rented better accommodations for the going rate of $35 to $37.50 a month," according to investigators.

As a rule, Head Start programs, like other anti-poverty measures, come under the direction of local groups overseeing all anti-poverty Community Action Programs. However, this is not true of the CDGM Head Start program. The Group supervises its own work in 28 countries and is responsible only to OEO.

Situation in Gulfport

Here's how Taylor Howard, President of the Harrison County Civic and Voters League of Gulfport, describes his local situation: "We have petitioned the Board of Supervisors of Harrison County to assist in creating a workable Community Action Committee . . . so we can bring all these poverty programs under one county committee. We feel that programs would be better managed. In our effort to help in this we have been vilified, and outright interference with public meetings has been one of the tactics used by CDGM personnel in . . . Harrison County . . ."

Meantime, CDGM is enthusiastic about its efforts. As noted, it wants to enlarge Head Start to a year-round program. It originally asked OEO for $41 million, but was persuaded to scale down the figure to $21 million.

So far, OEO appears to be succeeding beyond its wildest expectations in getting money from Congress for its nationwide Head Start Program. It requested $327 million for the program for fiscal 1967, but the Senate Labor Committee last week voted $527 million for Head Start, following a vote for $352 million by the House Labor Committee. The Senate Committee also approved $2.5 billion in spending authority for OEO—nearly $750 million more than the agency requested.

Head Start often has been called the most popular of the programs of the War on Poverty. Who, it is argued, can be against help for poor little children? But who, on the other hand, wants them to be taught by members of organizations charged with inciting riots? And who wants Head Start money to be used to finance riots?

Things started to pop immediately after publication of this article. On October 1, 1966 OEO representatives went to Jackson, Mississippi to meet with the CDGM Board, but found them "unavailable."

The following day, a Sunday, OEO mailed the board a report on its decision against further grants and publicly announced: "A decision was reached by OEO on September 27 that CDGM in its present organizational form, with its present administrative and operating personnel and record of management, cannot lawfully be refinanced by OEO."

At the same time the agency made public the findings of OEO reviews of CDGM of which the following is a condensation:

> Employees were listed as having worked and were paid when they were not in Mississippi. For example:
>
> At Cary, one employee was on the payroll and certified present for a period of at least six weeks, when, in fact, he was in Chicago.
>
> At Greenwood, a teacher was listed on the payroll for a two-week period during which she was, in fact, in New York.
>
> When he was a center chairman, one Board member listed two women on the payroll for several weeks, during which they did not work, and he certified records showing them present...
>
> Thirty-three teachers received both CDGM salaries and OEO stipends while attending training courses. Identified CDGM payments to teachers attending these courses totaled $3,984.
>
> A number of cashed payroll checks appeared to be endorsed by a person other than the payee. The total payments made on the basis of the questionable endorsements was about $1,000...
>
> Salaries paid on the basis of unapproved attendance records totaled about $31,500. At least five of the fifteen area administrators certified that employees were on the job when they were not.
>
> A review of a random sample of 300 personnel applications showed: ...
>
> Almost all applications appeared not to be reviewed or evaluated for authenticity of information.
>
> In three-quarters of the applications no effective date of hire was contained in personnel files.
>
> In one-quarter of the applications, salary justifications were difficult to evaluate since prior employment histories were often inadequate.
>
> Contracts for services and facilities have been awarded to

staff members and board members. In ten instances lessor was center chairman. In one instance lessor was board member. In 21 instances lessor appeared related to the agent acting for CDGM and/or center chairman. In three instances center chairmen hold transportation contracts.

Payments of $24,000 were made under at least 32 facility contracts totaling $19,500 and four transportation contracts totaling $4,500 awarded to parties having relationships that could be construed as conflicts of interest.

Some specific examples include: A member of the board of directors of CDGM signed the lease renting his church to CDGM for $240 a month. One individual appears as both the agent of CDGM and lessor on a facilities lease. Lessors on a lease appear to be related to the agent acting on behalf of CDGM who is center chairman. The center chairman also has a child transportation contract. The father of a paid assistant community organizer has a large transportation contract. One area administrator has the transportation contract for one center in his area, and a board member has another in the same area. The administrator's wife is committee chairman at a community center.

Seventy-two of the highest paid CDGM employees received salary increases in excess of 20 percent of their previous pay, a violation of OEO policy. These excess salary payments amounted to $64,000.

A number of cases of nepotism were identified. The member of the CDGM Board who serves in an unpaid capacity, has his wife on the CDGM payroll at a salary of $75.00 a week. One area teacher guide is the wife of a board member. Payments to CDGM board members and/or members of their families on the payroll totaled about $6,000 . . . The Assistant Community Organizer in another area is the son of the man who furnishes transportation for the Canton Center at $1,000 per week. At Cary Center, the center chairman has her mother, son and sister on the list of employees. In addition, the family is receiving $120 per month in rent for property she rented to CDGM.

CDGM management did not exercise close control over the usage of rental automobiles . . . The rental costs of automobiles used for non-grant purposes totaled about $3,000. A community organizer submitted gas receipts totaling $300. He obtained duplicate receipts and submitted the original with one voucher and a few days later the duplicate with another, collecting payments for the same bill. OEO found usage logs for two automobiles missing for periods of 3 consecutive months and in one case the log was missing for the major portion of a 2 month period. OEO questions the rental costs, totaling about $25,000 for automobiles during the unsupported periods.

Fifty-four of 134 contracts examined were awarded for the exact amount included in the approved budget amount indicating that the contract price negotiations were not in accordance with the grant provision that the budgeted amount was to be adjusted and documented based on local conditions. Contractors were paid on the basis of the total expected child enrollment regardless of the number of children actually transported. At Gulfport, both the area administrator and a CDGM board member have transportation contracts. At Belzoni, three teacher trainees' husbands are employed to furnish transportation. Seven payments were made under transportation contracts before the scheduled opening dates of classes.

Payments totaling some $104,000 to consultants under 14 of 19 consultant contracts examined were either unsupported or supporting invoices were inadequate. For example, invoices contained no details on work performed including dates, rates and exact descriptions of work. Where fixed-price contracts were awarded, payments were often based on contract provisions rather than detailed billings. Evaluation of final consultants' reports revealed the reports were not adequate proof of performance and/ or were not responsive to the requirements of the consultant contracts. For instance:

A consultant's contract contained a scope of work that appeared to be duplicated by several consultants subsequently hired by CDGM.

A consultant's report did not provide data on the evaluation of employees' qualifications and did not propose remedial actions, as required by the consultant's contracts.

A consultant was employed primarily for development of a management reporting system and for preparation of a follow-on grant application. At the time of audit near the end of the grant period the firm had not provided any written data on the management reporting system.

One CDGM consultant was also an employee receiving payroll checks and consultant payments concurrently ...

The refusal of the Board to face up to local CDGM committee resistance to using funds for professionals, because the committees preferred to spread the money among the poor, was a factor limiting the recruitment of a top staff ... The concern is that without proper supervision by qualified personnel, there is little prospect of improving the situation. CDGM seems unable to improve that supervision.

To insure efficient grant management, OEO attached conditions and received assurances from CDGM prior to awarding a six-month grant in February 1966 for $5.6 million. The specified conditions emphasized strengthening of fiscal management and program operation. CDGM officials have not fulfilled with resolution the measures on which the grant was based. It has been determined that serious programmatic, managerial and fiscal problems continue. This has led to serious program deficiencies, including inadequate classroom supervision of children, inadequate health programs, and sub-standard buildings and equipment.

OEO has, therefore, concluded that further funding of CDGM would not be in the best interest of a strong, well-managed Head Start program, of the type which OEO intends to see continued in Mississippi.

The day after issuance of this report, Richard W. Boone, Executive Director of the Citizens' Crusade Against Poverty, issued a press release in which he declared, "The people of Mississippi are deeply disturbed by this 'poor be damned' policy, and they will be coming together in Jackson next Saturday at a mass meeting to let their feelings be known."

Mr. Boone also revealed that CCAP was conducting its own investigation of CDGM. A few days later it issued its report which stated, "The program was of the highest calibre and must be considered a striking success."

Instead of examining the specific individual charges of misspending of federal funds, the CCAP Board of Inquiry declared, "The charges made—even if true—do not in the Board's opinion constitute grave enough defects to support a judgment to terminate the program." Then it grandly concluded, "The CDGM is a well-administered, carefully organized, creatively run organization, demonstrating integrity, fiscal responsibility and managerial competence."

In its next issue *Barron's* pointed out that the Board was suitably packed with members sympathetic to the "New Left" and that by suggesting that their report should take precedence over the finding of official auditors, Walter Reuther "presents his Crusade as an effort to substitute his judgment for orderly government."

The CCAP move, however, was just the beginning of a whole series of actions calculated to win new federal grants for CDGM. A half dozen students of Howard University, who had served the previous summer as temporary OEO employees, charged that the agency ordered them to disguise themselves as civil rights workers so they could spy on the CDGM in Mississippi.

On October 13 Senator Jacob K. Javits (R., N.Y.) took to the floor of the Senate to declare that OEO should not refuse to make further grants to CDGM without giving the group a public hearing in Washington. This appeared to be an attempt to establish a peculiar precedent—that those who ask the government to give them money are entitled to their day in court before being turned down.

On the same day Senator Javits spoke, members of the Ad Hoc Committee to Save the Children of Mississippi demonstrated their support for CDGM by picketing OEO headquarters.

The next day anti-poverty specialists of the United Church of Christ and the Episcopal and Presbyterian churches interrupted a meeting in Chicago to fly to Washington. While picketing OEO headquarters to protest the CDGM action, they threatened to halt the cooperation between their denominations and the War on Poverty.

An OEO official told me that when he went out to lunch that day, he was amazed to find the priest from his hometown church in the picket line. "What in the world are you doing here, Father?" he asked. "I got a phone call to fly here in a hurry to help the poor children," the priest replied.

The agency man persuaded him to go into the OEO offices with him and look at the OEO audit of the CDGM. After doing so, the priest told several of the other pickets about it, and they joined him on the next plane out of Washington.

Still the abuse of OEO continued. An editorial in the *Washington Post* on October 16 declared OEO "cannot break off all support to the Child Development Group without tarnishing its own credit and credibility throughout the nation." It said further, "One must assume that some of the federal money has been lost, or strayed. But the Mississippi case bears comparison with the history of Haryou-ACT in Harlem, which lost track of very large sums of money. But Haryou-ACT continues to get heavy grants."

By October 17, OEO was clearly on the defensive. That day Herbert Kramer, Assistant Director for Public Affairs, told the press that the General Accounting Office had submitted to the Senate Appropriations Committee a review of CDGM activities which concluded that OEO should never have provided the second grant of $5.6 million to CDGM. He said Congress might take the matter out of OEO's hands by specifically prohibiting funds for the Group.

The same day Mr. Shriver held a two-hour conference with several church officials and said he would confer with CDGM's Board of Directors to discuss possible continuation of the Head Start program.

A few days later the top brass of CCAP turned up on the newly organized National Citizens Committee for the Child Development Program in Mississippi which ran a full-page ad in the *New York Times.* "Say It Isn't So, Sargent Shriver," urged the headline. The ad then went on to depict the CDGM as the innocent victim of racists.

The same day Representative William F. Ryan (D., N.Y.) urged the House to keep giving money to the CDGM. Without discussing the specific documented charges against the Group, he said the basic question is "whether the Office of Economic Opportunity is willing to support local groups in areas where the political establishment is hostile to any semblance of power given to the poor."

The following week Mr. Shriver went to OEO's regional office in Atlanta, Georgia to meet with CDGM officials. Martin Luther King, Jr. showed up and called the CDGM program, "One of the finest in the country—a paragon of what a community action program should be." While the Atlanta meeting was in progress, some OEO employees in Washington told the press that OEO had pushed the panic button and cut off funds for the Group to insure Congressional passage of the bill continuing OEO for another year.

Three days later Mr. Shriver met in his office with CDGM and United Presbyterian officials and hinted that he might be willing to consider making a third grant to CDGM.

On November 3, Howard University picked up the ball and convened a two-day conference of one hundred legal experts to examine the controversy. Clarence Clyde Ferguson, Dean of the Howard Law School, declared, "CDGM and similar cases bring us to the frontiers of a major new realm of law—the relations of the rule of law to the treatment by government of recipients of federal largesse." He added that "the most basic rights of citizenship, protection of the individual, can be vitiated by mutilation of the group."

A week later Vice President Hubert H. Humphrey, after addressing the General Assembly of the National Council of Churches in Miami Beach, offered his services as an intermediary between OEO and CDGM. The *Washington Post* reported that the Rev. Truman B. Douglass, an official of the United Church of Christ and Rev. Kenneth G. Neight, National Missions Executive of the United Presbyterian Church, accepted an invitation to meet with Mr. Humphrey in Washington the following week.

Next to step into the fray was Carl T. Rowan, U.S. Information Agency Director turned columnist. In his November 9 column in the *Washington Star* he acknowledged that the GAO report "indicates a lot of administrative faults in CDGM but nothing like what you expect in a group of people, many poor and poorly educated, trying to lift themselves by their bootstraps even while acting like a government bureaucracy." He added the report "fairly convinced" him that violations did occur but that "people who have seen tax dollars used for a century to keep them in bondage have finally managed to use a tax buck or two to liberate themselves."

The same day the Rowan column was published, the picketing at OEO started again. That time it was fifty clergy and lay members of the United Church of Christ and Presbyterian and Episcopal Churches. The following day the picketing was taken up by those who said they represented the poor of Mississippi.

Then *Presbyterian Life*, a magazine distributed to congregations in Presbyterian churches across the country, ran an article in its December 1 issue which said United Presbyterian leaders are allied with CDGM and see it "as a landmark of what 'maximum feasible participation of the poor' in poverty projects means."

The magazine also said the following: "The future of the whole OEO appeared to be in question, and some writers were asking questions about Sargent Shriver's real influence as OEO head . . . The issue at stake, however, remains the same; to what extent does OEO intend to sustain its guidelines toward 'maximum feasible participation of the poor'? That this ideal has been carried out by CDGM has never been in question . . . The National Board of Missions authorized its general secretary and executive officers to take any appropriate action . . . in pressing for a successful conclusion of the campaign to obtain new funds for CDGM."

Also to the rescue came *Renewal Magazine*, supported by the Board of National Missions, United Presbyterian Church. It said withdrawal of OEO funds was the result of CDGM becoming "an encouraging example of the use of federal money to allow communities to shape the destiny of their own children." What happened to CDGM showed, it said, that "people in power do not really want to give up anything."

On December 10 the *New York Times* reported that CDGM was getting "some private nourishment" while it pressed its fight for OEO money. The Field Foundation, Inc., said the *Times*, had given the Group $20,000 with a promise of substantially more.

The next day Unita Blackwell spoke before the Washington Ethical Society on "A Crack in the Closed Society —Story of the CDGM." Miss Blackwell was a CDGM Community Organizer. I had watched her lead much of the pandemonium which broke loose when Sargent Shriver tried to address the Citizens Crusade Against Poverty in Washington earlier in the year. While he was still speaking, or trying to, she shouted, "This country is sick. Messes of speeches but no action." She later grabbed a microphone and warned of riots unless Washington did something for the poor.

Still I had not found one advocate of CDGM who had

responded to the specific findings in the reports of the General Accounting Office, Senate Appropriations Committee, or OEO audit. Nevertheless the campaign for the Group succeeded. On December 16, Mr. Shriver announced an "agreement in principle" which would result in giving more money to CDGM. On January 30, 1967, he formally announced a new grant of $4,927,100 with an additional $3 million "subject to the availability of funds in the new fiscal year." This opened up the prospect that in one year CDGM would get more than the $7.1 million of OEO money it had spent in two years.

Prior to the action, some members of Congress had questioned its propriety since the Justice Department still had under consideration possible violations of criminal law by CDGM. Mr. Shriver sought to meet this objection by writing into the grant agreement a provision under which the Presbyterian Board of National Missions assumed "full financial responsibility for any past, present or future disallowances of the program's expenditures which might be discovered by public auditors."

In this connection Professor Elwyn Allen Smith of Temple University's Department of Religion raised an interesting point. It was to avoid the Constitutional ban on church control of federally supported education that the Board of National Missions designated the church-affiliated Mary Holmes Junior College to set up the CDGM. He said he doubted that this was a sufficient expedient. In a letter to the *New York Times* he wrote, "We are astounded that the OEO should egregiously disregard even a minimal application of the First Amendment of the Constitution to anti-poverty programming." Moreover, he added that in 1963 the United Presbyterian Church laid down church-state guidelines wholly inconsistent with acceptance of the OEO condition of full financial responsibility for CDGM by the Presbyterian Church.

Another condition of the grant was that Mary Holmes Junior College would use part of the money to hire the management consultant firm of Klein and Saks "to assist the grantee [college], the Board of CDGM and the Director of CDGM in the following:

"A. Installation of suitable management control systems.

"B. Training of staff in operation of the systems.

"C. Consultation to the grantee, the Board of CDGM and the Director of CDGM in important management decisions relating to CDGM."

On January 5, 1967, the College, the Board of National Missions of the United Presbyterian Church and Klein & Saks, Inc. signed a contract which said the work done by Klein and Saks also would include "making an independent summary report and evaluation of the managing of the CDGM project for each week during the period of this contract, without interfering with the responsibility of the College, the Board of Directors of CDGM, and the Director of CDGM for the management decisions in connection with the project; and it is understood that all significant information relating to the managing of the CDGM project will be made available to the Contractor [Klein and Saks] by the College, the Board of Directors of CDGM and the Director of CDGM."

In other words the management consultants were to offer expert advice which those in charge of the CDGM project could take or leave. The contract specified that for this advice and "as compensation for the furnishing of five professional personnel in Mississippi and Washington for this purpose, the Contractor will be paid the fixed sum of Eighty-four Thousand Dollars for services commencing January 5, 1967 and ending July 31, 1967." It added, however, that "In the event of approval by the Office of Economic Opportunity of an extension of this grant, the College shall pay to the Contractor the additional sum of Sixty

Thousand Dollars for furnishing the services of the five professional personnel from August 1, 1967, through December 31, 1967."

To my knowledge, this was the first time that kindergartens had required management consultants. And, as the contract indicated, five of them for CDGM were to be paid at an annual rate for each of better than $28,000. Moreover, according to the CCAP whitewash study of CDGM, Klein and Saks already was working for the Group. The report issued in the fall quoted Richard Davies, President of Klein and Saks, as stating "On our arrival at CDGM we were happily surprised that remarkable progress in administration had been made, and since the opportunity of working with the project, we have witnessed additional improvement . . . We feel assured that the project will continue to be administered in a successful way in the future."

The previous summer CDGM had rejected General Electric Company as a management consultant, going so far as to threaten GE boycotts if the services of the firm were retained. Here's the way GE put it in a letter to me: "At the suggestion of consultants to the CDGM and the Office of Economic Opportunity, General Electric offered to provide CDGM with some business management consulting assistance on a fee basis . . . However, the board of directors of CDGM then decided it did not wish General Electric to undertake the administrative work proposed, and no contract was executed."

CDGM also apparently was opposed to having other Head Start groups operate in Mississippi. Shortly after it declared that it would not refinance CDGM, OEO announced grants to other Head Start groups in the Southern states—$1.2 million to Rust College, Holly Springs, Mississippi for a program for 600 children; $713,300 to Southwest Mississippi Opportunity, Inc., Woodville, Mississippi for 935 children, and $3 million to Mississippi Action for Progress, Inc. for 1,500 children. The Greenwood, Mississippi correspondent for *The Commercial Appeal* (Memphis, Tennessee) reported that CDGM hecklers broke up meetings in Greenwood and Ita Bena when the MAP was trying to get organized. "The CDGM group loudly protested," said the paper, "and began singing freedom songs. One youth shouted, 'This is black power. We'll get Stokely Carmichael back in here.'"

Months after publication of my aforementioned article, *Barron's* was still receiving letters regarding it. One from a Negro parent in Sharkey County in Mississippi said, "There has never been a group of people that has done so much harm to a community without going to jail. CDGM people have threatened the local Negro not to work with anyone but them. If we have a meeting and invite the whites, the CDGM group sends in their people to use profane language to drive the whites away . . . We have our Civil Rights, but CDGM is trying to make slaves out of us and demoralize our kids all they can . . . If you cannot help us, please get some paper somewhere in America to help us."

Another letter from Mississippi said, "We need your help to save our children from the CDGM. It looks like our community will deteriorate for another year, and we will be harassed in our community—the whites as well as the colored, thanks to Sargent Shriver."

16

Community Action and School Boycotts

As Representative Paul A. Fino (R., N.Y.) put it, "One of the more disturbing—yet amusingly ironic—things about the phony war against poverty is the way its dollar resources are being used to finance school boycotts, thus depriving many children of their best tool of advancement in life."[1]

Community action workers were proud of their roles in fostering organized unrest which resulted in school boycotts in Washington, Chicago, Rochester and New York City. Basically the platforms of the boycotters were the same in all four locations. In the name of the "poor," they wanted to abolish grades, hire non-teachers to teach, present history and social studies with what they regarded as the proper slant, and bus Negro children to schools in the suburbs. It looked like a program for chaos, and that may have been the idea. Melvin Moore, Assistant Director of the Near Northeast Neighborhood Development Program, a Washington CAP, told me, "It might be necessary to do away with the schools and start all over again."

The trouble in Washington began with Head Start. The

D.C. public school system was to run it with funds from the United Planning Organization. But the school system was not to be paid until UPO approved its final report at the end of the program. Thus the school system would not know until it completed the program whether it had approval and funding from UPO. Right away this engendered the opposition of the redoutable D.C. School Superintendent Carl F. Hansen, who had earned national acclaim as an educator.

Dr. Hansen said this was a poor way to do business and refused to sign such a contract. He also balked at accepting responsibility without authority and said UPO had saddled Head Start with conditions which made it impossible for the school system to run the program. UPO, it later developed, was only following orders from OEO which were later put in an official memorandum.

Dated November 7, 1966 and signed by Lawrence E. Williams, the memo said that any agency running a Head Start program must have policy set by a committee composed 50% of the parents of the enrollees. It said, "The remaining half of the committee should be drawn from (a) parents and community members of previous policy advisory committees; (b) representatives of public and private associations and organizations; (c) interested members of the community-at-large." The memo also said this committee must approve the selection of a Head Start director and all of the non-professional staff.

Joined by school superintendents in nearby Montgomery, Prince George's and Charles counties in Maryland, Arlington and Fairfax counties in Virginia, and the cities of Alexandria and Falls Church in Virginia, Dr. Hansen wrote to Sargent Shriver that such authority for the policy committee would contravene laws which gave school boards hiring and firing authority. Dr. Hansen won this point.

He also won the right to pay Head Start teachers salaries commensurate with those of other teachers, rather than the higher pay recommended by UPO. Nevertheless, the school system had an avalanche of requests for Head Start appointments on a political basis, and this led Dr. Hansen to lash out at "power-grabbers and politicians" for trying to build a new political patronage base with Head Start money.

Dr. Hansen also refused to put the so-called Model School Division under control of the Head Start Policy Committee. That was the name given to innovative educational processes tried at 24 D.C. schools. Included were new kinds of reading programs, tutor services, extension of the school day, teaching on Saturdays, volunteer services of college and university students and a parent education project. Altogether, the Model School Division accounted for about 5% of the total costs of the 24 schools. This 5% was supported by the UPO.

When the agency tried to get control of 95% of the budget of the 24 schools for this investment of 5%, however, Dr. Hansen said he would not ask Congress for money to run the schools unless the school system controlled the budgets.

From OEO came a suggestion that perhaps it was not such a good idea for UPO to split up the money for the Division among many schools. UPO's board of trustees went even farther on April 14, 1967 and voted ten to eight against supporting the Division at all. It decided to spend $242,000 previously earmarked for the Division for "education action teams" to organize Washingtonians to press for changes in the schools. This simply meant more money for activities upon which UPO already had embarked.

The formal organization in the forefront of the fight for control of the D.C. school system was the Committee for Community Action in Public Education (CCAPE). It was

established at an assembly on June 4, 1966 sponsored jointly
by the UPO and the Washington Urban League. UPO
gave money to the League which has as its Associate Director David Rusk, son of Secretary of State Dean Rusk.
This is what the young Mr. Rusk told an Urban League
meeting in Philadelphia in the summer of 1966:

> How much do you have to show your "black bour-
> geoisie" board member before he decides that it's about
> time to shelve this old, comfortable image of the Urban
> League, which didn't picket, boycott or organize strikes?
> . . . How much does the white businessman have to see
> before realizing that the Urban League should no longer
> be a moderating and reasonable influence?

Virtually all of Washington's multiplicity of federally
funded anti-poverty agencies were represented among the
450 persons at the assembly. As chairman of the CCAPE,
it selected Melvin Moore, Assistant Director of the Near
Northeast Neighborhood Development Program, funded
by UPO.

To accomplish the aims of the anti-poverty workers, the
CCAPE decided to work to abolish the appointed D.C.
Board of Education and obtain an elected one within six
months. If that could not be done, it planned to set up a
shadow board to make public the will of anti-poverty
forces, as their counterparts already had done in New
York. (After this proved more difficult than expected,
CCAPE decided to concentrate on getting rid of Superintendent Hansen.)

Mr. Moore, meantime, stepped down to Vice Chairman
after the UPO ruled that because of his anti-poverty post
he should not head the CCAPE. The Reverend Channing
E. Phillips took over as Chairman, giving up his job as Co-
Chairman of the D.C. Coalition of Conscience to do so.
Under him the Coalition had sponsored a bus boycott, a

boycott of Washington merchants and a sleep-in at the Anacostia-Bolling military complex in Southeast Washington.

The Rev. Phillips soon got anti-poverty funds, too. He also was Chairman of the Housing Development Corporation (HDC), set up to house poor people. In February 1966, OEO granted the corporation $294,294 for administrative purposes, and the Department of Housing and Urban Development promised an additional $100,000. HDC had told OEO it would use rent supplements to place low-income people in middle class housing and that "welfare recipients, persons with criminal records, alcoholics and men and women living out of wedlock will be welcomed."

The Rev. Phillips also was pastor of the Lincoln Temple Memorial Church in Washington. After he turned over the church's sanctuary to Stokely Carmichael, who held a rally there urging Negroes to resist the draft, the membership stripped the minister of his authority to let outside groups use the church.[2]

With all his activities, the Rev. Phillips found time to lobby against Dr. Hansen at the Board of Education. In his CCAPE capacity, the Rev. Phillips told the Board in November 1966 that Dr. Hansen was "incapable of implementing and administering decisions of the Board which may be inconsistent with his own thinking."

Other anti-poverty workers followed this up by picketing Dr. Hansen at his office on February 15, 1967 with signs saying such things as "Hansen must go."

Before that, anti-poverty workers tried to destroy the confidence of parents in the elementary schools. Melvin Moore organized and led parents who picketed Crummell School to protest its condition. In November 1966, UPO's Urban League Neighborhood Development Center distributed posters which said Perry and Seaton schools were in such poor condition that they constituted a danger to the pupils. Dr. Hansen ordered an immediate investigation which proved there was no substance to the charges.

After a tumultuous meeting on March 15, 1967, the Board of Education voted 5 to 4 to reappoint Dr. Hansen for a three-year term when his contract expired May 15, 1967.

The reaction was explosive. Julius Hobson immediately called for a one-day school boycott on May 1. He was employed by the Social Security Administration in Washington and also headed the Washington office of ACT, a civil rights group. However, Mr. Hobson failed to win the support of CCAPE and the Rev. Phillips, who explained to me that he preferred a boycott when school opened in the fall. This would give him more time for planning the logistics. It would be necessary, he said, to arrange for "freedom schools" like those conducted in New York, Chicago and Rochester to avoid running afoul of the truancy laws.

The National Park Service obligingly issued Mr. Hobson a permit to conduct a "freedom school" in the Sylvan Theater on the grounds of Washington National Monument. The May Day boycott then took place as scheduled, and an estimated 400 students at the monument grounds heard such volunteer teachers as James Bevel, who led the anti-Vietnam war demonstration in New York City earlier that spring.

Against a background of posters with such slogans as "Black History," Mr. Bevel declared, "The way you enslave people is to keep information away from them. The federal government is not about to educate Negroes unless you force them to do it." (A subtle way, indeed, to encourage federal control of education.)

While the boycott boosted absenteeism by only 2,000 pupils and could hardly be called a triumph of militancy, it focused attention on the interesting background of Mr. Hobson who obviously was in the vanguard of those fighting for control of public schools.

He was Chairman of CORE in the early sixties. At the time of the boycott, he had just lost a case at the D.C. Court of Appeals in which he charged that appointment of the D.C. Board of Education by judges was unconstitutional. Mr. Hobson said he planned to appeal to the U.S. Supreme Court. In another case, then still pending, he had asked the D.C. Court to give control of the public schools in Washington to the U.S. Commissioner of Education until racial balance was established.

Just prior to the boycott, the *Washington Post* quoted Mr. Hobson as follows: "You can't make Socialist promises within the Capitalist system. It won't work. I'm a Marxist, not a Communist, but I don't have any illusions that I can change the system, although I think I can improve it."

Mr. Hobson announced that supporters of his boycott included Ralph D. Fertig, Executive Director of UPO's Southeast Neighborhood House; Patricia Saltonstall, paid Director of Volunteer Services for UPO; Mrs. Willie Hardy, former Director of UPO's University Neighborhood Council; CORE, SNCC and Americans for Democratic Action.

The first three had picketed the home of Mrs. Ann H. Stults on March 20 because she was one of the Board of Education members who voted to reappoint Dr. Hansen.

In March, Mr. Hobson was one of those who went to the D.C. 13th precinct police station to protest "police brutality" when Marion Barry, former D.C. SNCC director and Lester McKinnie, then D.C. SNCC director, were arrested for disorderly conduct. Subsequently a Citizens' Committee for Equal Justice was formed which announced that Mr. Hobson would head its community action committee. The group gave the D.C. commissioners two days to suspend the two police officers accused of brutality, and then announced it would have a sound truck follow one of the policemen on his beat and broadcast warnings that he was armed and dangerous. After the group decided to use posters instead of sound trucks, Mr. Hobson resigned in disgust, charging that it was being intimidated by Congressional criticism. The *Washington Post* quoted him as saying, "We should go after the entire police department."

By April, Secretary of Defense Robert S. McNamara entered the school controversy, adding fuel to the fire of those who would destroy confidence in the schools. When the House Foreign Affairs Committee was questioning him sharply regarding defense spending, Secretary McNamara retorted, "I think the real disgrace is for you to sit here in the nation's capital, not two miles away from school children who lack textbooks because Congress won't appropriate the funds for them."

When Senator Robert C. Byrd (D., W.Va.) asked Dr. Hansen about this, the latter replied as follows: "From fiscal 1961 to fiscal 1967, Congress has appropriated $868,681 for textbooks, an amount 17.1% greater than requested by the Board of Education and 32.5% greater than approved by the Commissioners. In addition, the schools have applied $787,933 from other federal funds, including impact aid, to the meeting of textbook needs."

What happened in Washington, however, was only a variation on a theme, first begun in New York City with Mobilization for Youth. As noted in chapter nine, MFY aided New York's first school boycott in 1964.

The Rev. Milton A. Galamison led the boycott then and also those which have recurred in the big city each succeeding year. The Rev. Phillips called the Rev. Galamison "my counterpart in New York" and said they shared the same aims regarding public schools. The Rev. Galamison also was involved in the War on Poverty, being a member of New York City's Poverty Board, a policy-making group established by Mayor John V. Lindsay.

Another War on Poverty warrior and boycott leader was Preston Wilcox. In the spring of 1967, he ran the so-called Liberation Schools to keep from violating the truancy laws. (The Rev. Galamison had been jailed in 1965 for doing so.)

Mr. Wilcox was an Assistant Professor at Columbia University's School of Social Work. OEO gave the School $300,000 to train workers for Volunteers in Service to America (VISTA) and an additional $93,000 to evaluate the effectiveness of the workers it had trained. Mr. Wilcox was a paid consultant to OEO for the Upward Bound program, which was supposed to help impoverished high school students prepare for college. In addition he was a consultant to the Community Association of the East Harlem Triangle, Inc. (CAEHT), which received OEO money. He said he also was the author of two funded anti-poverty proposals, Massive Economic Neighborhood Development (MEND) and the United Block Association (UBA). Both received federal anti-poverty funds. So did the Manhattanville Community Centers where the Liberation Schools were conducted. Then too, school boycotters met in a UBA building.

As Mr. Wilcox outlined them, the aims of the boycotters were the same in New York as in Washington—control of the public schools.

Even though Negro parents may not be technically qualified to decide on school curricula and employment of teachers, they can learn, and in a democracy, the parents should have the same opportunity to make mistakes as anybody else, he declared. Given a choice between a Negro principal and a white one with much higher qualifications, he said he would choose the Negro without hesitation.

When I pressed for details on how this would improve

the quality of education, he replied that this alone would not be enough. "I have a superb education, and there are still places where I am not welcome because I am black," he declared. Then his eyes traveled upward to the poster on the wall of his office proclaiming "black power." He said, "I just wish we had more Stokely Carmichaels. What we need is more violence."

Even a quick glance at others involved in the New York student strikes turned up other anti-poverty workers. Alice Kornagay worked for CAEHT and was one of the leaders of the boycott to protest the opening of the $5 million air-conditioned Public School 201 in the fall of 1966. Other leaders included Babette Edwards, a paid worker for MEND, and Helen Testamark, employed as a teacher aide under a program financed with federal anti-poverty funds.

Mitchell Sviridoff, New York's Human Resources Administrator, told me that undoubtedly many of those involved in the boycotts might have been community organizers under the War on Poverty. He maintained, however, "the top leaders are not anti-poverty people."

Some New York public school officials who had been intimately involved in the boycotts were unable to agree with him. Said one, "I am sure that the boycotts never would have occurred without the War on Poverty."

17

Ramifications
of Community Action

The facets of community action were virtually inexhaustible, due largely to the broad legislative authority provided for it, and to the talents of OEO officials for innovation. OEO even gave away community action money for a program called Research and Demonstration, which could include almost anything, so long as there was any chance it might demonstrate a possible means of alleviating poverty. Even a cursory glance at the program indicates an aim to bolster a new base of political power.

For example, in Detroit a grant of $49,752 to the Mayor's Committee for Total Action Against Poverty was "expected to show that a CAA [Community Action Agency] can acquire a planning capability which enables it to serve as the local authority on human resource allocation and social program planning." Said OEO, "This capability should insure the CAA a decisive role in all future program planning and implementation efforts at the local level.

"This planning capability will equip the CAA to participate in planning efforts for the Department of Housing and Urban Development's Model Cities programs, provide information on local needs, and efforts and accomplishments and provide the poor with an opportunity to understand and participate in local decisions of resource mobilization."

A grant of $55,321 to the Oakland Economic Development Council, the CAA in Oakland, California, was to demonstrate the importance of providing CAA's "with the capability of assessing their needs, specifying program goals, strategies and priorities and evaluating programs."

Another facet of the attempt to take control of education away from local school boards was revealed in a grant of $34,360 to the Raleigh County Community Action Association, Inc., the CAA in Beckley, West Virginia. When OEO announced the grant April 10, 1967, it said it "will show that low-income people, when involved in an educational program as planners and participants, rather than recipients of a school-produced program, can be a positive force for improving the educational system in their county."

Legal services, according to OEO, provided: "(1) legal representation for the disadvantaged; (2) research into the legal problems of poverty; (3) education of the disadvantaged concerning legal rights and responsibilities and (4) advocacy of improvements in the law affecting those in poverty."

A study of the first 86 cases processed in upper Wisconsin showed that 72 had to do with divorce—63 suits for it —and nine cases of custody resulting from prior divorces.[1]

Elsewhere the early returns from the program were not any more encouraging. As noted earlier, the program was used to defend anti-Vietnam war demonstrators in a New York cathedral. In a story about the attack on the Washington police station described in an earlier chapter, the *Washington Post* reported, "Two citizens directly involved in the rock-throwing appeared ready to testify, but were persuaded not to by Julian Dugas, director of the Neighborhood Legal Services project."

Ted Bushman of the law firm of Clare, Bushman & Baldwin in Santa Maria, California wrote Senator George Murphy (R., Cal.) as follows to describe what was happening under the California Rural Legal Assistance Program funded by OEO: "The office here in Santa Maria has two receptionists, two legal secretaries and two attorneys. No private law office between Monterey and Santa Barbara has four secretary-receptionists. . . . Two of these legal secretaries earn $100 a month more than the highest paid legal secretary in the community.

"The attorneys on the staff are, without any experience, among the highest paid attorneys in the area.

"The spouse of one of the attorneys is on the Democratic Central Committee. The Democrat incumbent state senator is on their Board of Trustees.

"This organization appears to be formed more for political action than for rendering legal assistance."[2]

Mr. Bushman said the office had taken a case away from his firm involving an auto accident, a case in which the client was able to pay.

Aid to migrants, according to OEO, included grants, loans and loan guarantees "to states and localities and non-profit organizations . . . for housing, sanitation, education and day-care needs of migrants and their families [and for] . . . additional programs providing health, education, welfare, legal and other social services." Aid to Cesar Chavez and his striking grape workers under this program was described briefly in another chapter.

Upward Bound sent impoverished, under-achieving high school students to colleges for two or three summers of remedial tutoring to encourage them to attend college. Writing about the program in *The Reporter*, Mark Levy quoted a local Upward Bound director as saying, "I would be surprised if more than a half dozen of our 75 kids even tried to go on to college. Few of them have any special talents, and most just don't have the I.Q. however you measure it. We may be perpetrating a colossal fraud on them by making them believe they are college material."

Mr. Levy also reported that social studies teachers often took the daily newspaper as their text, "and a review of current events sometimes became a criticism of social ills." One instructor told him, "Maybe our discussion will help these kids realize that although society needs rules, not all of those rules are just. I hope that my students will come to understand that when the cops give them a rough time, something can be done about it. Maybe they'll learn that unjust laws don't have to be obeyed but can be changed."

At Trenton State College in New Jersey, Mr. Levy reported, the directors of Upward Bound allowed the students to determine the course content. At San Francisco State College, he said, a racial fight broke out after the students were "excited by a Black Nationalist lecturer who spoke at the invitation of Upward Bound officials."[3]

Medicare Alert sent community action workers out to encourage eligible people to sign up for voluntary health insurance for aged people. Apparently the campaign was highly successful. The Administration found it necessary to ask Congress for a supplementary 1967 appropriation of $91 million for payment to "Trust Funds for Health Insurance for the Aged." According to Representative Durward G. Hall (R., Mo.), "most of it was necessary because the original 1967 appropriation was based upon 15 million aged persons voluntarily enrolling in the supplementary medical insurance program, whereas over 17.5 million actually did enroll."[4]

The program called Foster Grandparents was just getting started as this was being written. The idea was to train elderly people to serve as substitute parents, primarily for institutionalized children.

Green Thumb employed elderly retired men with farming backgrounds "in community betterment and beautification projects," chiefly planting along highways. It was operated by the National Farmers Union, the only farm organization which served on the Task Force which drew up the first proposals for the War on Poverty.

In 1966 Congress specifically earmarked $12.5 million of OEO's appropriation for narcotics rehabilitation through community action. By the following May, OEO still hadn't figured out what it was supposed to do, and Herbert J. Kramer, OEO Assistant Director for Public Affairs, told me the agency was considering eleven different proposals. Since the money was put in the appropriation bill after the completion of hearings, OEO had little to guide it in the way of Congressional intent. The situation inspired Representative Robert McClory (R., Ill.) to comment, "It does not make sense to turn an important subject like this over to OEO without some ground rules or testimony as to what they contemplate doing."

18

Extra Weapons
in OEO's Arsenal

OEO's War on Poverty arsenal was filled with many weapons besides the Job Corps and community action. Most of them looked like duds for ending poverty, but like dynamite for dispensing political patronage.

The Neighborhood Youth Corps was administered for OEO by the Labor Department and offered part-time jobs with non-profit agencies to youngsters between the ages of 16 and 21. The idea was to provide income to the children of poverty to enable them to continue their high school education.

The *Providence Journal-Bulleton* found 63 ineligible youths enrolled in the program in Newport, Rhode Island. Included were the children of a Navy captain, a prominent surgeon, a store owner and a school administrator who also was an officer of an insurance and real estate firm. In Cranston, Rhode Island, it said that enrollees included the children of a dentist, doctor, vice president of a large bank, three high-ranking city officials and three state civil service employees who each earned more than $9,500 a year. The newspaper reported that in Jamestown, Rhode Island, everybody who applied was accepted without regard to financial need.

Under the program, millionaire Senator Hiram Fong (R., Hawaii) obtained summer post office jobs in Hawaii for his son, Rodney, and a niece, Carolyn Fong. His explanation, according to the *New York Daily News*, was that, "the Post Office Department never told me this was supposed to be a poverty program."[1]

But here's what Vice President Humphrey came up with: "While the emphasis should be on helping the poor and disadvantaged, some people are in need who are not poor in money. Some are poor in opportunity or poor in spirit, and the aim of this program is to help them as well as those in financial need."[2]

Volunteers in Service to America (VISTA) was the domestic version of the Peace Corps under which volunteers were supposed to live among the poor to help them combat poverty. Representative Harold Collier (R., Ill.) reported that training costs came to $15,000 per volunteer.

In Tulsa, Oklahoma, six VISTA workers circulated handbills among the city's Negroes which read as follows: "You are Negroes, not Tulsans. South side children play in beautiful parks, while Negro children play in streets. Does City Hall care? No parks, no movies, no recreation at all. Funny thing about North Tulsa, there's nothing for Negroes, nothing for nobody, just nothing. . ." It invited interested persons to attend a protest meeting and said, "Be prepared to take action." Mrs. Lena Bennett, Supervisor of VISTA workers, said, "This was to arouse people to become interested enough to attend the meeting."[3] The *Tulsa World* commented, however, that if racial agitation was the true aim of VISTA, "let us invite the OEO to de-VISTA our city."

The Farmers' Home Administration administered the rural loan program for OEO, and the cooperative aspects of it already have been discussed. However, the Economic Opportunity Act also authorized 15-year loans up to $2,500 "to any low-income rural family" to operate family-sized farms "or to finance non-agricultural enterprises which will enable such families to supplement their income."

What Congress really said here was that it would subsidize the operation of farms which already had been proved uneconomic, and many observers thought it merely was perpetuating poverty, instead of curing it, particularly in view of the maximum size of the loans.

Commenting on the program, an FHA official told me, "We'll take in anything that's legal, moral and rural, and rural doesn't mean it has to involve a farm; 46% of our loans to individuals are for non-farm activities.

"We don't say this program will pull them out of poverty. Credit is a vehicle through which we hope to get supervision and management assistance to the borrowers. For instance, maybe we'll advise them to send their children to Head Start or the Job Corps."

These, then, were the major OEO programs. An idea of the number of individual grants they involved can be obtained from a remarkable book on the status of OEO programs as of April 1, 1966. Put out by OEO, it is titled, *Poverty Program Information.* Each and every page, except the preface, lists separate OEO grants to local organizations, many of which redistributed the money to countless other groups. A typical page lists 18 to 20 separate grants, each ranging from several million to a few thousand dollars. The book has 705 pages.

This indicated that OEO's salesmanship succeeded—that the applications, indeed, were coming in for the anti-poverty money and that OEO was doling it out at a fast clip. But both the salesmanship and the administration of the federal largesse were expensive. Poverty really is where the money is for OEO's lavishly paid bureaucracy.

On public relations alone it spent $2.4 million a year,

including $450,000 in salaries, according to a study published in the *Columbia Journalism Review*. But that was only a small part of the expense of the OEO bureaucracy.

Sargent Shriver spent $43.8 million for personnel compensation in 1966, estimated it came to $73.3 million in 1967 and expected it to hit $86.2 million in fiscal year 1968.

Of his palace guard, 521 had annual salaries over $14,600, and 25 got over $25,000.[4] In addition, OEO had 211 consultants who received up to $100 per day, and 47 of them were full-time "consultants."[5]

On September 27, 1966 a *Republican Poverty Memo* declared, "A number of these 'consultants' have played prominent roles as full-time top-level functionaries since the Administration's anti-poverty program was launched. . . . Among these were Edgar Cahn, Special Assistant to the Director, and Lewis Eigen, as Associate Director of the Job Corps . . . When one realized that OEO has more personnel in supergrades than the Office of Education, which is budgeted for twice what OEO is, it is no small wonder that OEO tries to hide high-salaried people. The law and Civil Service regulations clearly provide that consultants may not be used when jobs call for full-time continuing employment."

The pay situation inspired Representative Bob Wilson (R., Cal.) to comment that "inflationary spending has been created by such ridiculousness as having more generals for the poverty war than there army generals in Vietnam—and at higher pay."

In addition, Representative William H. Ayres (R., Ohio) revealed that nearly half of the 2,350 OEO permanent employees in Washington and regional offices got $10,619 a year or more. He said that another 1,032 community action workers were paid $10,000 or more from federal funds and that an undetermined number of contract employees in fifteen privately-run Job Corps centers got over $10,000.

It is interesting to recall that when Sargent Shriver urged

Congress to start the War on Poverty, he declared, "It is also a prudent program. It is financially prudent . . . It is prudently planned in that every dollar allocated will be spent to help the poor. There will be no leakage. There is no contemplated huge new bureaucracy."

Despite the expense and OEO's frantic activities in giving money away, by May 1967 no one really was sure what it had accomplished, even though OEO had spent $31.4 million on research and evaluation of what it had done and had budgeted an additional $17.2 million for that purpose for fiscal year 1968.

Sar A. Levitan, who was making a study of OEO for the W. E. Upjohn Institute for Employment Research, noted that Mr. Shriver told the Senate Labor and Public Welfare Committee his program "affected the lives of 4 million impoverished Americans," but failed to particularize the ways in which it did so. Thus, said Dr. Levitan, " 'affected' could mean anything from giving a word of encouragement to providing a job or shelter."

Here's what Representative Glenn Andrews (R., Ala.) told Congress on September 28, 1966 about OEO's accomplishments: "Mr. Shriver a few weeks ago was asked how many people had been relieved from poverty by the program. His answer was about 50,000. This, gentlemen, is about the number of people employed by the government, directly or indirectly, under this great political fiesta."

Congress failed to follow up on how OEO was administering the complicated and broad legislation passed in such great haste. Senator Joseph S. Clark (D., Pa.), Chairman of the Employment and Manpower Subcommittee of the Senate Labor and Public Welfare Committee, told Congress, "We just did not have the staff or the equipment to go into the poverty program last year [1966]."[6]

While he was still Chairman of the House Education and Labor Committee, Representative Adam Clayton

Powell (D., N.Y.) obtained $200,000 for a thorough investigation of the poverty program. It was done very superficially and never made public officially.

By the spring of 1967, Senator Clark's subcommittee had started hearings on the poverty program in various locations, but so far had heard chiefly friendly witnesses who argued for enlargement of the War on Poverty.

19

OEO

and the Point

of No Return

As OEO's chamber of horrors increased almost daily, I was assured by Democrats as well as Republicans that Congress was becoming sufficiently aroused and would put a stop to the scandals. When I asked how it would do it, the answers were not convincing.

Acknowledging that laws regarding the hiring of leftists would be difficult to enforce, several Republicans said the answer might be to cut the funds for community action. Said one, "That will fix them; they can't operate without money."

It appeared unlikely, however, that Congress would soon terminate Head Start, and earlier chapters have demonstrated that this could be used to finance leftist groups. The same tactics could be employed in other OEO programs, and OEO had so many that it could shift emphasis from the notorious ones to the popular or unknown ones, or even think up new ones.

Even more important, community action had gone beyond the point of no return. The militant groups were organized, and the government could not un-organize them. Moreover, cutting off federal money entirely would not mean that they would be devoid of funds. National militant organizations already had begun to spring up as a direct result of the community action programs, and they had non-government financial support. Moreover, the militants organized by the War on Poverty became aligned with civil rights and church groups which were not dependent upon federal funds for survival.

The Citizens' Crusade Against Poverty was formed to forge a nation-wide network of the local anti-poverty groups put together under the community action programs, and to train them to agitate, demonstrate and otherwise participate in effective political action. The president was the United Auto Workers' Walter Reuther, and his union reportedly had contributed $1 million to the CCAP and promised more.[1]

After Mr. Reuther announced a "starter grant of $375,000" to the CCAP from the Ford Foundation on August 22, 1966, he said the CCAP would launch "an immediate start on a three-year $4 million program to train 1,000 leaders from the ranks of the poor." Assurances that the CCAP would be able to carry out the program, he added, had come from religious, civil rights, labor, academic, business, student and farm groups as well as foundations.

The Poverty Rights Action Center billed itself as the National Headquarters of the Welfare Rights Movement. It claimed the movement included 200 groups in more than 70 cities in 26 states and said that by mid-summer 1967 it hoped to have "a solid base of strong welfare recipient organizations in every major city in the country." Its aim was to bankrupt municipal and state welfare agencies so that the federal government would be forced to handle all welfare. Under such an arrangement, it was prepared to fight for a guaranteed income for everyone.

The center was headed by George A. Wiley, former Associate National Director of CORE, who said he had pulled out of the CCAP and formed his group because the CCAP wasn't moving fast enough for him. Unlike the latter, the center named only an impressive list of militant sponsors and did not make public its financial support. It had enough, however, to maintain headquarters in Washington and to conduct some sizeable demonstrations.

The close ties between anti-poverty groups and church and civil rights organizations have been shown in earlier chapters. As this was being written, a group of religious leaders announced an interfaith pact to seek funds from private secular foundations to pay for the creation and operation of militant organizations of the cities' poor.[2]

The Inter-Religious Foundation for Community Organization, representing ten national organizations with Catholic, Protestant and Jewish membership, said it would operate on an annual budget of $100,000.[3]

Father G. H. Woodard, an Episcopal Church representative to the group, said several foundations and wealthy individuals already had expressed interest in making contributions.[4]

Now for a closer look at the CCAP. Its Executive Director was Richard W. Boone, who, as noted in the first chapter, was in charge of the community action part of the Anti-Poverty Task Force which drew up battle plans for the War on Poverty. Subsequently, he became Director of Program Policy and Development for the community action program for OEO.

Serving on both the CCAP's Executive Committee and as Vice Chairman of its Commission on Public Information and Education was Bayard Rustin, Director of the A.

Philip Randolph Institute. Mr. Rustin rose to national prominence when he led the mammoth civil rights march on Washington in 1963. Here is what J. Edgar Hoover told Congress about his background: "Bayard Rustin was convicted for sodomy, a violation of the Selective Service Act and was an admitted member of the Young Communist League."[5]

Mr. Rustin has called the U.S. Senate "the most disgusting body in the Western world."[6] Though deploring violence, he told a Chicago audience during the hot summer of 1966, "Any Negro youngster who doesn't believe now that the way to get something is through violence obviously is not intelligent." Mr. Rustin said he favored guaranteed income, a complete overhaul of the whole welfare system and "training for which people are paid while they learn that which they need."[7]

Mr. Rustin also was a member of the CCAP's Interim Program Planning Group set up to map the aforementioned $4 million program to train 1,000 leaders from the poor. (His handling of the CCAP seminar on "maximum feasible participation" of the poor in community action was discussed in chapter nine.)

Stokely Carmichael also was a member of the Group. Martin Luther King, Jr. was a CCAP Vice Chairman and served on the Commission on Public Information and Education with Mr. Rustin. Michael Harrington, mentioned in the first chapter, was a member of the CCAP Executive Committee.

Also on the Executive Committee was Paul Potter as a representative of Students for a Democratic Society. J. Edgar Hoover told Congress that Communists were actively promoting and participating in the activities of the SDS and that "practically every subversive organization in the United States" was represented at the SDS national convention in 1965.[8]

As noted earlier, the CCAP came to national attention when it met in Washington in April 1966. In his opening address to the gathering of 550 persons, Mr. Reuther left no doubt of the organization's militancy. "We have now done the tooling for a crusade, and we are now on the march. . . . Our crusade has to create the climate to make bold action possible. People who are frustrated will cause riots, bitterness and bloodshed," he declared.

The meeting then broke up into smaller groups to listen to such speakers as Bayard Rustin and Michael Harrington. The next day the full assemblage convened to hear Sargent Shriver. He reminded his audience that the American Revolution began with the cry, "Taxation without representation is tyranny." Then he said that "Poverty programs without representation are tyranny."

Addressing an audience which had been harangued for a day and a half on how upset it should feel, he declared, "The discontent of the poor is explosive. The poor are dissatisfied—deeply dissatisfied. And in enacting the poverty program, this society said that the poor have a right to be dissatisfied in this rich nation of ours."

Then Mr. Shriver appeared genuinely surprised as his listeners began to boo when he suggested that they might not be able to get all they wanted as fast as they wanted it. Nevertheless, he doggedly continued his prepared speech advising the poor "to settle for less," even though he could not be heard above the boos and catcalls. As the screaming crowd began to converge upon him, many shaking their fists, Mr. Shriver blanched, said he would not take part in a riot, and beat a fast retreat through a side door.

Up to this point, people had been screaming into several microphones placed around the room and distorting the sound. Supposedly the meeting was completely out of control. By the time the TV camera crews arrived, however, a woman whom Bayard Rustin later admitted was a friend of his, persuaded the people to take turns at the mike in front of the TV cameras. (All the other mikes were turned off.)

The first one to do so was Unita Blackwell, a Community Organizer for the Child Development Group of Mississippi, discussed in chapter fifteen. I was attempting to interview her when a man who identified himself only as a professor from the University of California at Berkeley interrupted and said, "Don't just tell her; get in front of the TV cameras and tell everybody."

Miss Blackwell took his advice, and this is what she said: "We're tired of people pussyfooting and giving us the runaround all these hundred years. I'm not talking about what color they are; I'm talking about who's gonna do something. I'm tired of speeches. Don't tell us the guidelines and what is feasible and about the participation of the poor. Get up and do something about what you came here for. They're putting blacks and whites against each other so they don't fight the establishment."

She was followed at the mike by Lillian Craig of Cleveland who said, "In Cleveland, nothing has been done. Not one city in the United States with a program run by the poor has eliminated poverty. My kids are still going to a substandard school. Integration does not solve the problem. It's no longer gonna be race riots; it's gonna be integrated riots about you people out there who don't give a damn about us."

This prompted another woman from Cleveland to take the mike and say, "A poverty program is to help the poor. What are you doing keeping us this way? We're still poor!"

The next speaker wore a jacket with the words "Rebels with a Cause" emblazoned on it. The Rebels were an anti-poverty youth group supported by OEO. Said this Rebel, "We're not gonna wait. We're gonna get ours today."

A young girl from Harlem who was next at the mike

declared, "We need a voice. We're youth. When you're gone, we're gonna take over. It's gonna be a long hot summer. We're gonna have this voice or else. White men should be ashamed to have black men beg for something the white man has had for so long. The money for poverty is ours, not these bourgeois people who come running down here from agencies."

The speakers followed in rapid succession, without benefit of introductions, except those they sometimes provided themselves, telling where they were from—Watts, Selma, Harlem, Mississippi and Washington, D.C.

Said one, "We don't have to ask anybody for a damn thing when our brothers are in Vietnam. We're just gonna take it."

Said another, "We're tired of people speaking for us. We've got a voice, and we're gonna be heard. I was thrown out of school. There's nothing in school to interest anybody. They ain't learnin' nobody nothin'."

Then came the suggestion, "We should form a basic foundation to solve our problems because we all have the same problems. We've got to build a foundation based on these grievances." Subsequently the CCAP announced that it would open a grievance center in Washington, to be followed by others at different, as yet undetermined locations.

Next a young girl told her TV audience, "You old people ought to sit down or get out of the way and let the youth speak. You don't know what poverty is. You've probably never been to the Harlem ghetto because you're afraid."

Her successor at the mike said, "I'm not saying that riots are good, but that gets action, and if that's what it takes, that's what we'll do."

The next speaker asked, "How come Shriver couldn't stay to answer questions? He's no better than the other people who answered. He must have something to hide.

Why can't he face the people he's supposed to serve? Shriver wants to talk to a delegation in a corner. I don't want no damn corner."

This prompted OEO Assistant Director Hyman Bookbinder to take a turn at the mike, a move which undoubtedly required a good deal of courage. "Any appropriate technique for further dialogue and communication will be honored, and we are not going to run away from you," he declared.

Then Mr. Bookbinder flung out the challenge, "Now you goons who created this fiasco today—let's see you take the stand and see how much guts you have." Before stepping down, he added, "This demonstration is a help to Sargent Shriver. It will help him to get things done."

Next at the mike was Marjorie King, an anti-poverty worker from Syracuse, who made a plea for saving the CCAP "because it's all we've got at this point."

In the early part of Sargent Shriver's speech, before he was interrupted, he made a statement which might have been prophetic. This is what he said: "We have started a movement. No one can stop it; OEO can't. The Citizens' Crusade can't, and you can't, even if you wanted to."

A few days after the meeting, Mr. Shriver told the *Washington Post* that the mental processes of people like those who attended the CCAP meeting could best be summed up by the following syllogism which he had considered using in his speech: "A real War on Poverty requires a social revolution. Government cannot subsidize a social revolution. Therefore, the War on Poverty is a fraud."⁹

The story of how the CCAP successfully brought pressure on the government to obtain funds for a highly questionable Head Start program in Mississippi has been detailed in another chapter.

The Poverty Rights Action Center was a newer organization, and at this writing had not chalked up any such success. The December 1966 issue of *Trans-action*, however, pointed up the potential when it said, "If a movement of welfare recipients should, in fact, take form and gather strength, the ghetto and the slum will have yielded up a new political force. And it is conceivable that such a force could eventually be turned to the objective of procuring federal legislation for new programs of income re-distribution . . ."

The Center is the brain-child of Dr. Richard A. Cloward of the School of Social Work of Columbia University who also provided the inspiration for Mobilization for Youth, as noted in an earlier chapter. He said he believed the welfare system should be dismantled "brick by brick until there is nothing left but rubbish." He added that one of the principal afflictions of American society is the Calvinist concept that work is virtue and that without work there can be no virtue.[10] By spreading the idea of "Poverty Rights," he hoped to have every person who qualified for relief demand relief. He figured this would double the number of those on welfare and bankrupt the systems across the country. Then he wanted to replace the present welfare system with a guaranteed annual income.

Center Director George Wiley told me he thought this idea was so simple that it was brilliant. He said he wanted all welfare programs run by the federal government because Washington would be more liberal, and had more money. For one thing, it would get around the problem of the poor and conservative Southern states, he explained.

The Counsel for the Center was Carl Rachlin, who was also Counsel for the CORE Scholarship, Education Defense Fund, Inc. and former General Counsel for CORE. Mr. Rachlin also had served on Norman Thomas's 80th Birthday Committee, a vehicle to raise funds for Socialistic purposes.[11] In addition, he was a member of the American

Civil Liberties Union which had called for abolition of the House Un-American Activities Committee and the Internal Security Act.

Members of the Center's Board of Sponsors included Dr. Cloward; James Farmer, former Director of CORE; Val Coleman, Director of Public Relations for Mobilization for Youth; and Alan Gartner, Executive Director of the anti-poverty program in Suffolk County, New York and former Director of Public Information for CORE.

This is the Center's version of how the National Welfare Rights Movement began. "On June 30, 1966, [welfare] recipients in Pittsburgh began the day with a vigil in front of the State Welfare Department. As the sun rose, demonstrations spread from Boston to San Bernadino. By the end of the day, over 6,000 recipients had participated. It was the first such nation-wide demonstration of poor people in over 30 years. A new movement had been born."[12]

Along with two other organizations, the City-Wide Community Action Group of New York and Grass Rooters Interested in Poverty Education, the Center managed the so-called Poor People's March on Washington on September 27, 1966. While the Center had predicted that 5,000 people would take part, and only 500 did so, it still was an impressive spectacle as the demonstrators trooped through the rain to Capitol Hill that day to lobby for enlargement of the War on Poverty.

Mr. Wiley said that because the CCAP was a tax-exempt organization, it could not engage in the militant lobbying techniques that would mark the work of his Center.[13] Moreover, he explained that he made no attempt to obtain federal funds because he didn't want to be "fettered by political liabilities."[14]

Mr. Wiley did not hesitate, however, to take advantage of the work done by anti-poverty community organizers and to welcome anti-poverty groups into his organization.

For instance, the United Planning Organization, Washington, D.C.'s anti-poverty agency, organized the Washington Welfare Alliance and the Barry Farms Welfare Movement, both of which belonged to the Center.

In testimony before the Senate District Appropriations Subcommittee, Annie McLean, Chairman of the first group, declared, "We are living worse than criminals. Our [welfare] allotment is so small it is impossible to survive off of it."[15]

Etta Mae Horn, Chairman of the latter group, said before the same subcommittee, "Why is it that when you are on welfare, you are treated worse than a criminal?"[16]

Bettye McKenzie, community action coordinator for the anti-poverty agency in Suffolk County, New York, distributed pamphlets of the Poverty Rights Action Center during a demonstration of welfare recipients in the offices of the county's Welfare Department.[17] According to the *New York Times*, the Economic Opportunity Commission denied that Miss McKenzie "had urged mothers to take their children in rags to the welfare office and have them urinate in the halls."[18]

By May 1967, the Center was operating from its Washington headquarters with a budget of $5,000 a month and had managed to raise $50,000.

The following month, on June 3, a riot resulted from a sit-in of women welfare recipients at a district welfare building in the Roxbury section of Boston. According to the *New York Times* of June 4, 1967, the demonstration was planned by Mothers for Adequate Welfare (MAW). MAW is a member organization of the Poverty Rights Action Center.

Here, in part, is how the *Times* described the disturbance: "At least 25 stores were looted during the height of the violence, which Mayor Collins called 'the worst manifestation of disrespect for the rights of others that this city has ever seen.'

"The 1,700 policemen—many armed with submachine guns and bayonets—were mobilized to quell the jeering, cursing waves of rioters who flung stones, bottles and beer cans from rooftops and side streets.

"Among the 75 persons injured were 30 policemen, fire-fighters and newspapermen, who were treated at the city hospital."

At the end of that same month, on June 30, the Center celebrated the establishment of a permanent national organization of welfare recipients with coordinated demonstrations across the country. On July 1, 1967 the *New York Times* said the largest single demonstration occurred in New York City where more than a thousand pickets marched around City Hall. It added that the new organization could develop considerable political weight since there are more than eight million persons on welfare. Center Director Wiley participated in the New York City Hall demonstration.

In Washington hundreds of demonstrators staged a sit-in at the Welfare Department office at 500 First Street, N.W. and blocked the exit from the Department's underground parking lot. Among other things, they demanded bargaining recognition for the welfare alliance, according to the *Washington Star* of July 1, 1967.

Washington also saw a significant straw in the wind in May 1967 when the United Givers Fund announced that it was giving money to two anti-poverty agencies of the UPO. Southwest Community House got $23,267, and Southeast Neighborhood House, $65,000. As noted earlier, the latter had been implicated in an attack upon a police station, and Ralph Fertig, Director of the House, had supported the D.C. school boycott. In addition, the UGF gave $57,954 to the Washington Urban League which operated a community action center for the UPO.[19]

While it is too early, as this is being written, to determine the accomplishments of the various anti-poverty groups, it is apparent that Michael Harrington already has realized his dream of giving a political voice to the poor, a voice which Congress would not be likely soon to mute. OEO has reached the point of no return.

20

Special Projects
in the
War on Poverty

Vast as its operations are, OEO makes up only part of the total War on Poverty package. It has billed itself as the catalyst and coordinator for federal aid to the poor which President Johnson put at $22 billion for 1967 and budgeted at $25.6 billion for 1968.

Here is the breakdown the President gave for that $22 billion: education and training, $3.1 billion; health, $3.6 billion; cash benefit payments, $12.8 billion; and "services, economic and community development and other," $3.1 billion. Tucked in there were OEO expenditures of $1.6 billion for 1967. Out of that $25.6 billion request for 1968, $1.9 billion was for OEO.

Instead of coordinating the War on Poverty, however, OEO appeared to be merely another layer on an unwieldy bureaucracy. *The Wall Street Journal* counted "upward of 70 agencies operating several hundred programs to uplift people, communities or regions." The *Washington Post* found 300 federal programs dealing with education, poverty, physical environment and community development, with responsibility for administration scattered through 150 major bureaus and offices in Washington and 400 regional and subregional offices in the field.

Here is the picture *The Wall Street Journal* painted as an example of the confusion and lack of coordination: "Nowadays a school drop-out can get help from the Juvenile Delinquency and Youth Offenses Control Act, the Manpower Development and Training Act, the Vocational Education Act, the Job Corps, the Neighborhood Youth Corps, a variety of welfare programs . . . community action grants, and from the new billion-dollar school aid law. Fifteen programs authorize aid for acquiring teaching equipment, nine provide teacher training, and four . . . include funds to promote basic adult literacy. Needy students can reach for loans or scholarships offered by eight, including President Johnson's higher education bill."

Some educators told me, however, that they feared OEO would manage to coordinate tightly enough with the Office of Education to use Title I of the Elementary and Secondary School Assistance Act of 1965 to bolster the aim of further federal control of public schools. Their fears seemed to be justified by the federal budget for 1968 which declared, "Special efforts will be made in 1968 to develop close ties between the programs supported under Title I and the Head Start and other community action programs of the Office of Economic Opportunity."

Under Title I, Congress provided a billion dollars a year to the Office of Education to help impoverished pupils. The money was distributed to local school districts on the basis of their number of students from low-income families. The money could be spent for an almost limitless list of purposes including health tests, school breakfasts, cultural trips, clothing, family counseling, psychiatric help and classroom instruction.

Senator Edward W. Brooke (R., Mass.) said Title I established a highly inequitable system because grants were based solely on the number of poor children in a district without reference to the nature of the district or the calibre of its school system. Here's how he explained the results: "Grants are being awarded to wealthy communities with excellent school systems in which a few poor children who attend the public schools are already receiving quality education. Such communities use poverty program funds to make outstanding school systems even more outstanding. On the other hand, some other communities are so badly off that federal education funds must be used to provide food for hungry children."

Garth L. Mangum and the aforementioned Dr. Levitan surveyed federal manpower programs for the Institute of Industrial Relations of the University of Michigan and Wayne State University and reported that the personnel director of a large retail firm complained that representatives from 70 different federally funded programs visited his office regularly seeking jobs for their disadvantaged clients. The researchers also found that operators of federally financed job training programs bid against each other to persuade employers to establish programs and even offered training subsidies to employers who already were conducting training programs at their own expense.

Some of the other significant parts of the War on Poverty conducted outside OEO are so huge and complicated that only a cursory glance is possible within the confines of a single volume. The Appalachian Regional Development Act of 1965 authorized a billion-dollar program. The money was to be spent over a six-year period in a dozen states, and $840 million was earmarked for roads. Commented the U.S. Chamber of Commerce, "There is a real question as to whether these expenditures will in fact reduce poverty. . . . It is conceivable that if the present plans are carried out, five years from now we will have seen the injection of vast amounts of concrete into the areas, but little reduction in poverty."

Very popular in Appalachia was the Work Experience Program administered by the Department of Health, Education and Welfare. Writing in the *Washington Star*, Haynes Johnson found it was known as the "Happy Pappy" program in twelve counties of Kentucky which received $1 million a month under it. "As unemployed fathers, they get up to $250 a month, tax exempt, which makes them very happy pappies indeed," he reported. In addition, they could stretch the money by purchasing food under the U.S. food stamp program. They also received free education and medical care.

Mr. Johnson reported, "Some of the projects provide an introduction to job training, but most of the work is done on the roads and hills. Men work in teams of ten supervised by a 'Happy Pappy' like themselves who has been appointed foreman by the magistrate of the district. The foreman turns in the work time sheets.

"There is no effective way to check on his figures. Consequently, there are reports of men sitting home in the hollows when they choose, and continuing to draw full pay . . .

"Many criticisms can be leveled at such a program. Inevitably, it lessens incentive and glorifies the welfare dole system. One measure of that effect can be seen in recent reports that a labor shortage now exists in some areas of Eastern Kentucky, particularly in the coal mines."

To be eligible for the program, a man had to be unemployed for 90 days, have one or more children, be willing and able to work and not be eligible for unemployment compensation. He could own an auto and farm or homestead, but he couldn't have over $1,000 in the bank.

At the time Congress put the program into law, the Council of State Chambers of Commerce said it "adds nothing but additional funds and an additional supervisory layer to three programs that already exist. They are the work-training programs under the 1962 Social Security amendments, and the Manpower Development and Training Act and the Vocational Education Act. . . ."

The Department of Housing and Urban Development (HUD) also contributed substantially to the cost of the War on Poverty. The 1965 Act creating the new department authorized upwards of $8 billion for urban renewal, public housing (including a highly controversial program of rent supplements) and subsidized private housing. In 1966 Congress gave HUD close to another $1 billion.

Not counted in the budget was $2.2 billion the President allocated from his Special Assistance Fund to HUD's Federal National Mortgage Association to buy 3% mortgages on housing built for persons of moderate income (too rich to qualify for public housing but too poor to afford private housing available).

By 1967, however, the legislature was beginning to have second thoughts about rent supplements. It voted $10 million for that program in response to an Administration request for $40 million. The National Association of Real Estate Boards may have explained one of the reasons for Congressional displeasure. The Association pointed out that rent supplements were not for persons who qualified for public housing or welfare, but for those with annual incomes of between $4,000 and $10,000, depending upon family size, who lived in substandard housing.

NAREB said, "There are 18.8 million families whose incomes are in the $4,000-$8,000 range. Of these, only 8.4% or 1.5 million families live in substandard housing. Thus, 17.3 million families, who through the exercise of their own effort and a degree of frugality pay for their own shelter, will pay the taxes for the few of whom may be living in substandard housing because of personal preference as to the allocation of income."

Also waging the War on Poverty was the Economic

Development Administration, successor to the discredited Area Redevelopment Administration. Like ARA, it gave grants and loans to businesses to persuade them to locate in economically depressed areas, and, as with ARA, this sometimes meant subsidizing unfair competition with companies already in the depressed areas. For instance, EDA put up $975,000 toward a $1.5 million clay pipe plant at Seminole, Oklahoma. A special subcommittee of the House Public Works Committee had this to say: "The existing plants [in the area] have indicated that statistics will show that existing facilities serving the area have more than sufficient capacity of products available to serve the needs of the area and that the Administration did not properly investigate the markets before granting the loan."

Under its poverty loan program, the Small Business Administration focused a disproportionate part of its aid on racially troubled areas for reasons unrelated to economics or even poverty. The consequences of paying insufficient attention to the economic soundness of the loans were that SBA's "help" put some borrowers further into poverty.

A case in point was one in which President Johnson took a personal interest. Lawrence Young, a Chicago cab driver, wrote to the Chief Executive and asked his help in getting started in the fried chicken business. The result was that Mr. Young obtained an SBA poverty loan for $19,500. However, the business failed, SBA seized the restaurant equipment and furniture, and Mr. Young was $6,000 in debt, in addition to the $18,000 he still owed SBA.

21

Reaction to the War on Poverty

Many members of Congress were not surprised when they saw the War on Poverty lose battle after battle. They had known it was a fraud from the beginning and voted for it only because politicians who want to stay in office don't usually oppose doling out federal funds to their constituents.

But Congress got more than it bargained for when the War on Poverty first organized a revolutionary lower class in a heretofore stable society and then created a highly volatile situation by raising the expectations of these people and frustrating them.

Since Negroes made up a large part of this class, civil rights groups far to the left of the NAACP were able to use the anti-poverty program in their attempt to change the entire direction of the civil rights movement, employing tactics described in earlier chapters. Unlike the NAACP, they were not interested in racial integration and equal opportunity for all. They wanted new power for Negroes, and did not hesitate to urge violence to acquire it.

After seeing one race riot after another, the Administration never once publicly connected them with the War on Poverty. Indeed, as leftist civil rights leaders threatened more violence and a long hot summer in 1967, government officials, led by Vice President Humphrey, said the answer was an intensification of the War on Poverty. They really were calling for more fuel for the fire. They didn't bother to note that the War on Poverty wasn't ending poverty and that, even if it was, there was no assurance that it would decrease crime and violence, since both were at only a fraction of present rates during the Great Depression.

The Republicans, supposedly the last remaining champions of private enterprise, failed to attack the basic fallacy of the premise that it was up to the government to end poverty with monumental federal programs. Few suggested that the answer was for the government to promote a healthy economy in which private enterprise could continue to lift people out of poverty in the way which made America the most affluent country in the world. Rarely did they insist that society should care only for those unable to help themselves. Congress accepted the idea that in an affluent society everyone has a right to a decent standard of living, regardless of his lack of industriousness.

Instead of challenging this, the Republicans pushed their own version of the War on Poverty. Their Opportunity Crusade, they said, would do essentially the same thing, only better.

In attacking the War on Poverty, Republicans confined themselves essentially to citing cases of maladministration. Most of them deliberately avoided mentioning how the War had been used to aid leftists. Such exposure, they believed, would reflect on the entire program and probably kill it, and this they did not want to do.

One Republican on Capitol Hill even told me: "Attacking Communists is old hat; that went out with McCarthyism. Politicians have been afraid to attack Communism ever since the demise of Senator McCarthy. Besides, how can you do it? The Communist Party has become very sophisticated and doesn't even issue membership cards now. Members don't even have to take leading roles in community action because others do it for them—pave the way, so to speak.

"Even if you get anything on Communist involvement in the War on Poverty, what have you got? There are no votes in anti-Communism. Besides, the line of both the Administration and businessmen is to do business with the Soviet bloc. Also, if we topple the War on Poverty by condemning Communist or leftist influence, we'll lose the Negro vote because Negroes are playing such a great role in the program."

What he neglected to mention, however, was that not all businessmen were interested in doing business with Communists. Furthermore, it was not logical to conclude that those who favored it were willing to use their tax dollars to finance the subversion of the way of life under which they had prospered in the United States.

This defeatist attitude also very likely underestimated the intelligence of Negroes and poor people. It did not follow that they would believe the War on Poverty was helping them just because the government's high-powered and expensive propaganda said so.

Back in the fall of 1966, *The Wall Street Journal* commented, "The so-called War on Poverty has spent lavishly and accomplished little . . . If such spending were reduced, therefore, it does not automatically entail injury for the poor, since they are getting scant help as it is."

One leading Republican privately predicted soon thereafter that the American public was sane enough not to let a thing like the War on Poverty go on indefinitely. "Sooner or later," he said, "there's going to be such a backlash as this country has never seen or even envisioned." Another Republican said he hoped it would not take a disaster of the dimensions of Pearl Harbor to wake up the public to what was happening.

In the spring of 1967, the Knoxville *News Sentinel* sagely commented, "Any man who thinks he is going to be happy and prosperous by letting the government take care of him should take a close look at the American Indian."

The warning of the New York State Senate Committee on Affairs of the City of New York continued to be just as pertinent as when it was issued at the beginning of the War on Poverty. Here it is:

"The mere fact that a program is designated as 'anti-poverty' and is described in 'new professional jargon' is no assurance that it will be beneficial to the people it is alleged to be helping.

"Information on how new projects are expected to work, criteria by which their effectiveness is to be judged, and yardsticks for measuring the worth of the projects and their operating results have to be developed.

"Otherwise, the anti-poverty program may find itself in the same position as the Emperor in the fairy tale of *The Emperor's New Clothes:*

> *His treasury empty,*
> *Naked before his citizens, and*
> *Exposed as a fool."*

On December 15, 1967, moments before it adjourned, Congress appropriated $1.773 billion for OEO to continue the War on Poverty in fiscal year 1968. This compared with an appropriation of $1.687 billion the previous year and an Administration request for $2.06 billion for 1968.

The Senate voted for the appropriation 69 to 3. In the more conservative House, members did not stand up to be counted and passed the measure with a voice vote.

Epilogue

During the third fateful week of July 1967, wide-scale riots exploded in cities throughout the country with accompanying death and destruction.

Newark came first—725 injured, at least 25 dead and property damage over $10 million. Before the five days and nights of shooting, looting and burning in Newark ended, Detroit burst into flames—324 injured, at least 43 dead and property damage put at $500 million.

After that, violence in the cities erupted with such frequency that some newspapers took to running a daily tally, citing the riot areas and the facts available. The list of 26 cities included Cambridge, Maryland; Chicago, Illinois; Toledo, Ohio; Milwaukee, Wisconsin; Riviera Beach, Florida; Providence, Rhode Island; Portland, Oregon; Elgin, Illinois and Newburgh, New York.

Initially, at least, Washington played politics in responding to a shocked nation which was demanding some answers. President Johnson emphasized that he sent federal troops to Detroit only because of the total inability of Michigan Governor George Romney to cope with the situation; and Governor Romney berated the President for delaying 24 hours in meeting his desperate plea for troops.

While several Congressional committees vied with each other to start investigations, President Johnson started his own, and his majority leader said this made it unnecessary for Congress to do anything. Sargent Shriver started to go to Newark to look into the trouble but at the last moment retreated to the Kennedy compound in Hyannis Port, Massachusetts. Vice President Humphrey put the blame on Congress for not enacting enough anti-poverty measures. For anyone who would look, however, evidence abounded that the War on Poverty's community action programs were deeply involved in the riots.

During that first week while the cities burned, SNCC's Stokely Carmichael visited Communists in Havana, openly called for revolution and praised Cuban Communism,[1] thus giving new significance to the participation of SNCC members in community action programs. H. Rap Brown, Mr. Carmichael's successor as national chairman of SNCC, was arrested for inciting the riot in Cambridge.

Almost unbelievably, during that same week, the District of Columbia's top anti-poverty agency hired a former national chairman of SNCC as a $50-a-day consultant. He was Marion Barry, and his new employer was the United Planning Organization discussed in chapter eleven. Less than a week after UPO hired him, he said, "Riot power or rebellion power might make people listen now."[2]

In 1961 Mr. Barry became national chairman of SNCC, according to the *Daily Worker* of July 1, 1962. According to page H15180 of the *Congressional Record* of November 4, 1967, Representative Joel T. Broyhill (R., Va.) told the House that Mr. Barry took over direction of the SNCC office in Washington in June, 1965, and two months later was arrested for disorderly conduct while leading demonstrators onto the Capitol grounds.

The Capitol demonstration was part of a so-called Washington Summer Action Project from August 6 through

August 9, 1965 in which Mr. Barry took an active part. FBI Director Hoover told Congress the Project was sponsored by Students for a Democratic Society, an organization in which Communists were taking an active part; the W.E.B. DuBois Clubs, a youth project of the Communist Party; SNCC and the Committee for Nonviolent Action.[3]

Mr. Hoover described the Project as follows: "This demonstration included picketing of the White House and a sit-in at the White House gate entrance, and workshops on Vietnam, the draft, Puerto Rico and South Africa. On August 9, the demonstrators marched to the Capitol grounds for the purpose of staging a 'Congress of Unrepresented People' to declare peace in Vietnam. The sponsors of the demonstration had previously announced their intention of actually occupying Congressional seats; however, they were stopped at the boundary of the Capitol grounds. As with other demonstrations, the Communist Party and other subversive organizations supported and participated in the Washington Summer Action Project. Among the Communist Party members noted were James Jackson, a member of the party's national committee, and Michael Zagarell, the national youth leader of the party. Demonstrations were held throughout the United States during this period in support of the Washington Summer Action Project."[4]

In addition, Mr. Barry took an active part in boycotts of D.C. merchants and Capital Transit buses, both in January 1966. (Indeed, as noted in chapter 11, he told a UPO meeting he wanted to run Capital Transit out of business.)

The SNCC member's job with UPO was to draw "alienated youths" into the anti-poverty program, according to Ted Parrish of the agency.

Representative Joel T. Broyhill (R., Va.) said Rufus Mayfield was Mr. Barry's "back-up man"[5] and the *Wash-*

ington Post explained that Mr. Mayfield helped Mr. Barry draw up a proposal for organizing the city's youths—a plan which prompted UPO to hire Mr. Barry.[6]

According to page H5350 of the *Congressional Record* of May 11, 1967, Representative Joel T. Broyhill (R., Va.) told the House that Rufus Mayfield had been running afoul of the law since the age of 12 and had spent much time in reform schools. Representative Broyhill said that Mr. Mayfield spent "27 months at the Lorton Youth Center for auto theft, where, as a source of constant trouble, he spent much time in the special treatment unit." The Congressman added, "Since his parole in January of last year [1966] he has been booked twice for disorderly conduct—the latest occasion a month ago today."[7]

To top it all, both D.C. and federal government officials kept urging Congress to pour more and more money into UPO to keep Washington cool that hot summer of 1967 and avert the riots predicted by the Rev. Martin Luther King and other civil rights leaders.

Just preceding that hot summer—in May 1967—Hal Witt became Acting Director of UPO. The following October he was named to the permanent UPO post of Deputy Director at $21,000 a year.

Here is what Virginia's Representative Broyhill said about Hal Witt, and other UPO employees, according to page H15180 of the *Congressional Record* of November 14, 1967:

> Mr. Witt is the son of Nathan Witt, a member of the Communist Party, USA. He is on the Executive Board of SANE, a regular sponsor of anti-war demonstrations . . . He is on the Washington Area Committee to abolish the House Un-American Activities Committee . . . His police record reveals that when charged with disorderly conduct in 1960 he chose as his attorney Joseph Forer, the leading attorney for the Communist Party, described by a mem-

ber of the National Committee of the Communist Party, USA, as one of the most important Communists in D.C. According to information from FBI files, Mr. Witt has close and frequent association with many known Communist Party members as well as financial backers of the Communist Party.

"I do not say Mr. Witt is a Communist, Mr. Chairman. I do not know. I do know that a very real question as to his loyalty should prohibit his employment by a public agency."

Later that day, according to the *Washington Post* of November 15, 1967, Mr. Witt admitted being the son of Nathan Witt. He also admitted he had been on the board of SANE but said he no longer is. Mr. Forer called Representative Broyhill a liar for calling him (Forer) a Communist.

In his same address in the Congressional Record, Representative Broyhill declared the following:

"We all know the antics of Hubert Geroid Brown, known as Rap Brown. He was a UPO employee from March 1965 until June 1966 when he resigned to take the SNCC chairmanship from Stokely Carmichael.

" . . . Gaston Thomas Neil, a UPO worker in the Cardoza area, runs the New School of Afro Thought. He has spent time in St. Elizabeth's Hospital [for the mentally ill] after being found not guilty by reason of insanity on a number of narcotics charges. He now has other charges pending against him not yet resolved. Meanwhile he and a companion bought two Russian-type carbines in Alexandria in August, for what purpose we can only guess."

Riots began in Washington in the early morning hours of August 1, 1967. Gangs roamed the streets in the middle of the city, shouted black power slogans, burned, looted and threw rocks and bottles. The *Washington Star* reported that cries of black power "could be heard ringing from the cellblock of the 13th [police] precinct, where most of the [33] arrested persons were taken."[8]

Julian Dugas, Director of the Neighborhood Legal Service, funded by OEO through UPO, immediately tried to obtain the release of those arrested. According to the *Washington Star* of August 2, 1967, he was on the scene of the riots, complained about the presence of too many policemen and declared, "I saw police display a very callous use of weapons, waving shotguns and poking them in kids' stomachs."

The riot was preceded by a meeting called by Sterling Tucker of the Washington Urban League to discuss setting up an interracial commission to study racial problems in Washington. The *Washington Star* said the spokesman for SNCC at the meeting was a man it identified only as Kimani. The newspaper reported he said, "The thing you are not addressing yourself to . . . the real issue is that we [the blacks and the whites] are involved in a war. Black people consider it a war of liberation. Until you deal with that, you can sit here all night and nothing will happen."[9]

The day after the outbreak of violence in Washington, Rufus Mayfield, Mr. Barry's "back-up man," popped up and publicly declared he admired H. Rap Brown 100 percent.[10] The same day the D.C. commissioners met with Mr. Mayfield and a group of D.C. youths. (According to the *Washington Post* of August 2, 1967, some of them were members of SNCC.) As leader and spokesman for the youngsters, Mr. Mayfield presented a two-page list of grievances to the commissioners, which included inadequate recreation facilities, lack of vocational training in city high schools and scarcity of job opportunities for youths.

Later the youths shouted threats at the commissioners. On August 2, the *Washington Star* reported as follows:

"We feel that if the youths arrested . . . are not released, Washington is going to have some justice tonight.

"You have no power. You ought to know what black power is.

"You should have done something by three o'clock, and it's six now."

By the next day the federal government did something. With War on Poverty funds from the Labor Department, it set up a $300,000 corporation, Pride, Inc., to pay youths $56 a week to participate in neighborhood cleanup and rat control projects. The pay was $80 a week for 121 team captains and $100 for 21 supervisors.

Members of the Neighborhood Youth Corps (discussed in chapter 17) and the Youth Committee for Equal Justice elected Rufus Mayfield chairman of the board. The Committee was organized by Mr. Mayfield and Marion Barry. The *Washington Star* reported on August 3, "Mayfield will be salaried, but his pay rate was not immediately known." It added, "Working in conjunction with Pride, Inc., will be the Washington Urban League, United Planning Organization and other agencies. These groups will name some staff members to work under the board."

On the same date, the newspaper also reported that the D.C. commissioners "wrote the Rev. Everett A. Hewlett, President of the [D.C.] Board of Education, asking the board to meet with Rufus Mayfield, 20, a youth leader who has criticized the quality of education and the attitudes of teachers and administrators." It revealed further that "Commissioner Walter N. Tobriner wrote the school board that he was quite impressed with the sincerity of the Mayfield group, the cogency of its arguments and the constructive character of the ideas proposed for improvement in the school system."

Washington was not the only spot where the federal government organized and financed the militants during the riotous summer. Elsewhere it repeated the sorry spectacle, with gorier results.

On May 25, well in advance of Newark's disaster, the city's police director wired Sargent Shriver that Newark faced riots and anarchy because of agitation by federal anti-poverty workers and urged him to take immediate action. According to Representative James C. Gardner (R., N.C.), "After a three-week delay, Mr. Shriver gave his usual inept reply and strongly denied that any such activity was occurring and attempted to whitewash the whole matter."[11]

OEO had poured $7 million into the United Community Corporation (UCC), its community action agency in Newark. Representative Gardner told the House that one of UCC's community organizers had stated that for four months it was deeply involved in demonstrations which directly led to the riots.[12] On July 13, 1967, the organizer said, the agency sponsored a rally and picketing at the 4th Precinct of the Newark Police Department to protest the arrest of a Negro cab driver the previous night. The organizer explained, "A rumor was started at the rally that the taxi driver was dead. A spontaneous reaction followed which resulted in the Newark riots. . ."[13]

Here is a report on the harangue at the rally by an anti-poverty worker, according to an affidavit by Detective Junius Hedgepeth, in the possession of Representative Gardner: "He told them that the black man was in a position to seize power in Newark. The crowd responded with yells, 'We came here to fight.' Whereupon, someone in the crowd threw a bottle that hit the wall of the precinct station, and almost instantly was followed by other bottles. Then a barrage of rocks and bottles were thrown through the station doors and windows. The windows of all the police cars outside were smashed."[14]

Representative Gardner revealed that a few days before the rioting an anti-poverty worker on the OEO payroll told the Newark City Council, "There is going to be blood running in the streets of Newark like there has never been anywhere else in America." After the riots, he still remained on the payroll, according to the Congressman.[15]

Belatedly, OEO asked UCC to suspend Willie Wright as a trustee pending investigation of a report that he told a rally of Newark Negroes to buy guns and keep them until the rioting started again. OEO also asked UCC to disavow any sympathy with statements that precipitate violence. UCC turned down both requests, and its president, Timothy Still, said he agreed with Mr. Wright that Negroes should arm themselves to defend their homes from police.[16]

On August 1 the Associated Press reported that, in addition to holding his UCC post, Willie Wright also was the leader of a band of Negro volunteers who were prowling Newark at night looking for evidence of police brutality. According to the Associated Press, Mr. Wright had warned that unless conditions change in a very few weeks, he planned to test the law in all kinds of ways as far as arms are concerned.

On August 7 Leonard Kowalewski, a Newark jailer and president of a fraternal order of policemen, told the Senate Judiciary Committee that anti-poverty workers paid by OEO helped bring about the Newark riots. He testified that for the last five years CORE had made "vicious, insidious" attacks on the Newark Police Department, calling it a Gestapo that was both brutal and sadistic.[17] Robert Curvin was one of the CORE leaders who took part in these attacks, and he also was a director of the UCC, according to Mr. Kowalewski.[18]

Chapter ten described how LeRoi Jones's Black Arts Theater obtained $115,000 in anti-poverty funds. On July 14, Mr. Jones was arrested in a riot-torn area of Newark and charged with carrying two loaded .32 calibre pistols. But within four days he was released on $25,000 bail and attended a black power conference in Newark on July 23. Afterwards he told a press conference, "We will govern ourselves in Newark or no one will govern."[19]

The head of the Legal Services Project (LSP) in Newark (an organization funded by OEO) also joined the outcry. LSP Administrator Oliver Lofton blamed the riots on "lousy homes, lousier jobs and the lousiest schools" and on "racist, brutal white cops and a mayor who refused to work with poor, helpless, frustrated people." He added that the riots would be "a solidifying factor for the Negro community."[20]

At the taxpayers' expense, Mr. Lofton served as the attorney for John W. Smith, the cab driver whose arrest touched off the riots. OEO money also defended those arrested in connection with the riots. Said the *Washington Star* on July 16, "Lofton's staff of 14 is handling the cases of hundreds of adults and teenagers jailed in the burning, shooting and looting."

A few days later LSP Attorney Harrison David endorsed the feasibility of a CORE move to gather signatures for a petition to oust Newark Mayor Hugh J. Addonizio. Earlier the mayor had charged that organizers of Students for a Democratic Society inflamed conditions by printing leaflets calling for organized protest.[21]

At the black power conference in Newark shortly after the riots, the role of CORE in the War on Poverty took on new significance when CORE enthusiastically endorsed a resolution supporting "the right of black people to revolt when they deem it necessary and in their interests."[22]

After the conference, CORE Director Floyd B. McKissick told the press that people have a constitutional right to revolt or use violence if they are victims of intolerable conditions.[23] A few days later the AP quoted him as saying that the civil rights movement was passé and that the riots were the beginning of a black revolution. AP further reported the following: "McKissick said in a news conference yesterday that not only the demands of integrationists should be met, but those of black separatists who want to establish communities in Africa and demand financial reparations from the federal government for past wrongs to Negroes. He also demanded that the ownership of all ghetto businesses be turned over to Negroes and that they be given charge of all public facilities in black communities."[24]

A man who led demonstrators, composed in part of antipoverty workers, within the halls of Congress on August 7, 1967 apparently shared some of these views.[25] He was Jesse Gray (mentioned in chapter nine), founder of the Organization for Black Power, according to the *Washington Star*.[26]

FBI Director Hoover told Congress that literature of the Organization states that membership "shall be of organizations and individuals who accept the perspective of black power and the discipline of the Organization in the struggle for this power." Mr. Hoover declared, "The Organization states it 'is part of the revolutionary struggle of people all over the world to liberate themselves from the determination of the United States to impose its way of life on the whole world and to build a new world free from exploitation.' "[27]

This is what Representative Watkins M. Abbitt (D., Va.) said about Mr. Gray in a speech in the House: "Jesse Gray is a dedicated Communist who has been active in subversive, anti-American work for a long time. Back in the mid-1950's, Jesse Gray was working actively under the direction of the notorious Communist, Benjamin Davis. Under Davis' orders, he directed efforts to start Communist youth organizations in Harlem among Negroes and also among Puerto Ricans . . . When young Albert Gaillard testified before the House Un-American Activities Committee in 1960, he identified Jesse Gray as one who, along with known Communist Hunter Pitts O'Dell, directed his activities in organizing Harlem youths for Communism."[28]

According to the *New York Times* of August 8, 1967,

some of the participants in the Gray-led demonstration represented Harlem Backstreet Youth, an organization which had a federal anti-poverty grant of $10,633.

The demonstrators forced their way into the gallery of the House of Representatives to fight for a bill to provide federal funds for rat control—and fight they did. They battled with Capitol police, and one of the latter was admitted to a hospital after coughing up blood. The *Washington Post* reported "Rep. Roman C. Pucinski [D., Ill.] said he saw a razor pulled on a police officer during the melée in the Capitol corridors."[29]

When the demonstrators first forced their way into the House, they chanted, "Rats cause riots." What they didn't mention was that riot-wracked Detroit had a $1.8 million rat extermination project which had been heralded as a model for the rest of the nation.[30]

New York's federally financed anti-poverty warriors were busy elsewhere too. On July 27, 1967, three of them were arrested for looting stores on Fifth Avenue. A fourth youth arrested with them recently had been on a federal anti-poverty payroll. Of the three then in the pay of Uncle Sam, two worked for the Neighborhood Youth Corps and one for Harlem Youth Unlimited, a junior division of Haryou-ACT.[31]

Farther north, in Rochester, City Manager Seymour Scher charged that leaders of the federally funded anti-poverty agency there were making statements designed to inflame rather than to calm racial disorders which broke out July 23, 1967. After bottles, rocks and fire bombs had been thrown, city police set up check points in the trouble areas. The agency, Action for a Better Community, called for the suspension of and murder charges against whatever policeman it was who had fatally shot a Negro when he ran a car through a police check point, the *New York Times* reported on July 27, 1967.

I asked County Executive Edwin G. Michaelien about reports that federally paid community action workers had arranged a demonstration in White Plains, New York of welfare recipients from Yonkers in March 1967. Here, in part, is his reply:

"While indications are that the funds for hiring the buses were not anti-poverty funds, personnel of the Community Action Center, who are paid by federal moneys, in whole or in part, organized the demonstration, accompanied the demonstrators and, presumably were paid their wages and salaries, they having assumed that this was part of their duties. There is no evidence whatsoever to indicate that this had been done on their own time."

The problem of OEO-financed trouble was not confined to the North, however. In hearings during the first week of August, the Senate Judiciary Committee revealed that a few weeks earlier a federally funded anti-poverty agency in Nashville, Tennessee had signed a contract to support a "liberation school" run by Fred H. Brooks, the head of the Nashville chapter of SNCC who also was identified as a leader of an April 1967 riot in that city.[32]

Captain John Sorace and Lieutenant Robert Hill of the Nashville police force testified that the school taught hate of the white race and that some of the teachers were members of SNCC.[33] When they raided the local SNCC headquarters, the two men said they found the fingerprints of a former teacher at the school on a Molotov cocktail.[34]

The following day the Associated Press quoted Mr. Brooks as saying, "I think Sorace is a racist. He should be killed."[35]

The Rev. J. Paschall Davis, Chairman of Nashville's Metropolitan Action Commission (MAC), told the Committee the Commission had signed a contract giving $7,700 for seven summer projects, one of which was the liberation school for 10- to 13-year-olds. OEO contributed $5,000 of the full amount, knowing that part of it would go to the liberation school.[36]

The Rev. Davis testified on August 4 that MAC had disbursed no money under the contract and that if the school was teaching hate, it would violate an anti-discrimination provision of the contract and make it void.[37]

Four days later, however, the Rev. Davis wired Senate Judiciary Chairman James O. Eastland (D., Miss.) that his testimony was "not exactly correct."[38] MAC, he admitted, had contracted to pay up to $20 a week each toward the rent of four women employed by the school "and one is a member of SNCC." He added that the first of the payments was made July 27 and that they were to continue for six weeks. He also said that Mr. Brooks had used a station wagon rented with anti-poverty funds.[39]

And in Durham, North Carolina automobiles leased with OEO money were used to transport people to a July 12 meeting which ended in a rock-throwing melée. OEO announced, "The misuse of these automobiles is an extremely isolated, if not an unprecedented incident." It added, "No persons paid with federal funds can be permitted to engage in partisan political activities or in any form of direct social action which could lead to violence."[40]

Nevertheless, OEO supported the North Carolina Fund. After Robert R. Monte resigned as director of the War on Poverty for the Craven County area of North Carolina, he wrote Representative David N. Henderson (D., N.C.) in part, as follows:

> I found that I could no longer stomach the verbal directives from Washington, the Office of Economic Opportunity or the rantings of the people of the North Carolina Fund.
> I believe that the programs cannot succeed when they are headed by people in OEO who have on numerous occasions stated that what we needed in our area were a

few good demonstrations and when the North Carolina Fund openly attacks our elected representatives to the Congress and the Senate plus actively supporting the civil rights groups in a so-called "drive for a change in local power structure" which is, in essence, a shield for the so-called "black power" struggle. It appears to me that they have forgotten what the programs were originally designed for, that being to help people help themselves out of poverty.[41]

In addition, Mr. Monte told the governor of North Carolina, "The management of the North Carolina Fund has endorsed and supported a doctrine of racism or racial polarization which could fall within the popularized category of 'black power.' "[42]

According to the *Northampton County Times-News* (Rich Square, North Carolina) the Fund financed a North Carolina "grass roots" organization known as the Peoples' Program on Poverty (PPP). The newspaper reported that Willie Riddick, director of Craven Operation Progress in New Bern, addressed a meeting of 500 members of the PPP in Woodland on July 29, 1967. "Riddick, after condemning the white 'power structure,' said he is 'surprised fire bombs haven't been thrown in eastern North Carolina,' " the *Times-News* said.[43]

Another speaker was Jim McDonald, associate director of New Careers Training Laboratory of New York who, according to the *Times-News*, said the following:

> White power is a Congressman voting against funds for controlling rats which attack Negro children and voting for more money so white policemen can shoot black people.
> White power is that which keeps us on dusty roads, and keeps us in the kitchen where we cook for white people, yet can't cook for our own black children.
> If the United States of America is to be saved—it will not be saved by white power, but black power.[44]

One mayor thought he had the answer for saving his city. On March 15, 1967 he told a Senate subcommittee his city "avoided the civil disorder that has beset our other major cities for the past few summers. This didn't happen by chance; it is the result of careful planning and the implementation of programs made possible through the Economic Opportunity Act." He added, "These programs contributed to an orderly community and aided in the reduction of crime." The speaker was Detroit Mayor Jerome P. Cavanagh, a few short months before Detroit exploded.[45]

As noted in the first chapter, Detroit had the first community action program and was the first city to receive OEO money. By the time of the July riots the agency had pumped $41 million into it as a War on Poverty showcase.[46] Counting contributions from the Department of Labor and the Department of Health, Education and Labor, Detroit had an annual federal anti-poverty budget of $18 million,[47] not including $112 million already spent for urban renewal.[48]

Mayor Cavanagh praised an OEO program in Detroit under which persons arrested for a first offense were turned over to community action teams for "intensive counseling." The name of the program slipped his mind. "We have so many programs that I lose track of the names we have given some of them," he explained to the senators.[49]

One program which Mayor Cavanagh credited with contributing to Detroit's tranquility was a six-week OEO training program for the 1,800 Detroit policemen assigned to the ghettos and slums.[50] But when the violence came, not those policemen, nor all the rest of Detroit's police force, nor 8,000 National Guardsmen could stop it. They finally got the help of 4,700 federal troops.

End Notes

End Notes

CHAPTER 1

1. Houghton Mifflin Co., Boston, 1958, p. 323.
2. *Ibid.*, p. 327.
3. Study titled *Automation: Its Impact on Employment and Unemployment*, prepared by General Electric Company for the National Commission on Technology, Automation and Economic Progress and submitted August 20, 1965.
4. *Ibid.*
5. Letter dated March 26, 1958, from Representative Francis E. Walter (D., Pa.), then Chairman of the House Un-American Activities Committee, to the Secretary of the Treasury.
6. Jacket of the book, *The Other America*.
7. *Hearings*, 1938, House Special Committee on Un-American Activities, Vol. I, p. 678.
8. Address of Walter W. Heller at the Seventh Annual Public Affairs Forum of Indiana State College, Indiana, Pa., March 25, 1965.
9. Paper by Robert J. Lampman titled *Population Change and Poverty Reduction, 1947-75.* Delivered at Morgantown, W. Va., May 4, 1965.
10. Remarks of the President to a group of leaders of organizations of senior citizens in the Fish Room of the White House, January 15, 1964.
11. *The Concept of Poverty.* First report of the Task Force on Economic Growth and Opportunity of the U.S. Chamber of Commerce, 1965.
12. *Congressional Record*, August 21, 1964, p. 20039.
13. *Congressional Record*, August 21, 1964, p. 20179.
14. *Ibid.*
15. Debate between Mr. Bookbinder and Saul Alinsky, organizer of the poor, at a meeting of the Baltimore League of Women Voters, Baltimore, Md., April 19, 1966. Excerpt published by OEO.
16. *Congressional Record*, September 27, 1966, p. 23029.
17. *Health, Education and Welfare Indicators*, February 1964. Published by the Department of Health, Education and Welfare.
18. *Social Security Bulletin*, January 1965.
19. *Ibid.*, May 1966.
20. Statement to press at CCAP meeting April 14, 1965, International Inn, Washington, D.C.
21. *Washington Post*, December 14, 1966.
22. *The Wasted Americans*, by Edgar May. Published by Harper & Row, 1964, p. 203.
23. *Washington Post*, December 14, 1966.
24. *Congressional Record*, May 6, 1964, p. 9941.
25. *Ibid.*, June 24, 1964, p. 14436.
26. *Ibid.*, May 6, 1964, p. 9941.
27. *Ibid.*, May 26, 1964, p. 11584.
28. *Congressional Record*, May 26, 1964, p. 11584.
29. *Ibid.*, August 21, 1964, p. 20179.
30. *Ibid.*
31. *Ibid.*, May 6, 1964, p. 99431.
32. *Ibid.*, September 29, 1966, p. 23468.

CHAPTER 2

1. *Republican Poverty Memo*, April 22, 1966.
2. The following is the text of the robotyped letters:

EXECUTIVE OFFICE OF THE PRESIDENT
WASHINGTON, D.C. 20506

OFFICE OF ECONOMIC
   OPPORTUNITY

Poverty strikes early!

It is now well on the way toward engulfing a million deprived children who will be starting to school this fall.

There is still time to launch a major rescue effort for these children. And an exciting new weapon has been developed by some of America's leading authorities so that communities all over the nation can strike back. This weapon is known as Project Head-Start, a nation-wide pre-school program which is part of the War on Poverty. This summer it is estimated that more than 100,000 four and five year olds from pockets of poverty in 300 communities will be enrolled in eight-week sessions aimed to:

     —improve their health and physical abilities
     —develop their self-confidence
     —provide a wide range of classroom and field trips
     —establish joint activities with their parents

In short, help these children overcome the obvious deficiencies imposed on them by poverty and prepare them to face life and school with a better chance of success.

The widest possible participation of communities and public and private agencies will be necessary if this plan is to succeed. More than 20,000 professional, neighborhood and volunteer workers will need to be recruited. The coordinated action of public health, welfare and public and private school officials on an unprecedented scale at all levels will be required. The Office of Economic Opportunity will pay for 90% of the cost where local communities organize and operate such a two-month program this summer. The local community will furnish the remainder in either cash or kind. The average cost per child is estimated at $85.00 per month. A guidebook and application form are ready so that you can immediately take the necessary action to put Project Head-Start in operation in your community. There are less than 100 working days left before the sessions should start. Please fill in and mail to me the enclosed return card or wire my office. If there are duplicate requests from a single community we will advise you. The important thing is to start your planning now so that the children in your community will get this chance to start their private war on poverty.

Sincerely,
Sargent Shriver
Director

P.S. Attached is a reease which contains a summary of Project Head-Start and biographical data on the authorities who developed it.

3. *Congressional Record*, June 2, 1966, p. 11623.
4. *Republican Poverty Memo*, March 22, 1966.

CHAPTER 3

1. U.S. Chamber of Commerce Study, *The Disadvantaged Poor: Education and Employment*, p. 94.

2. Memorandum from Mr. Yarmolinsky to Presidential Assistant Joseph A. Califano, June 13, 1964, as quoted in *Congressional Record*, September 26, 1966, p. 22813.

3. *Congressional Record*, January 24, 1967, p. H 516.

4. Statement on House floor by Rep. Charles E. Goodell (R., N.Y.), February 10, 1966.

5. *Ibid.*

6. Article in *National Review*, October 10, 1965, by Don E. Cope, former official at Camp Atterbury, Indiana.

7. Joint statement in the House by Representatives Quie and Goodell, February 7, 1966.

8. *New York Times*, July 3, 1966.

9. *Phoenix Republic*, November 18, 1965.

10. *Indianapolis Star*, January 8, 1966.

11. *San Antonio Express*, March 10, 1966.

12. *Virginian-Tennessean*, Bristol, Virginia, January 21, 1966, and *Herald-Courier*, Bristol, Tennessee, January 21, 1966.

13. *Virginian-Tennessean*, January 21, 1966.

14. *Congressional Record*, September 27, 1966, p. 23025.

15. *Hearings on Supplemental Appropriation Bill for 1967* before Subcommittee of the House Appropriations Committee, Part 1.

16. *Congressional Record*, March 30, 1966, pp. 6938 through 6946.

17. *Wall Street Journal*, May 17, 1966, and *Republican Poverty Memo*, May 13, 1966.

18. *Hearings before House Appropriation Subcommittee on Supplemental Appropriation Bill, 1967, Part 1*, p. 59.

CHAPTER 5

1. *Senate Labor and Public Welfare Committee Hearings*, June 21 through June 24, 1966, on Amendments to the Economic Opportunity Act, pp. 417-418.

2. *Congressional Record*, October 4, 1966, p. 24123.

3. *Baltimore Sun*, January 25, 1966.

4. *Congressional Record*, June 29, 1966, p. 13996.

5. *Ibid.*, February 6, 1967, p. H1038.

CHAPTER 6

1. *Republican Poverty Memo*, June 16, 1966.

2. *House Republican Poverty Subcommittee Report*, April 21, 1966.

3. *Congressional Record*, September 26, 1966, p. 22809.
4. *Republican Poverty Memo*, March 21, 1966.
5. *Congressional Record*, April 25, 1966, p. 8395.
6. *Ibid.*, September 26, 1966, p. 22809.
7. *Supplemental Appropriation Bill Hearings for 1967*, House Appropriation Subcommittee. Part 1, p. 594.
8. *Ibid.*, p. 591.
9. *Ibid.*, p. 592.
10. Letter to the author, dated February 23, 1967, from John Crow, Associate Director, Bureau of Land Management.
11. *Supplemental Appropriation Bill Hearings for 1967*, House Appropriation Subcommittee. Part 1, p. 351.
12. *Republican Poverty Memo*, March 16, 1966.
13. *Supplemental Appropriation Bill Hearings for 1967*, House Appropriation Subcommittee. Part 1, pp. 592 & 593.
14. *Supplemental Appropriation Bill Hearings for 1967*, House Appropriation Subcommittee. Part 1, p. 247.
15. *Congressional Record*, January 12, 1967, p. S204.
16. *Ibid.*
17. *Supplemental Appropriation Bill Hearings for 1967*, House Appropriation Subcommittee. Part 1, p. 247.
18. *Congressional Record*, September 27, 1966, p. 23025.
19. *House Education and Labor Committee Report on Economic Opportunity Act Amendments of 1966*, p. 95.
20. Statement by Senator Strom Thurmond, May 23, 1966.
21. *Republican Poverty Memo*, May 13, 1966 and *Congressional Record*, April 26, 1966, p. 8691.
22. *Congressional Record*, September 29, 1966, p. A5017.
23. *Ibid.*, September 28, 1966, p. 23187.

CHAPTER 7

1. *Washington Post*, November 17, 1966.
2. *Ibid.*
3. *Supplemental Appropriation Bill Hearings for 1967*, House Appropriation Subcommittee. Part 1, p. 599.

CHAPTER 8

1. *New York Times*, July 24, 1966.
2. *Huntington Advertiser*, April 16, 1966.
3. *Associated Press*, August 4, 1966.
4. *New Bedford Standard Times*, March 27, 1966.

CHAPTER 9

1. *Hearings on 1966 Amendments to the Economic Opportunity Act*, House Education and Labor War on Poverty Subcommittee, Part 1, p. 496.

2. *Congressional Record*, September 29, 1966, p. 23505.

3. *Report of the New York (State) Senate Committee on Affairs of the City of New York on Mobilization for Youth, Inc.* Also, interview with Richard Boone.

4. *Human Events*, June 25, 1966.

5. *Report of the New York (State) Senate Committee on Affairs of the City of New York on Mobilization for Youth, Inc.*

6. *Ibid.*

7. *Ibid.*

8. *Ibid.*

9. *Ibid.*

10. American Arbitration Association study, *Representation Elections and Voter Participation in Community Action.*

11. *Congressional Record*, September 29, 1966, p. 23467.

12. *Hearings on 1966 Amendments to the Economic Opportunity Act*, House Education and Labor War on Poverty Subcommittee, Part 1, pp. 149 & 485 and *Human Events*, March 19, 1966.

13. *Hearings on 1966 Amendments to the Economic Opportunity Act*, pp. 149 & 485.

14. American Arbitration Association study, *Representation Elections and Voter Participation in Community Action.*

15. *Hearings on 1966 Amendments to the Economic Opportunity Act*, p. 149.

16. *The Reporter*, May 5, 1966.

17. *Congressional Record*, September 29, 1966, p. 23505.

CHAPTER 10

1. *Office of Economic Opportunity Memo 23.*

2. *Congressional Record*, October 4, 1966, pp. 24133 & 24134.

3. *Ibid.*, February 8, 1967, p. A 544.

4. *Ibid.*, April 3, 1967, p. A 1533.

5. *Exclusive*, April 19, 1967.

6. *Chicago Tribune*, February 11, 1966.

7. *Chicago Sun Times*, February 23, 1966.

8. *New York Times*, October 9, 1966.

9. *Counterattack*, December 31, 1965.

10. *Congressional Record*, October 4, 1966, p. 24132.

11. *Washin. ton Star*, February 4, 1966.

12. *Nation's Business*, May, 1966.

13. *Congressional Record*, February 27, 1967, p. H 1795.

14. *Ibid.*, February 16, 1967, p. A 694.

15. *Ibid.*, October 4, 1966, p. 24132.

16. *Ibid.*, September 28, 1966, p. 23149.
17. *Ibid.*, September 28, 1966, p. 23148.
18. *House Education and Labor Committee Report on Economic Opportunity Amendments of 1966*, June 1, 1966, p. 130.
19. *Ibid.*
20. *Record-American*, March 3, 1966.
21. *House Education and Labor Committee Report on Economic Opportunity Amendments of 1966*, June 1, 1966, p. 131.
22. *Congressional Record*, April 3, 1967, p. A 1545.
23. *House Education and Labor Committee Report on Economic Opportunity Amendments of 1966*, June 1, 1966, p. 130.
24. *New York Times*, August 7, 1966.
25. *House Education and Labor Committee Report on Economic Opportunity Amendments of 1966*, June 1, 1966, p. 132.
26. *Ibid.*
27. *New York Post*, June 1, 1966.
28. *Congressional Record*, September 29, 1966, p. 23506.
29. *Ibid.*
30. *New York Times*, August 21, 1966.
31. *Ibid.*, March 14, 1967.
32. *Ibid.*, March 21, 1967.
33. *Ibid.*, September 24, 1966.
34. *Wall Street Journal*, August 29, 1966.
35. *Associated Press*, February 4, 1966.
36. *New York Times*, February 28, 1966.
37. *Congressional Record*, April 17, 1967, p. H 2418.

CHAPTER 11

1. Report issued by the General Accounting Office, October 1964, and titled *Inadequate Policies and Practices Relating to the Relocation of Families from Urban Renewal Areas, District of Columbia, Redevelopment Land Agency and Housing and Home Finance Agency.*
2. Memo from Mr. Banks to UPO Executive Committee, September 8, 1966.
3. *UPO Review*, Ford Foundation Panel, May 18, 1966.
4. *Washington Post*, October 7, 1966.
5. *Washington Star*, December 11, 1966.
6. *Washington Post*, October 7, 1966.
7. *Ibid.*, February 17, 1967.
8. *Washington Star*, March 16, 1967.
9. *Washington Post*, April 24, 1967.
10. *Washington Star*, March 30, 1967.
11. *Ibid.*, September 10, 1966.
12. *Ibid.*, August 16, 1966.
13. *Ibid.*, September 10, 1966.
14. *Congressional Record*, September 29, 1966, p. 23505.
15. *Washington Post*, October 8, 1966.

16. *Ibid.*
17. *Ibid.*, November 28, 1966.
18. *Ibid.*, August 27, 1966.
19. *Ibid.*, August 3, 1966.
20. *UPO Review*, Ford Foundation Panel, May 18, 1966.
21. *Washington Post*, May 28, 1966.
22. *Ibid.*, June 15, 1966.
23. *Ibid.*, December 13, 1966.
24. *Ibid.*
25. *Washington Star*, December 11, 1966.
26. *Washington Post*, December 19, 1966.
27. *Ibid.*
28. *Ibid.*
29. *Ibid.*, January 11, 1967.
30. *Congressional Record*, April 3, 1967, p. H 3407.
31. *Washington Post*, July 30, 1966.
32. *Washington Star*, May 25, 1967.
33. *Fiscal Year 1967 Hearings, District of Columbia Subcommittee of
Senate Appropriations Committee*, pp. 145 & 147.
34. *Washington Post*, May 10, 1967.

CHAPTER 12

1. *Washington Star*, December 8, 1966.
2. *New York Times*, December 4, 1966.
3. *Washington Post*, April 17, 1967.
4. *New York Times*, March 5, 1967.

CHAPTER 14

1. *Republican Poverty Memo*, March 30, 1966.
2. *Ibid.*, March 28, 1966.
3. *Ibid.*
4. *Ibid.*
5. *New York Times*, April 6, 1966.
6. *The Top of the News with Fulton Lewis, Jr.*, June 27, 1966.
7. *Senate Supplemental Appropriations Hearings for 1967*, pp. 458-459.
8. *New York Times*, November 13, 1966.
9. *Washington Post*, December 7, 1966.
10. *Ibid.*, August 31, 1966.
11. *Washington Star*, January 29, 1967.

CHAPTER 16

1. *Congressional Record*, May 23, 1967, p. A 2528.
2. *Washington Post*, May 29, 1967.

CHAPTER 17

1. *Washington Star,* September 7, 1966.
2. *Congressional Record,* September 28, 1966, pp. 23154 & 23155.
3. *The Reporter,* October 6, 1966.
4. *Congressional Record,* May 3, 1967, p. H 4986.

CHAPTER 18

1. *New York Daily News,* September 9, 1965.
2. *Human Events,* April 23, 1966.
3. *Tulsa Tribune,* March 17, 1967.
4. *House Education and Labor Committee Report on Economic Opportunity Act Amendments of 1966,* p. 142.
5. *Ibid.*
6. *Congressional Record,* February 20, 1967, p. S 2303.

CHAPTER 19

1. *Human Events,* March 26, 1966.
2. *Washington Post,* May 11, 1967.
3. *Ibid.*
4. *Ibid.*
5. *Congressional Record,* September 27, 1966, p. 23083.
6. *New York Times,* August 23, 1966.
7. *Ibid.*
8. *Congressional Record,* September 27, 1966, p. 23080.
9. *Washington Post,* April 19, 1966.
10. *New York Times,* August 2, 1966.
11. *Human Events,* November 21, 1964.
12. *Congressional Record,* March 16, 1967.
13. *Washington Post,* June 9, 1966.
14. *Milwaukee Journal,* March 3, 1967.
15. *Washington Star,* October 4, 1966.
16. *Ibid.*
17. *New York Times,* January 15, 1967.
18. *Ibid.*
19. *Washington Post,* May 13, 1967.

FOOTNOTES FOR THE EPILOGUE

1. *Washington Post*, August 2, 1967.
2. *Ibid.*, July 27, 1967.
3. *Congressional Record*, July 27, 1966, p. 23079.
4. *Ibid.*, September 27, 1966, p. 23079.
5. *Congressional Record*, July 24, 1967, p. H 9188.
6. *Washington Post*, July 21, 1967.
7. *Congressional Record*, May 11, 1967.
8. *Washington Star*, August 2, 1967.
9. *Ibid.*
10. *Ibid.*
11. *Congressional Record*, July 27, 1967, p. H 9543.
12. *Ibid.*, July 27, 1967, p. H 9543.
13. *Ibid.*
14. *Ibid.*
15. *Ibid.*
16. *New York Times*, August 4, 1967.
17. *New York Times*, August 8, 1967.
18. *Ibid.*
19. *Washington Star*, July 23, 1967.
20. *Ibid.*
21. *Washington Post*, July 19, 1967.
22. *Washington Star*, July 23, 1967.
23. *Ibid.*
24. *Ibid.*
25. *New York Times*, August 8, 1967.
26. *Washington Star*, August 8, 1967.
27. *Congressional Record*, September 27, 1966, p. 23079.
28. *Ibid.*, August 9, 1967, p. H 10214.
29. *Washington Post*, August 8, 1967.
30. *Washington Daily News*, August 1, 1967.
31. *New York Times*, July 28, 1967.
32. *Washington Star*, August 3 and August 5, 1967.
33. *Washington Post*, August 4, 1967.
34. *Ibid.*
35. *Washington Star*, August 5, 1967.
36. *Washington Post*, August 4, 1967.
37. *Ibid.*, August 5, 1967.
38. *Washington Star*, August 8, 1967.
39. *Ibid.*
40. OEO press release, July 20, 1967.
41. *Congressional Record*, June 27, 1967, p. H 8105.
42. *Ibid.*
43. Issue of August 3, 1967.
44. *Ibid.*
45. *Hearings, Examining the War on Poverty, Part 1*, Subcommittee on Employment, Manpower and Poverty of the Senate Labor and Public Welfare Committee, p. 99.
46. Figure furnished by Marshall Peck, OEO information officer.

47. *Hearings, Examining the War on Poverty, Part 1,* Subcommittee on Employment, Manpower and Poverty of the Senate Labor and Public Welfare Committee, p. 91.

48. *Congressional Record,* August 7, 1967, p. A 3976.

49. *Hearings, Examining the War on Poverty, Part 1,* Subcommittee on Employment, Manpower and Poverty of the Senate Labor and Public Welfare Committee, p. 116.

50. *Ibid.,* p. 109.